FYODOR DOSTOEVSKY'S
CRIME&PUNISHMENT

A GRAPHIC NOVEL

ILLUSTRATED BY
ALAIN KORKOS
ADAPTED BY
DAVID ZANE MAIROWITZ

STERLING

New York / London
www.sterlingpublishing.com

Published by Sterling Publishing Co., Inc.
387 Park Avenue South, New York, NY 10016

© 2008 SelfMadeHero

First published 2008
by SelfMadeHero
A division of Metro Media Ltd
5 Upper Wimpole Street
London W1G 6BP
www.selfmadehero.com

Illustrated by Alain Korkos
Translated and adapted by David Zane Mairowitz
Cover Designer: Jeff Willis
Designer: Andy Huckle
Dostoevsky biography: David Zane Mairowitz
Proofreader: Nick de Somogyi
Originating Publisher: Emma Hayley

Distributed in Canada by Sterling Publishing
c/o Canadian Manda Group, 165 Dufferin Street,
Toronto, Ontario, Canada M6K 3H6

        Library of Congress Cataloging-in-Publication Data

Korkos, Alain.
    Crime and Punishment: A graphic adaptation of Fyodor Dostoevsky's novel. Illustrated
by Alain Korkos; translated and adapted by David Zane Mairowitz.
        p. cm.—(Illustrated Classics)
    ISBN: 978-1-4114-1594-2 (pbk.)
1. Graphic novels. I. Mairowitz, David Zane, 1943- II. Dostoyevsky, Fyodor, 1821-1881.
Prestuplenie i Nakazanie. III. Title.
PN6727. K664C75 2008
741.5'944—dc22

                                                        2007049166

Printed in the United States

10 9 8 7 6 5 4 3 2 1

For information about custom editions, special sales, premium and corporate
purchases, please contact Sterling Special Sales Department at 800-805-5489 or
specialsales@sterlingpub.com.

"Can I really do it? Smash her skull with an axe, watch the blood rush out of her, steal her money?"

These questions haunt an impoverished student, Rodion Romanovich Raskolnikov, in the beginning of *Crime and Punishment*. The next day he carries out the murder based on an idea he is obsessed with: If he kills a greedy old woman, he will do society a service. He thinks this act will also make him into a man no longer bound by the common morals that keep the masses enslaved to their suffering.

Murder is never simple though, and Raskolnikov struggles with his guilt and paranoia. He wanders feverishly through the streets of a city that is as lost as he is. Dostoevsky's Petersburg teams with corruption, self-destruction, prostitution, cruelty, and the belief that anything and anyone can be bought or sold. A lecher vies with a businessman to buy the affection of Raskolnikov's sister, a bureaucrat drinks himself to death and leaves his widow and her children to beg on the streets, and a prostitute with a Bible offers the only hope.

Dostoevsky draws a grim portrait of nineteenth century Russia, a society divided into the depraved rich and the helpless poor. Hunted by a police inspector and his own conscience, Raskolnikov is driven toward confession. He despairs that only by turning himself in will he find reprieve from his agony or, maybe, he will find salvation.

This graphic adaptation transplants Dostoevsky's psychological drama to today's Russia. The transition is eerily seamless. Autocracy, greed, and limitless capitalism keep a stranglehold on the new Russia. How many Raskolnikovs walk the streets of St. Petersburg today? Watch the old Russia and the new Russia meet as one in these vividly drawn pages.

AT THE BEGINNING OF JULY, DURING A HEATWAVE, TOWARD EVENING, A YOUNG MAN LEFT THE TINY ROOM HE RENTED IN S-----Y LANE IN ST. PETERSBURG, WALKED OUT INTO THE STREET, AND SLOWLY, ALMOST INDECISIVELY, MADE FOR THE K-----N BRIDGE.

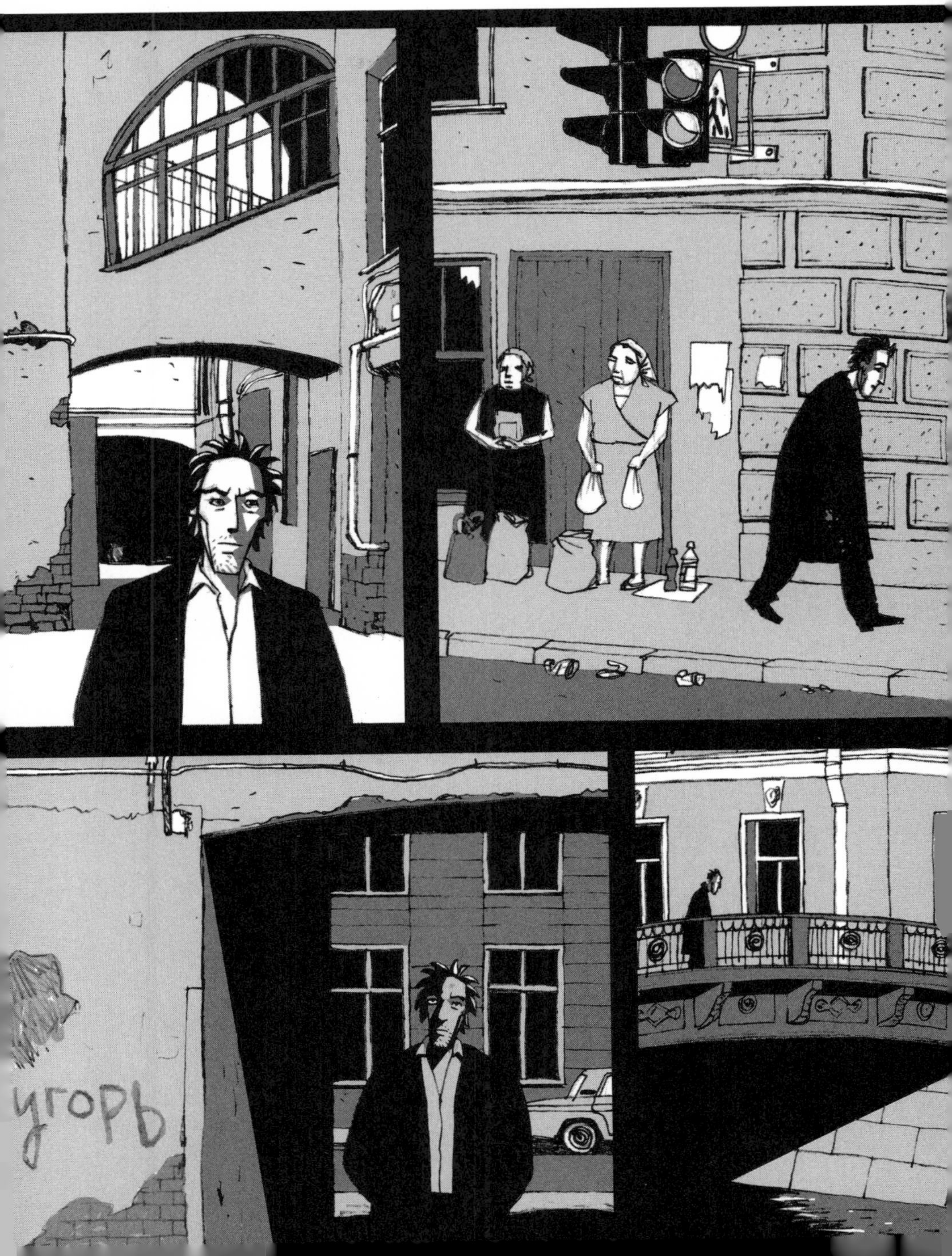

угорь

FOR A LONG TIME NOW HE HAD BEEN IN AN IRRITABLE STATE AND SUFFERED FROM HYPOCHONDRIA. HE WAS INCREDIBLY POOR AND HAD STOPPED DEALING WITH HIS DAILY LIFE. HE WAS LOST INSIDE HIMSELF AND AFRAID OF MEETING ANYONE, CREEPING LIKE AN ANIMAL DOWN THE STAIRS.

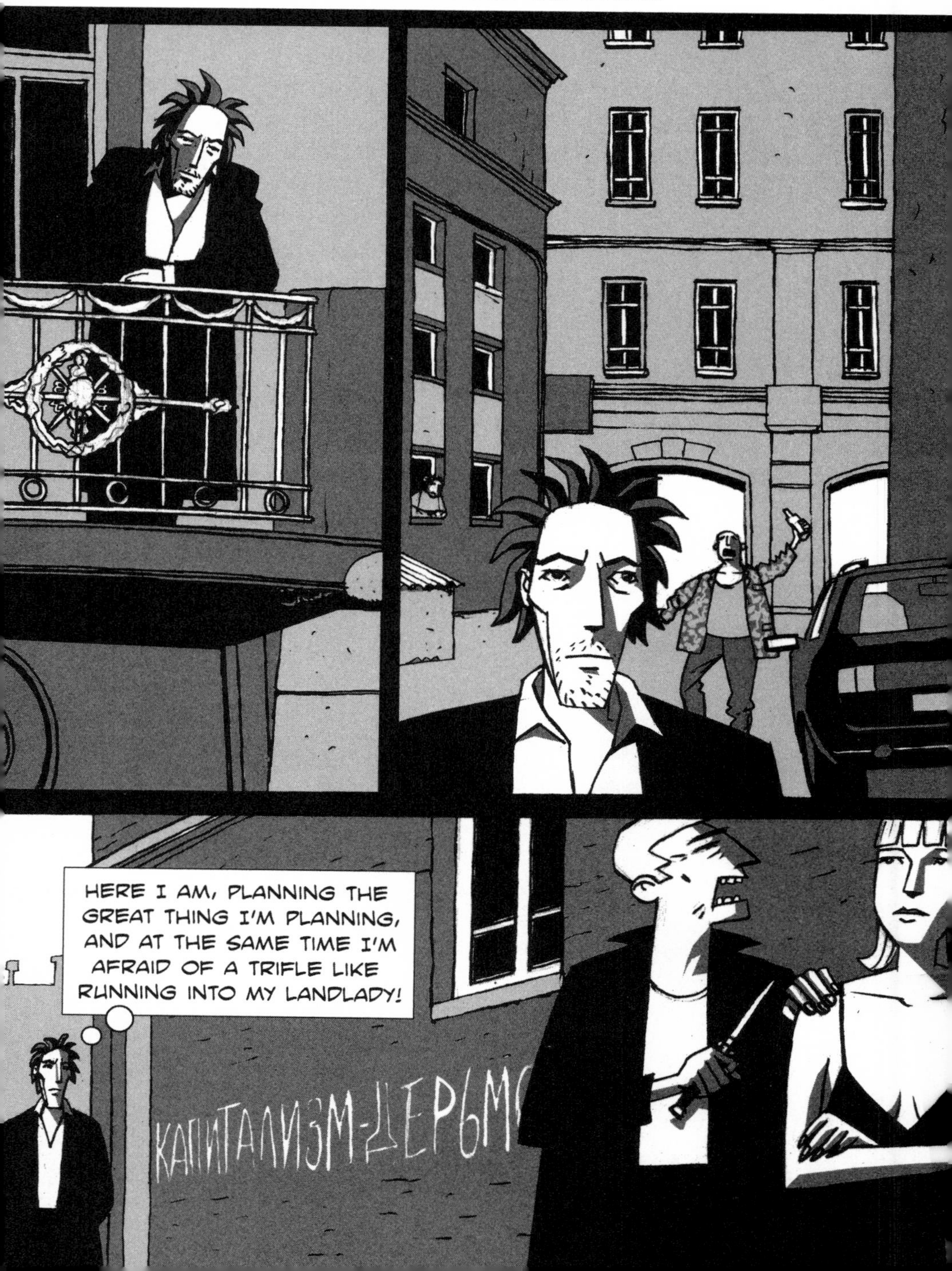
HERE I AM, PLANNING THE GREAT THING I'M PLANNING, AND AT THE SAME TIME I'M AFRAID OF A TRIFLE LIKE RUNNING INTO MY LANDLADY!
КАПИТАЛИЗМ-ДЕРЬМ

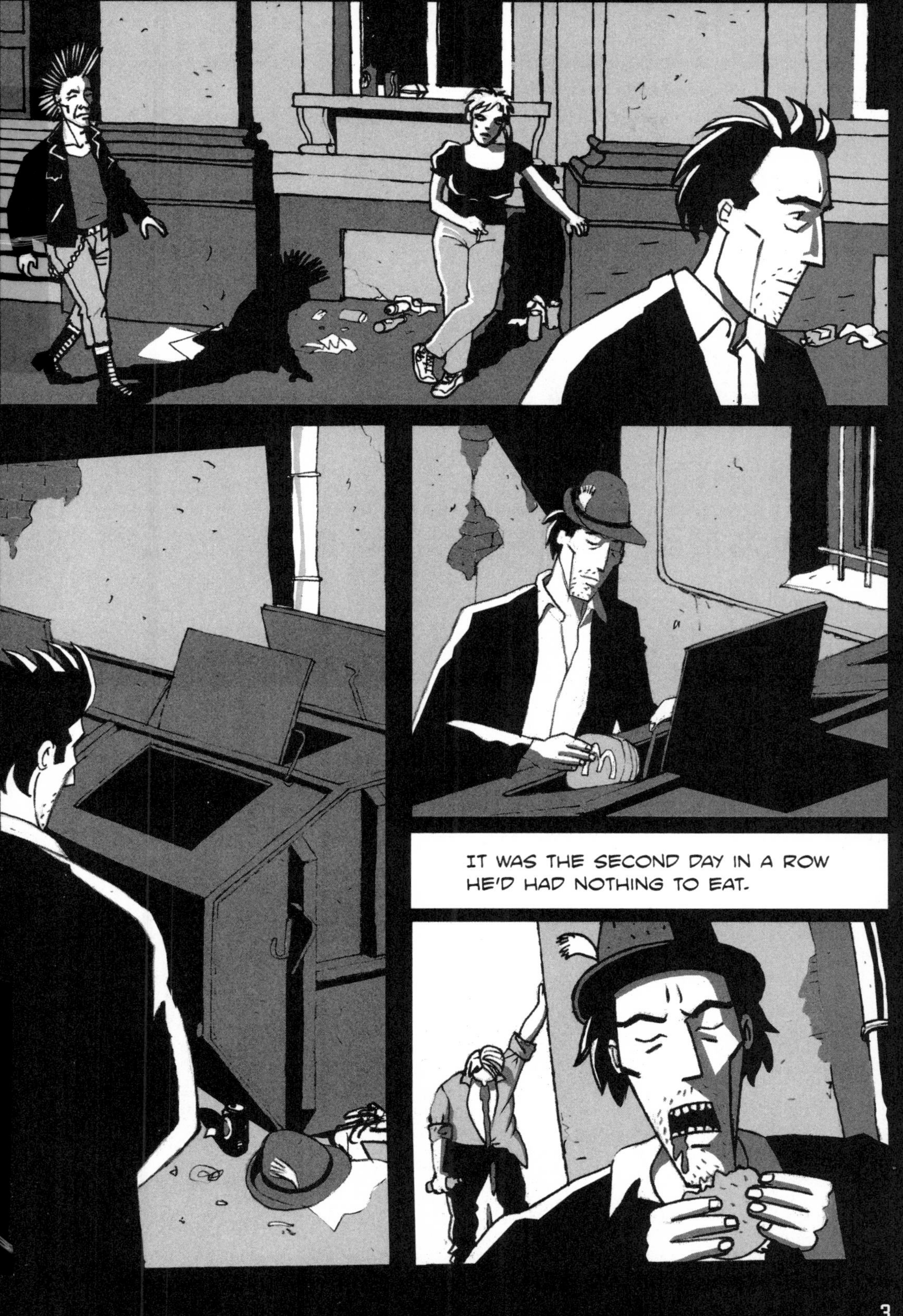
IT WAS THE SECOND DAY IN A ROW HE'D HAD NOTHING TO EAT.

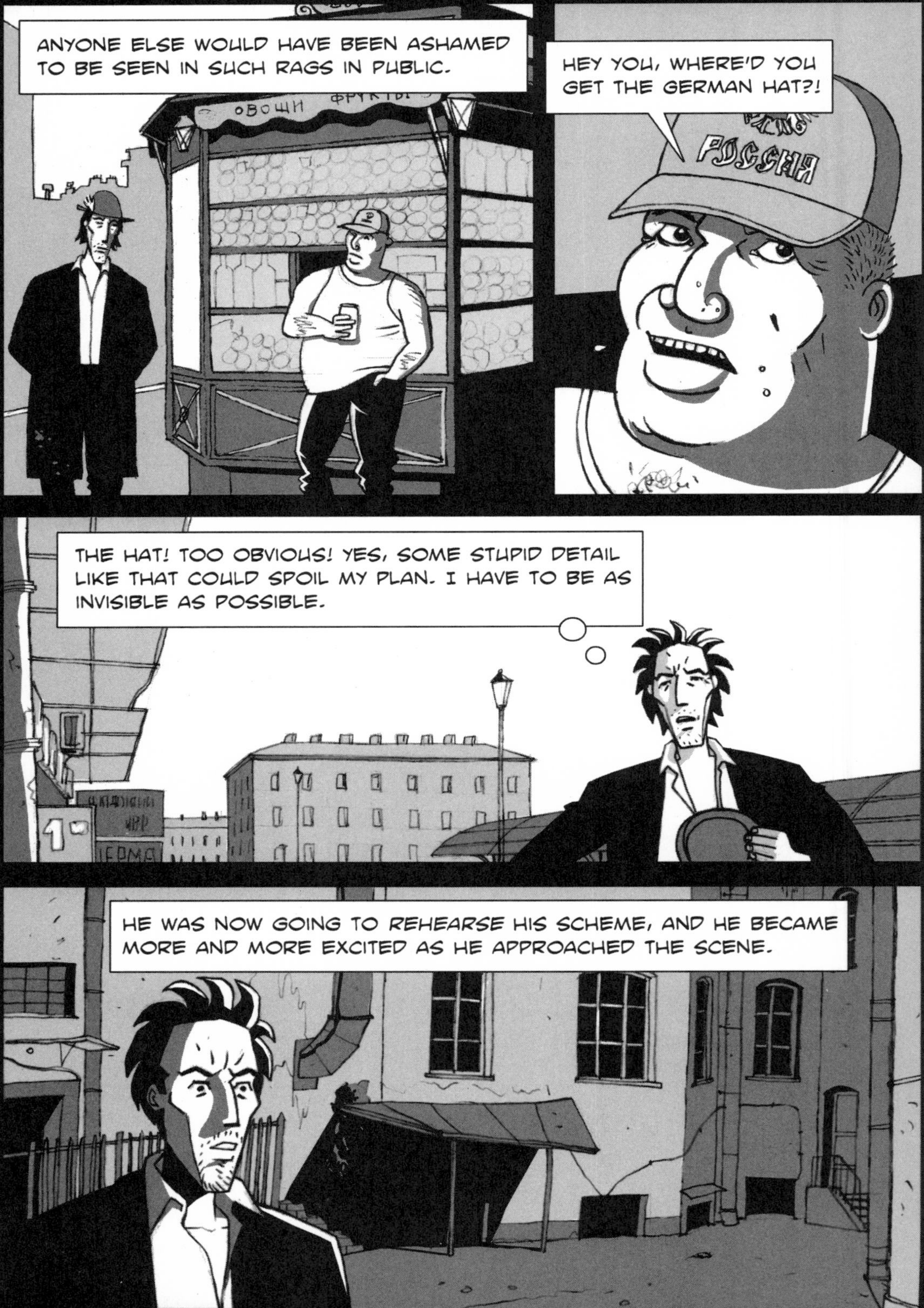
ANYONE ELSE WOULD HAVE BEEN ASHAMED TO BE SEEN IN SUCH RAGS IN PUBLIC.
ОВОЩИ
HEY YOU, WHERE'D YOU GET THE GERMAN HAT?!
РОССИЯ
THE HAT! TOO OBVIOUS! YES, SOME STUPID DETAIL LIKE THAT COULD SPOIL MY PLAN. I HAVE TO BE AS INVISIBLE AS POSSIBLE.
HE WAS NOW GOING TO *REHEARSE* HIS SCHEME, AND HE BECAME MORE AND MORE EXCITED AS HE APPROACHED THE SCENE.

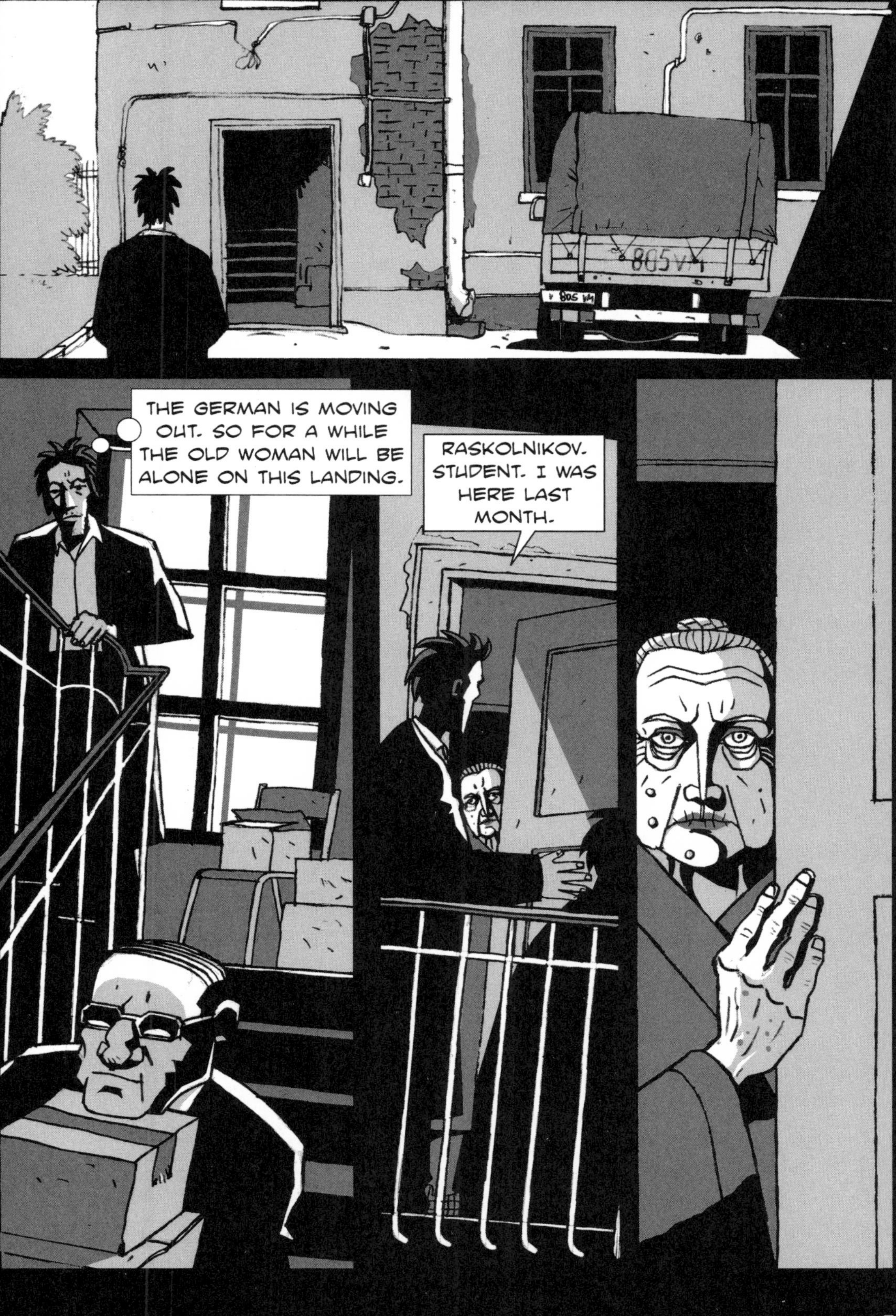
THE GERMAN IS MOVING OUT. SO FOR A WHILE THE OLD WOMAN WILL BE ALONE ON THIS LANDING.
RASKOLNIKOV. STUDENT. I WAS HERE LAST MONTH.

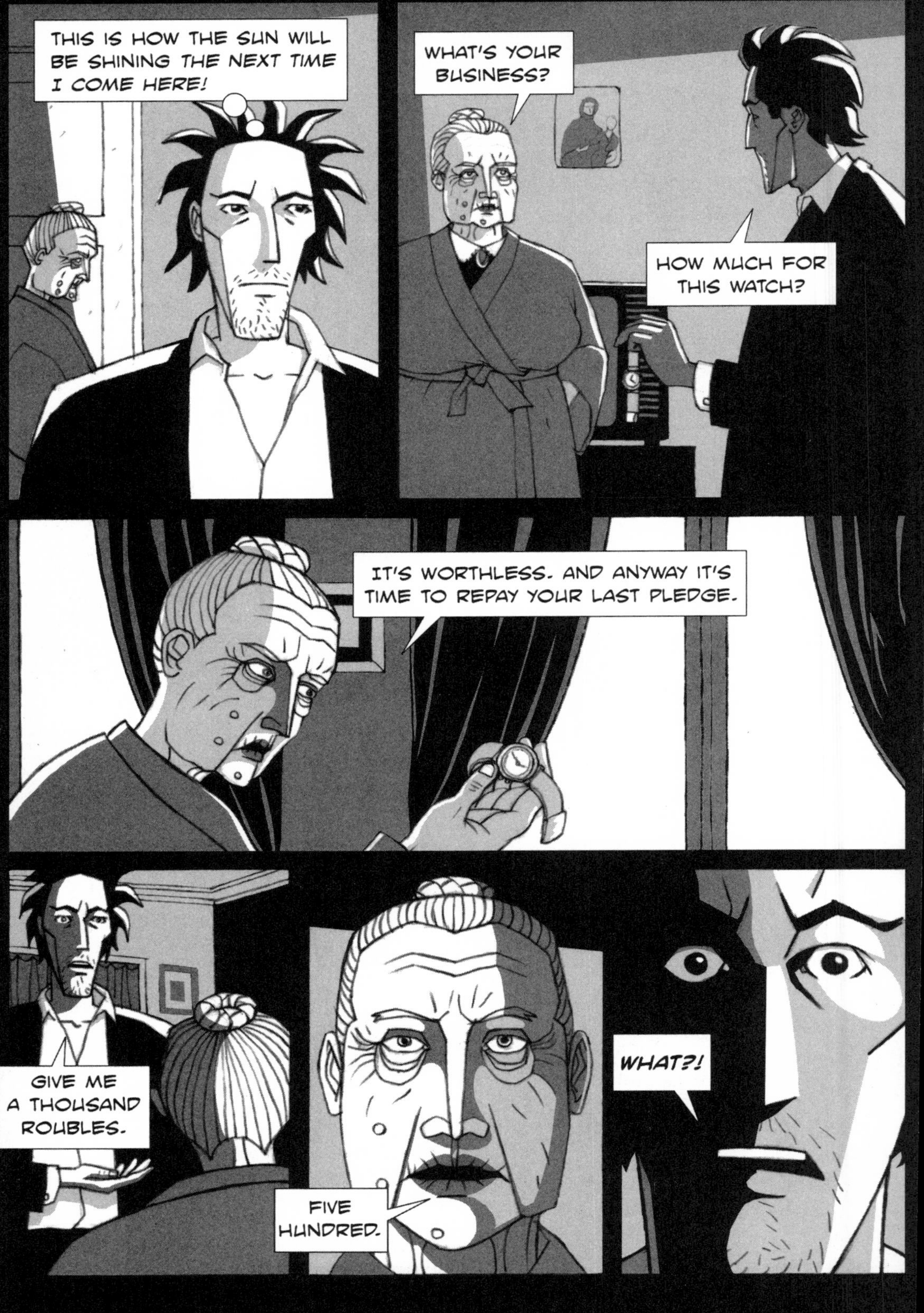
THIS IS HOW THE SUN WILL BE SHINING THE NEXT TIME I COME HERE!
WHAT'S YOUR BUSINESS?
HOW MUCH FOR THIS WATCH?
IT'S WORTHLESS. AND ANYWAY IT'S TIME TO REPAY YOUR LAST PLEDGE.
GIVE ME A THOUSAND ROUBLES.
FIVE HUNDRED.
WHAT?!

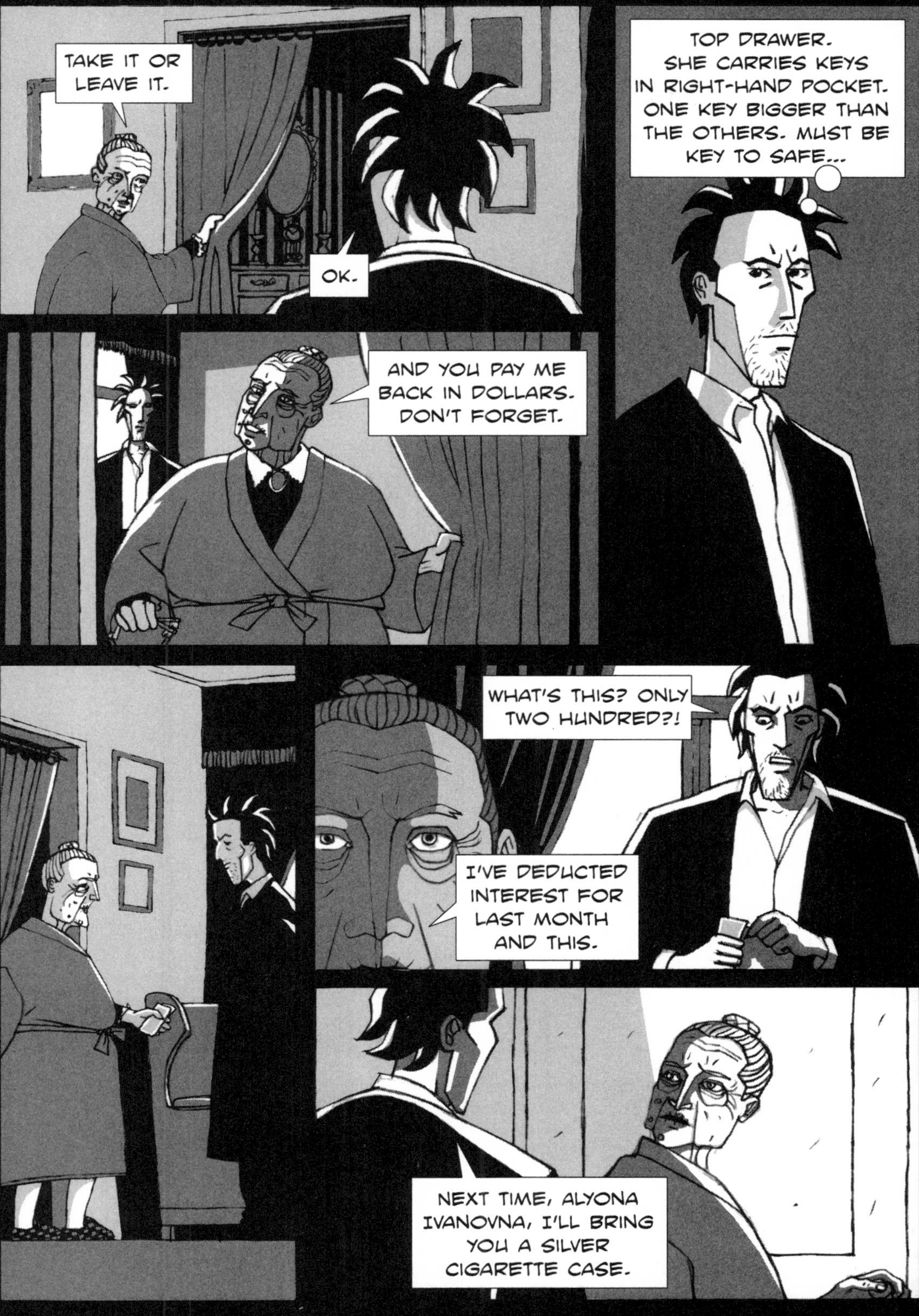
TAKE IT OR LEAVE IT.
OK.
TOP DRAWER. SHE CARRIES KEYS IN RIGHT-HAND POCKET. ONE KEY BIGGER THAN THE OTHERS. MUST BE KEY TO SAFE...
AND YOU PAY ME BACK IN DOLLARS. DON'T FORGET.
WHAT'S THIS? ONLY TWO HUNDRED?!
I'VE DEDUCTED INTEREST FOR LAST MONTH AND THIS.
NEXT TIME, ALYONA IVANOVNA, I'LL BRING YOU A SILVER CIGARETTE CASE.

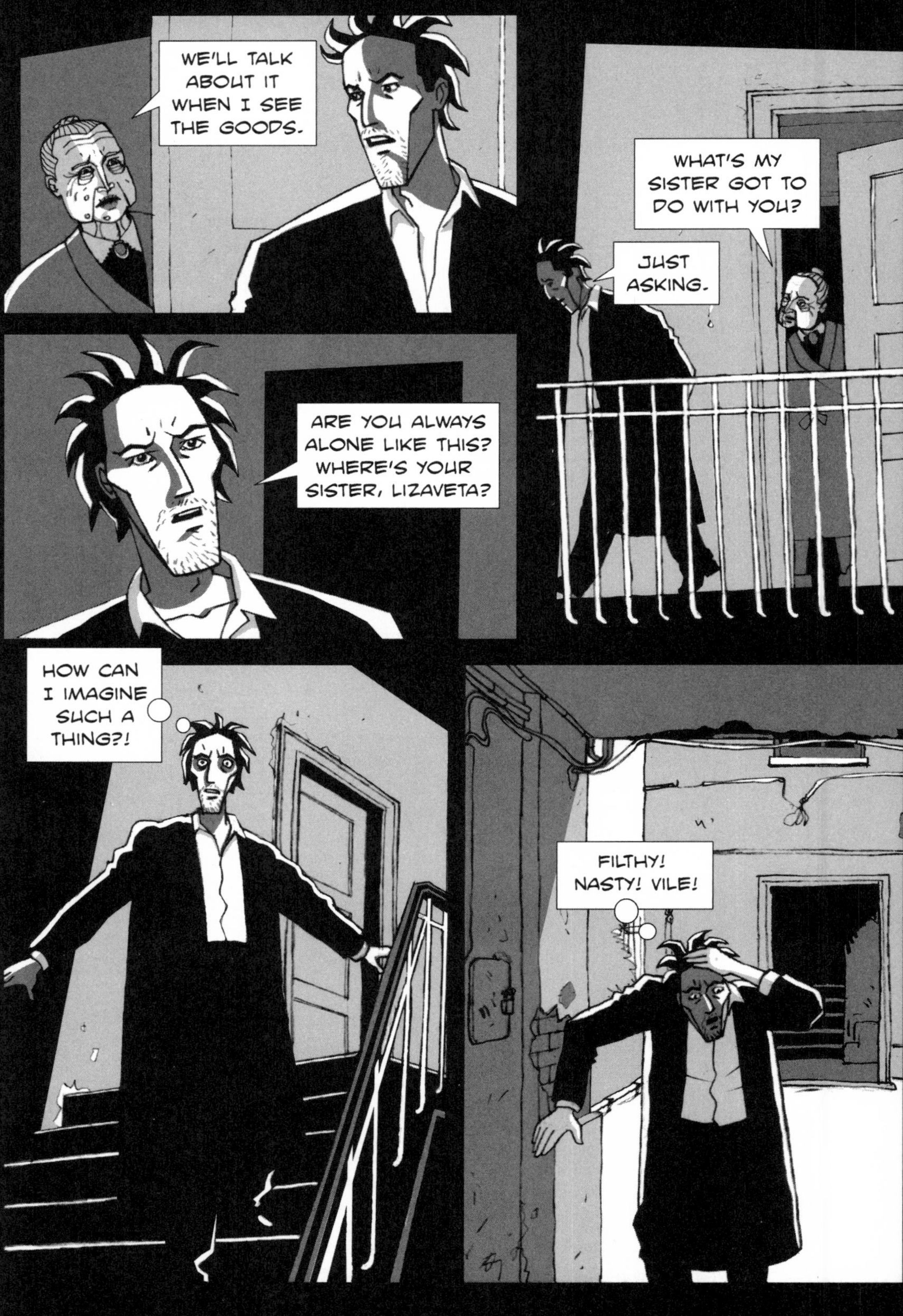
WE'LL TALK ABOUT IT WHEN I SEE THE GOODS.
ARE YOU ALWAYS ALONE LIKE THIS? WHERE'S YOUR SISTER, LIZAVETA?
WHAT'S MY SISTER GOT TO DO WITH YOU?
JUST ASKING.
HOW CAN I IMAGINE SUCH A THING?!
FILTHY! NASTY! VILE!

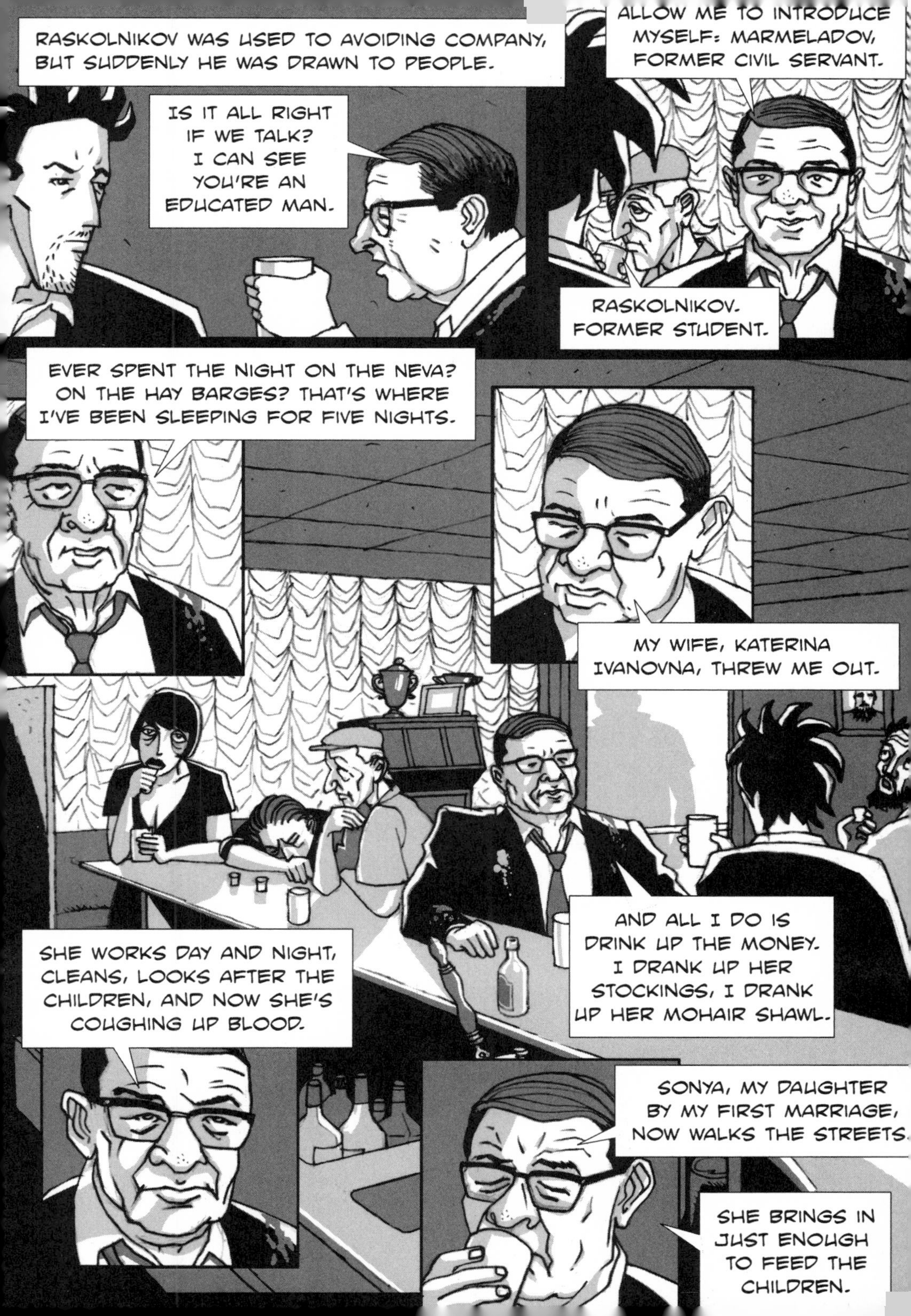
RASKOLNIKOV WAS USED TO AVOIDING COMPANY, BUT SUDDENLY HE WAS DRAWN TO PEOPLE.
IS IT ALL RIGHT IF WE TALK? I CAN SEE YOU'RE AN EDUCATED MAN.
ALLOW ME TO INTRODUCE MYSELF: MARMELADOV, FORMER CIVIL SERVANT.
RASKOLNIKOV. FORMER STUDENT.
EVER SPENT THE NIGHT ON THE NEVA? ON THE HAY BARGES? THAT'S WHERE I'VE BEEN SLEEPING FOR FIVE NIGHTS.
MY WIFE, KATERINA IVANOVNA, THREW ME OUT.
AND ALL I DO IS DRINK UP THE MONEY. I DRANK UP HER STOCKINGS, I DRANK UP HER MOHAIR SHAWL.
SHE WORKS DAY AND NIGHT, CLEANS, LOOKS AFTER THE CHILDREN, AND NOW SHE'S COUGHING UP BLOOD.
SONYA, MY DAUGHTER BY MY FIRST MARRIAGE, NOW WALKS THE STREETS.
SHE BRINGS IN JUST ENOUGH TO FEED THE CHILDREN.

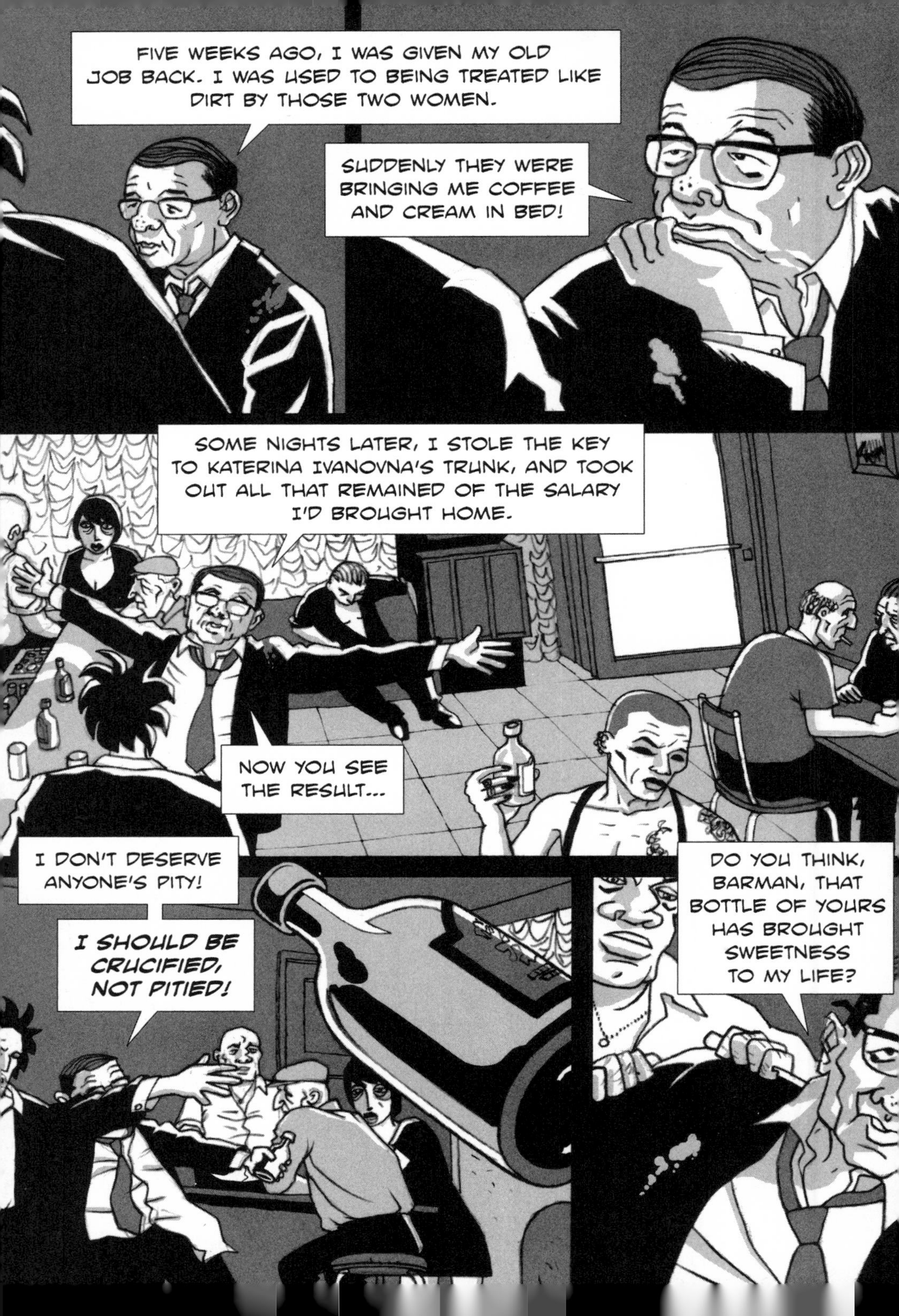
FIVE WEEKS AGO, I WAS GIVEN MY OLD JOB BACK. I WAS USED TO BEING TREATED LIKE DIRT BY THOSE TWO WOMEN.
SUDDENLY THEY WERE BRINGING ME COFFEE AND CREAM IN BED!
SOME NIGHTS LATER, I STOLE THE KEY TO KATERINA IVANOVNA'S TRUNK, AND TOOK OUT ALL THAT REMAINED OF THE SALARY I'D BROUGHT HOME.
NOW YOU SEE THE RESULT...
I DON'T DESERVE ANYONE'S PITY!
I SHOULD BE CRUCIFIED, NOT PITIED!
DO YOU THINK, BARMAN, THAT BOTTLE OF YOURS HAS BROUGHT SWEETNESS TO MY LIFE?

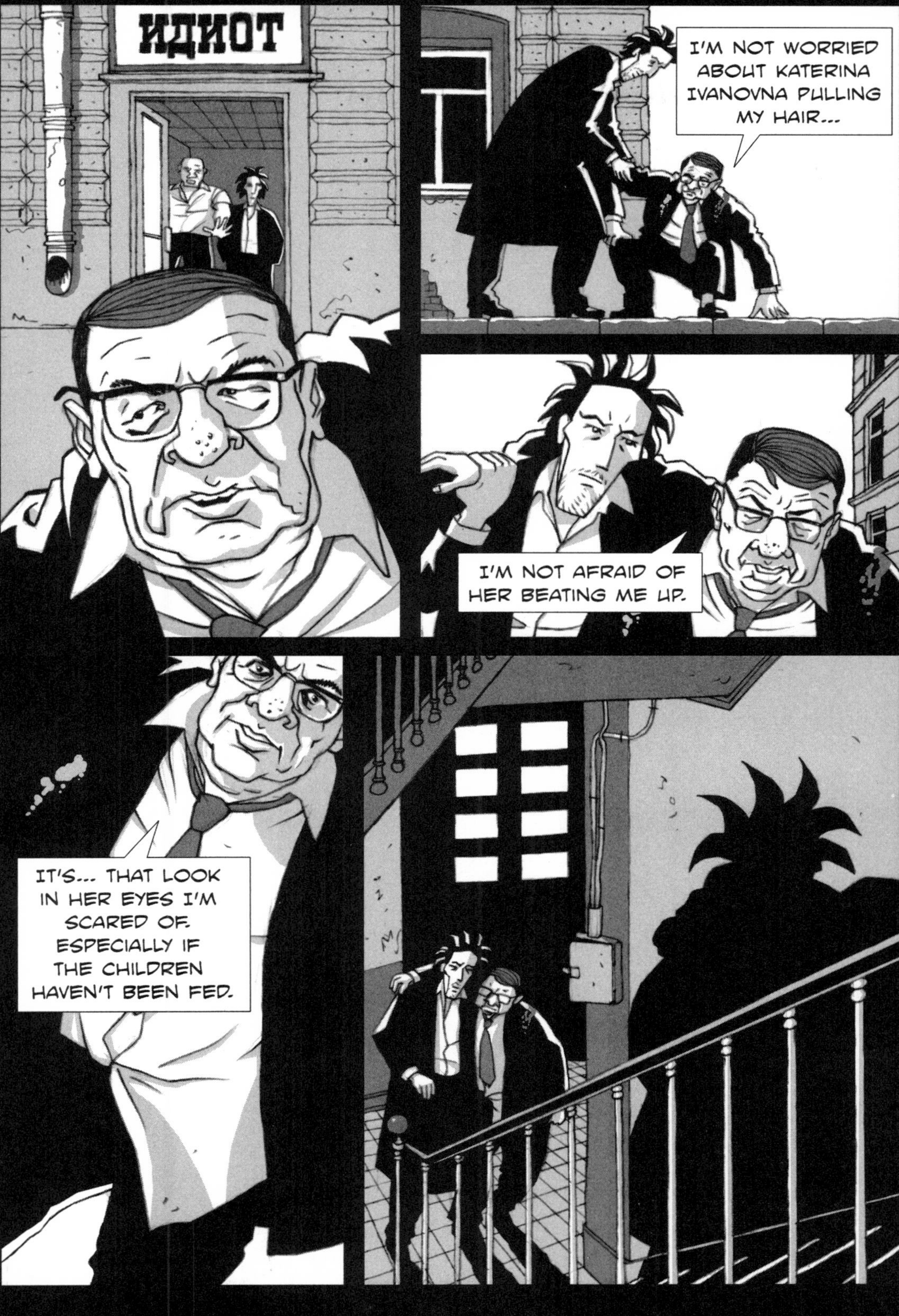
ИДИОТ
I'M NOT WORRIED ABOUT KATERINA IVANOVNA PULLING MY HAIR...
I'M NOT AFRAID OF HER BEATING ME UP.
IT'S... THAT LOOK IN HER EYES I'M SCARED OF. ESPECIALLY IF THE CHILDREN HAVEN'T BEEN FED.

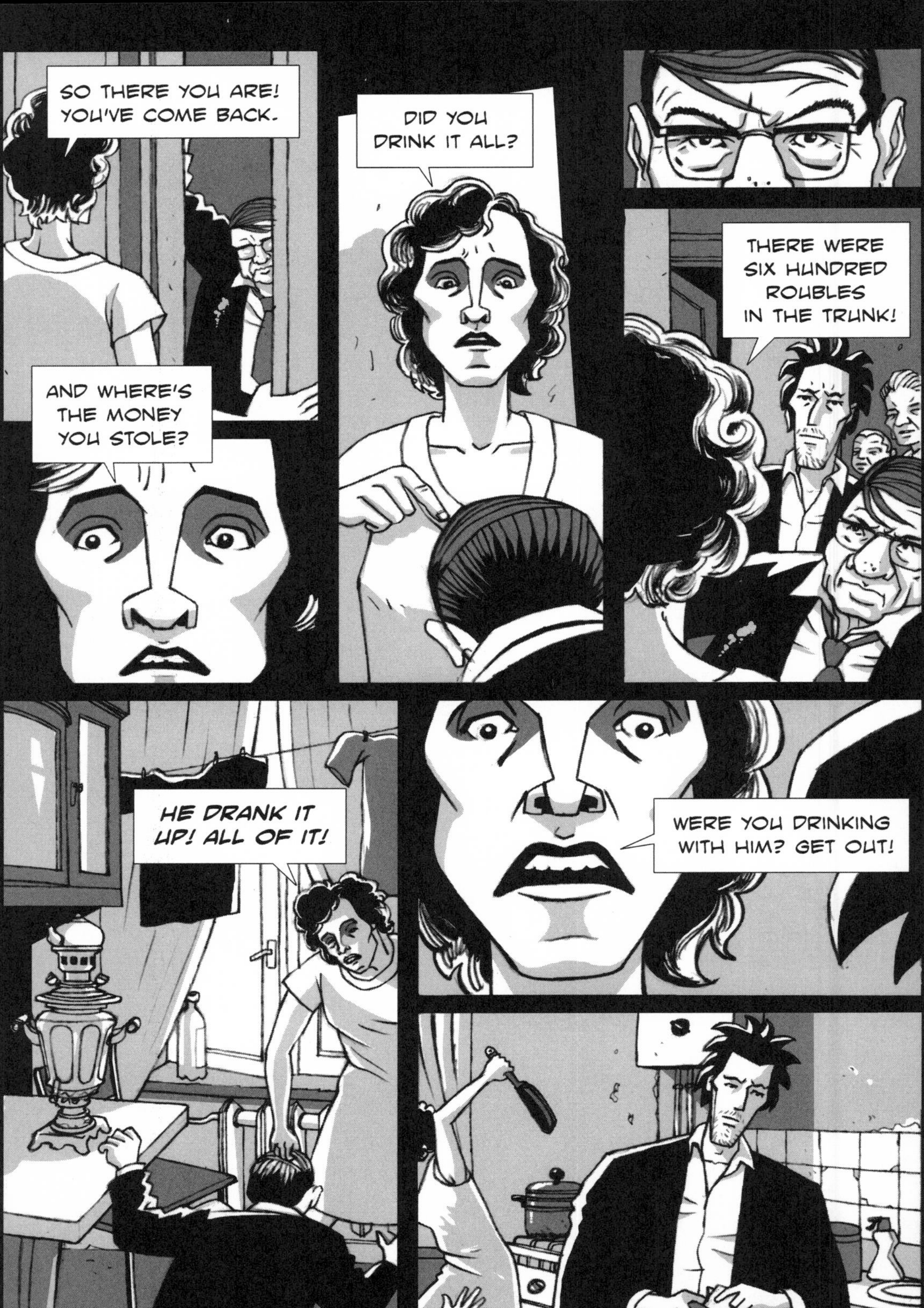

SO THERE YOU ARE! YOU'VE COME BACK.
AND WHERE'S THE MONEY YOU STOLE?
DID YOU DRINK IT ALL?
THERE WERE SIX HUNDRED ROUBLES IN THE TRUNK!
HE DRANK IT UP! ALL OF IT!
WERE YOU DRINKING WITH HIM? GET OUT!

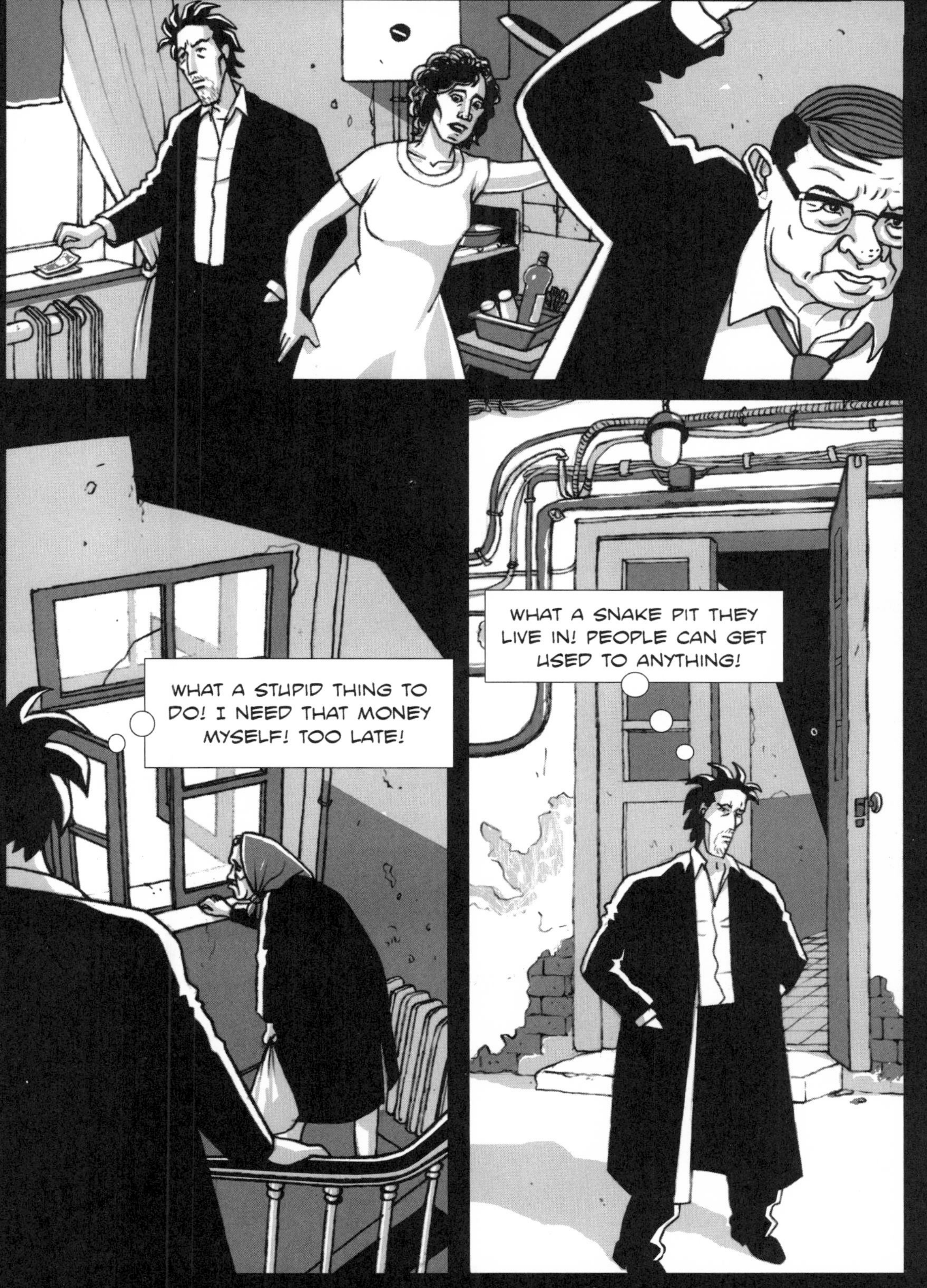
WHAT A STUPID THING TO DO! I NEED THAT MONEY MYSELF! TOO LATE!
WHAT A SNAKE PIT THEY LIVE IN! PEOPLE CAN GET USED TO ANYTHING!

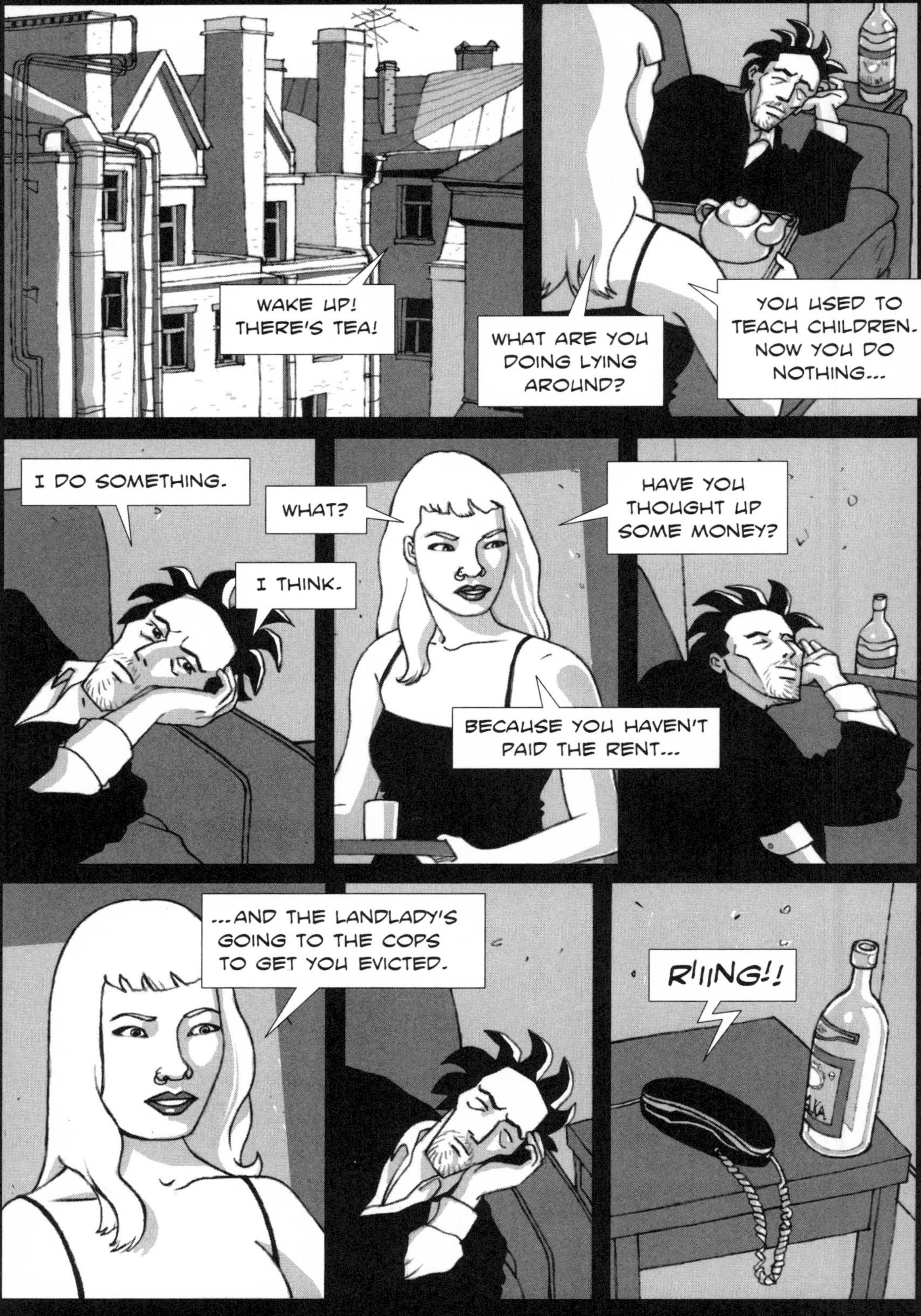
WAKE UP! THERE'S TEA!
WHAT ARE YOU DOING LYING AROUND?
YOU USED TO TEACH CHILDREN. NOW YOU DO NOTHING...
I DO SOMETHING.
WHAT?
I THINK.
HAVE YOU THOUGHT UP SOME MONEY?
BECAUSE YOU HAVEN'T PAID THE RENT...
...AND THE LANDLADY'S GOING TO THE COPS TO GET YOU EVICTED.
R!!ING!!

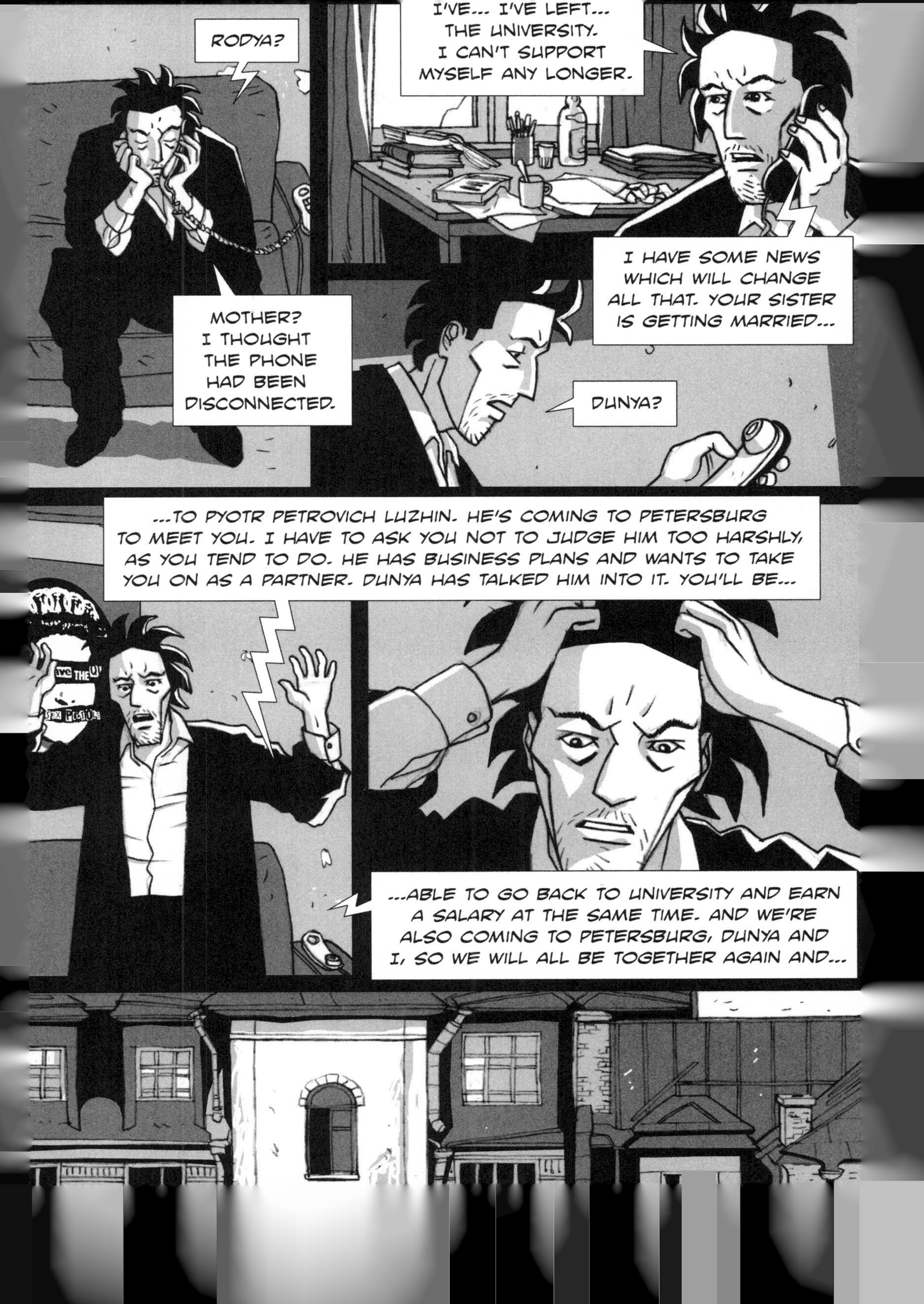
RODYA?
MOTHER? I THOUGHT THE PHONE HAD BEEN DISCONNECTED.
I'VE... I'VE LEFT... THE UNIVERSITY. I CAN'T SUPPORT MYSELF ANY LONGER.
I HAVE SOME NEWS WHICH WILL CHANGE ALL THAT. YOUR SISTER IS GETTING MARRIED...
DUNYA?
...TO PYOTR PETROVICH LUZHIN. HE'S COMING TO PETERSBURG TO MEET YOU. I HAVE TO ASK YOU NOT TO JUDGE HIM TOO HARSHLY, AS YOU TEND TO DO. HE HAS BUSINESS PLANS AND WANTS TO TAKE YOU ON AS A PARTNER. DUNYA HAS TALKED HIM INTO IT. YOU'LL BE...
SEX PISTOLS
...ABLE TO GO BACK TO UNIVERSITY AND EARN A SALARY AT THE SAME TIME. AND WE'RE ALSO COMING TO PETERSBURG, DUNYA AND I, SO WE WILL ALL BE TOGETHER AGAIN AND...

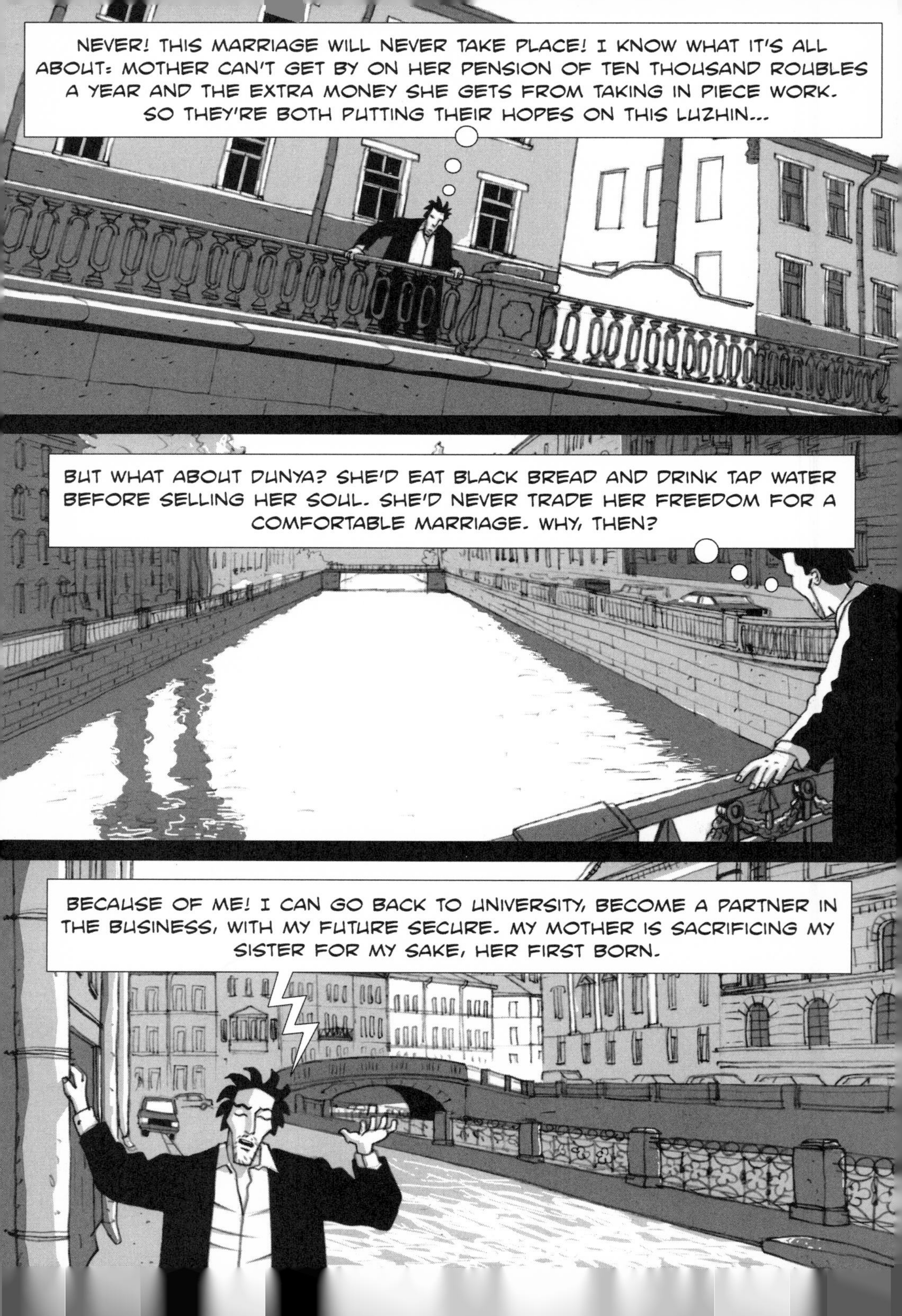
NEVER! THIS MARRIAGE WILL NEVER TAKE PLACE! I KNOW WHAT IT'S ALL ABOUT: MOTHER CAN'T GET BY ON HER PENSION OF TEN THOUSAND ROUBLES A YEAR AND THE EXTRA MONEY SHE GETS FROM TAKING IN PIECE WORK. SO THEY'RE BOTH PUTTING THEIR HOPES ON THIS LUZHIN...
BUT WHAT ABOUT DUNYA? SHE'D EAT BLACK BREAD AND DRINK TAP WATER BEFORE SELLING HER SOUL. SHE'D NEVER TRADE HER FREEDOM FOR A COMFORTABLE MARRIAGE. WHY, THEN?
BECAUSE OF ME! I CAN GO BACK TO UNIVERSITY, BECOME A PARTNER IN THE BUSINESS, WITH MY FUTURE SECURE. MY MOTHER IS SACRIFICING MY SISTER FOR MY SAKE, HER FIRST BORN.

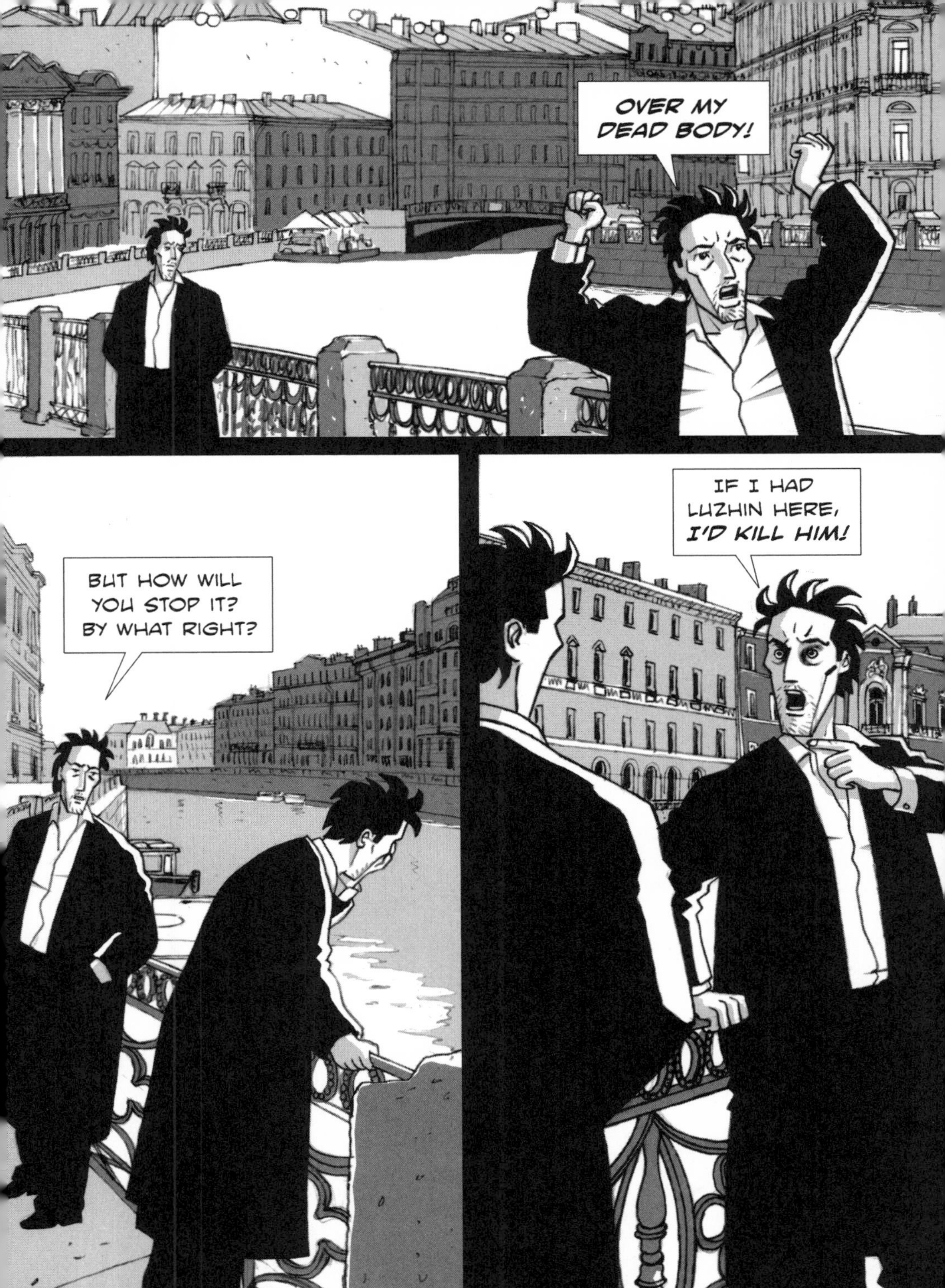
OVER MY DEAD BODY!
BUT HOW WILL YOU STOP IT? BY WHAT RIGHT?
IF I HAD LUZHIN HERE, I'D KILL HIM!

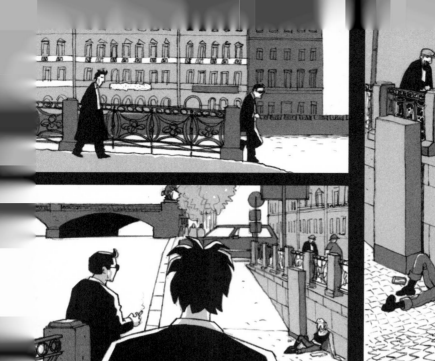

WHAT DO YOU WANT HERE?

WHAT'S IT TO YOU?

BEAT IT, PERVERT!

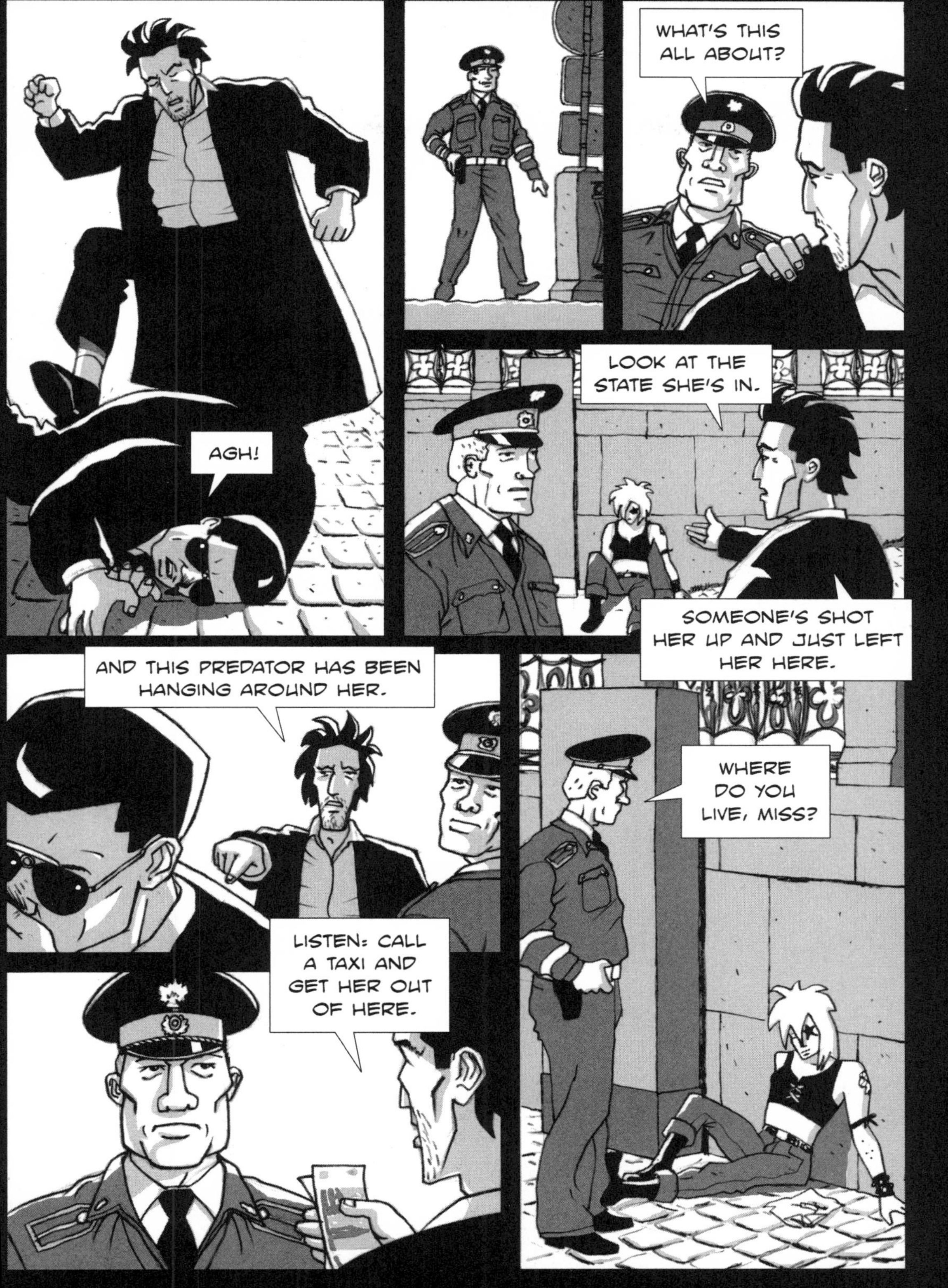
AGH!
WHAT'S THIS ALL ABOUT?
LOOK AT THE STATE SHE'S IN.
SOMEONE'S SHOT HER UP AND JUST LEFT HER HERE.
AND THIS PREDATOR HAS BEEN HANGING AROUND HER.
LISTEN: CALL A TAXI AND GET HER OUT OF HERE.
WHERE DO YOU LIVE, MISS?

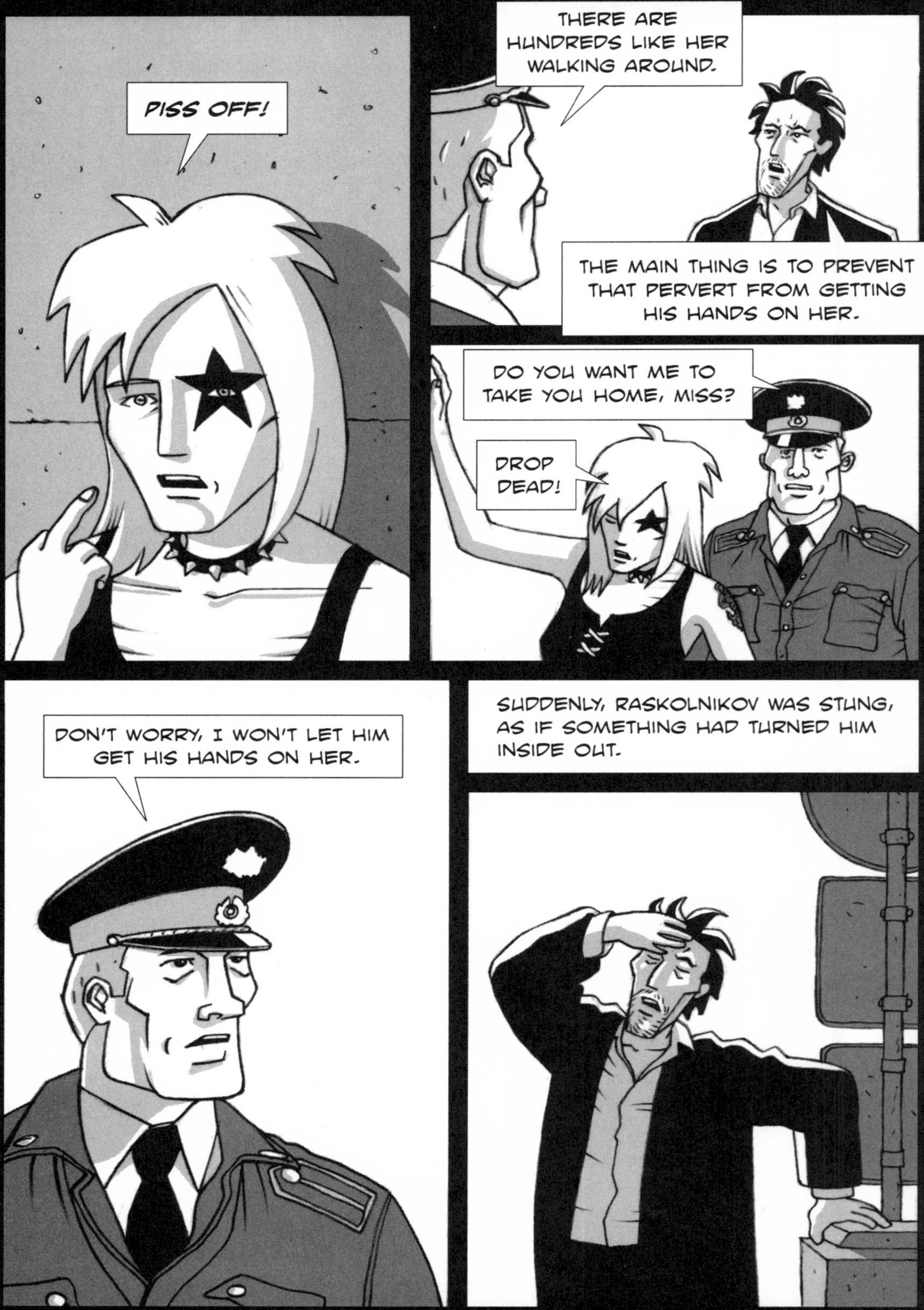
PISS OFF!
THERE ARE HUNDREDS LIKE HER WALKING AROUND.
THE MAIN THING IS TO PREVENT THAT PERVERT FROM GETTING HIS HANDS ON HER.
DO YOU WANT ME TO TAKE YOU HOME, MISS?
DROP DEAD!
DON'T WORRY, I WON'T LET HIM GET HIS HANDS ON HER.
SUDDENLY, RASKOLNIKOV WAS STUNG, AS IF SOMETHING HAD TURNED HIM INSIDE OUT.

FORGET IT! WHO CARES?
LEAVE THEM BE!
LET HIM HAVE FUN WITH HER.
WHAT'S IT TO YOU?

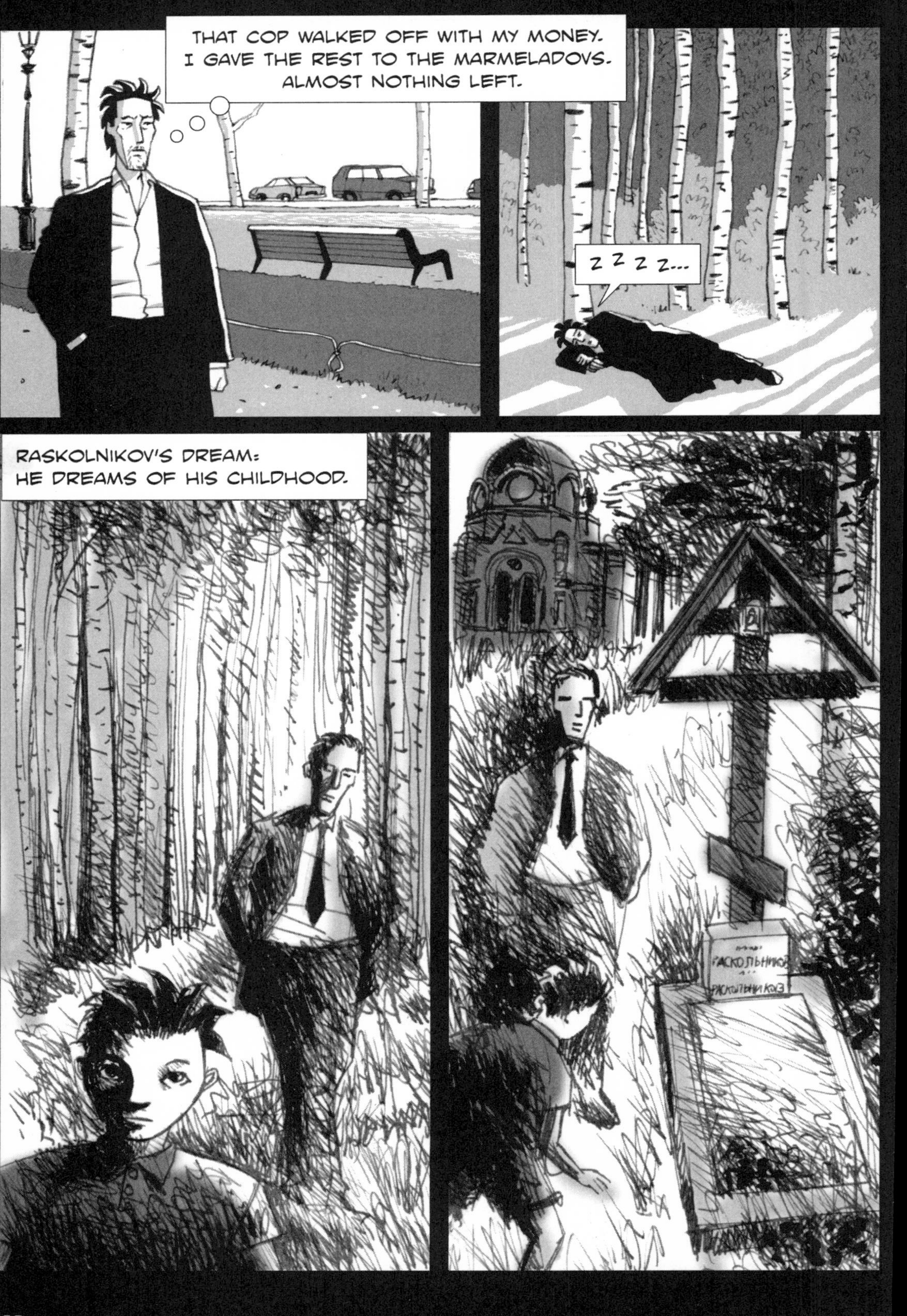
THAT COP WALKED OFF WITH MY MONEY. I GAVE THE REST TO THE MARMELADOVS. ALMOST NOTHING LEFT.
Z Z Z Z...
RASKOLNIKOV'S DREAM: HE DREAMS OF HIS CHILDHOOD.

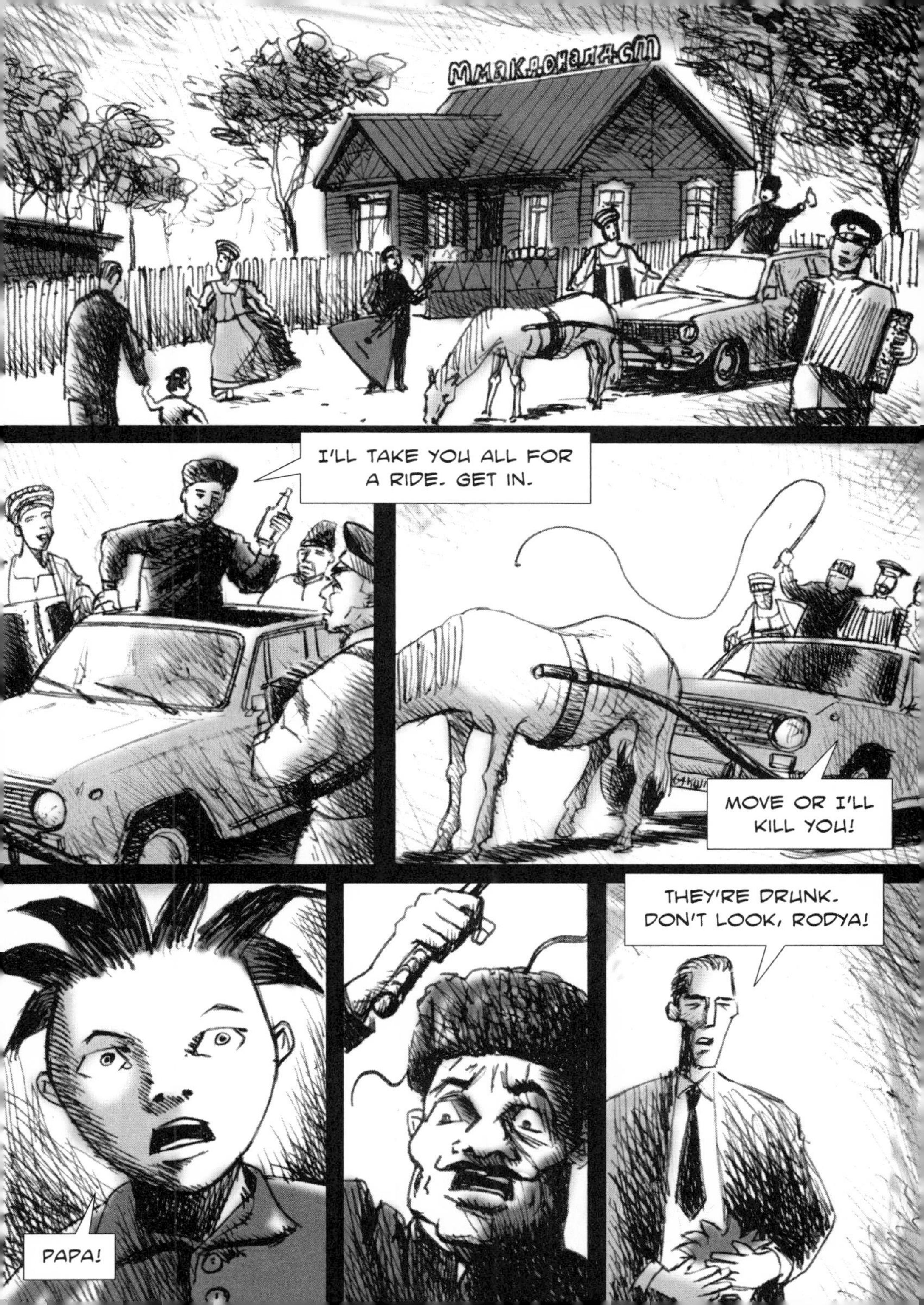
I'LL TAKE YOU ALL FOR A RIDE. GET IN.
MOVE OR I'LL KILL YOU!
PAPA!
THEY'RE DRUNK. DON'T LOOK, RODYA!

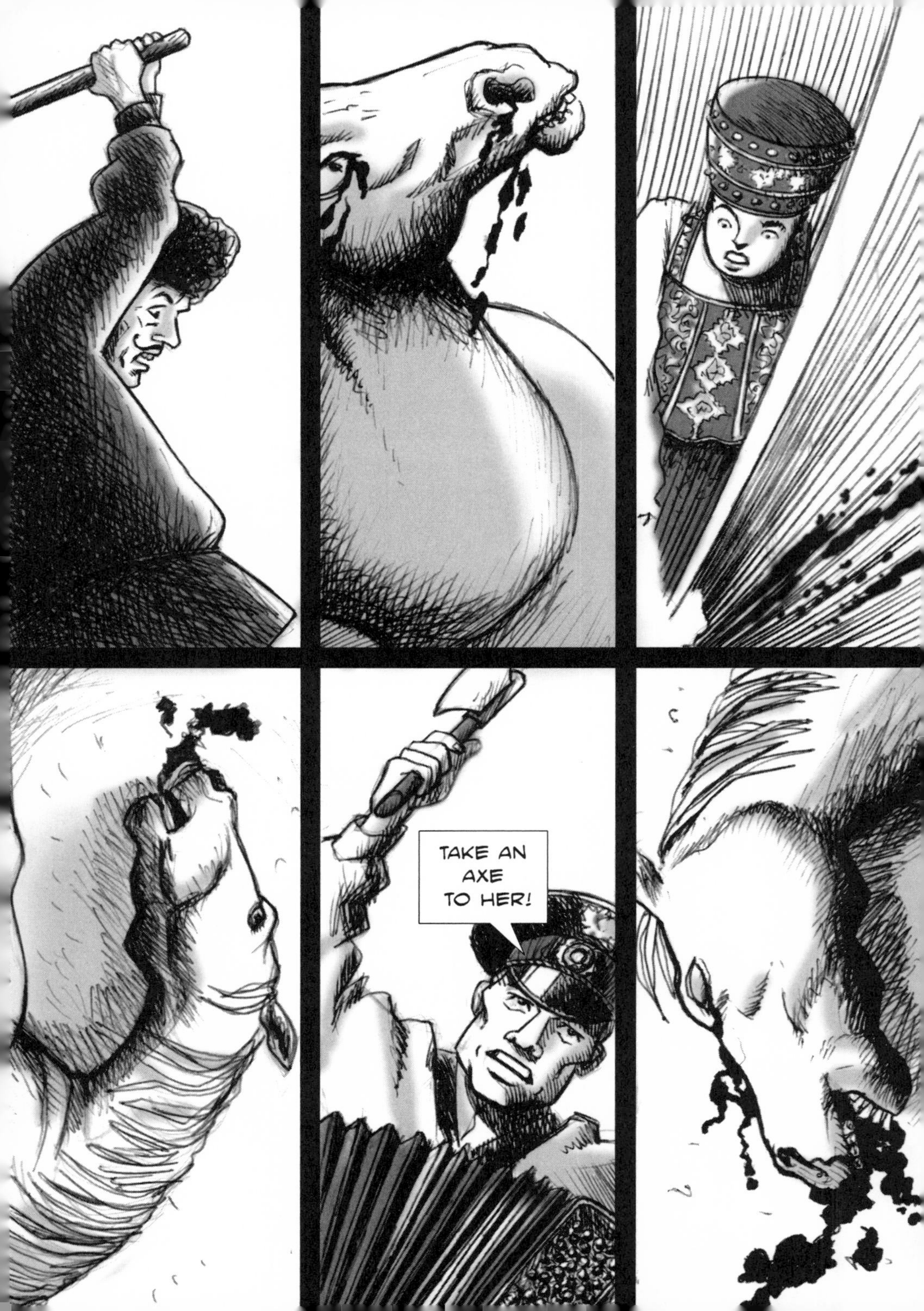
TAKE AN AXE TO HER!

CAN I REALLY DO IT? SMASH HER SKULL WITH AN AXE, WATCH THE BLOOD RUSH OUT OF HER, STEAL HER MONEY?

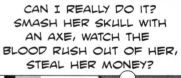

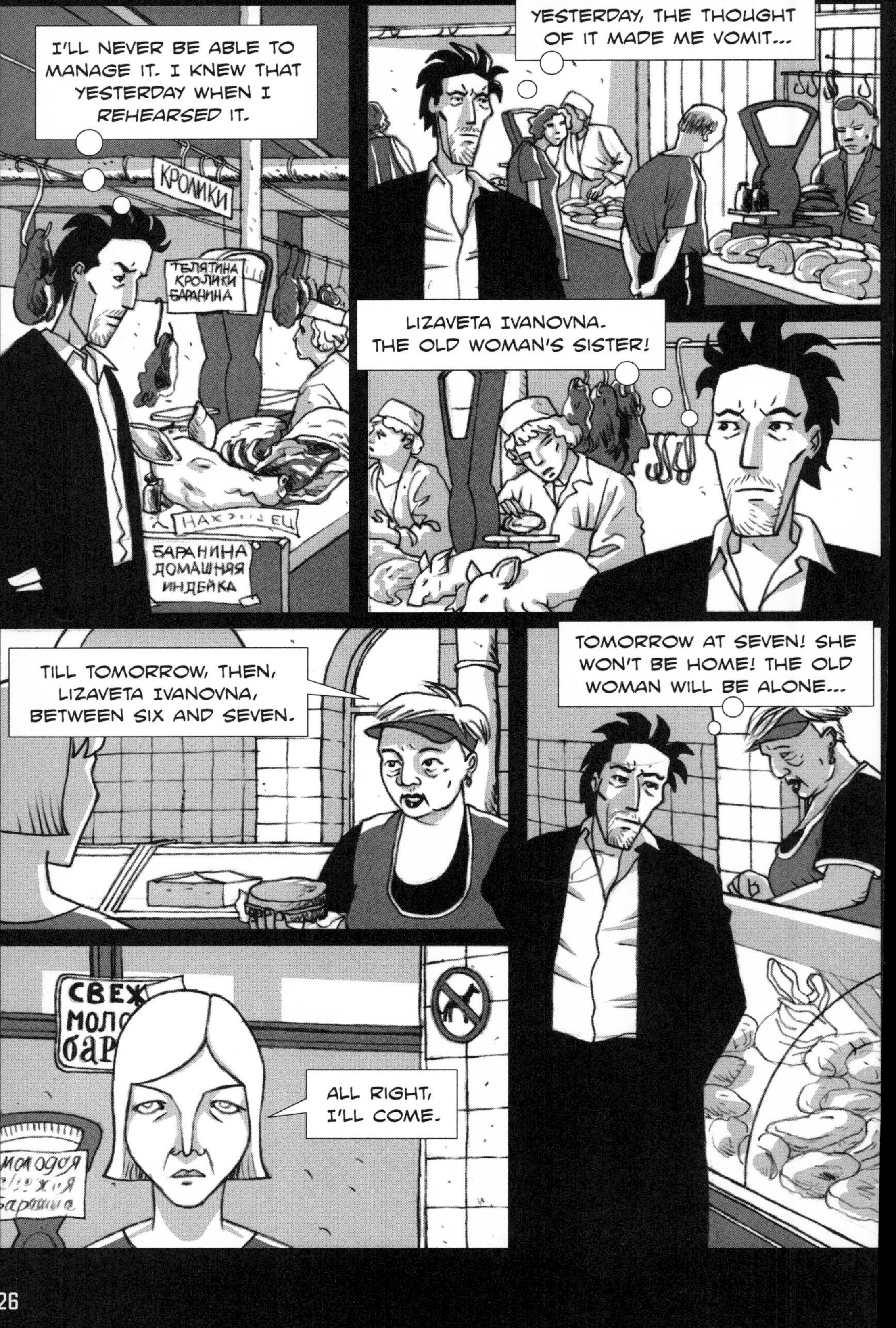

I'LL NEVER BE ABLE TO MANAGE IT. I KNEW THAT YESTERDAY WHEN I REHEARSED IT.
КРОЛИКИ
ТЕЛЯТИНА КРОЛИКИ БАРАНИНА
БАРАНИНА ДОМАШНЯЯ ИНДЕЙКА
YESTERDAY, THE THOUGHT OF IT MADE ME VOMIT...
LIZAVETA IVANOVNA. THE OLD WOMAN'S SISTER!
TILL TOMORROW, THEN, LIZAVETA IVANOVNA, BETWEEN SIX AND SEVEN.
TOMORROW AT SEVEN! SHE WON'T BE HOME! THE OLD WOMAN WILL BE ALONE...
ALL RIGHT, I'LL COME.

LIZAVETA WAS ALYONA IVANOVNA'S HALF-SISTER, AND WAS TOTALLY UNDER HER THUMB. EVERY KOPECK SHE EARNED WENT TO THE OLD WOMAN, WHO GAVE HER NOTHING IN RETURN AND EVEN EXCLUDED HER FROM HER WILL.

LIZAVETA WAS UNMARRIED, AWKWARD, AND UNUSUALLY TALL, AND HAD THE DISTINCTION OF BEING CONSTANTLY PREGNANT...

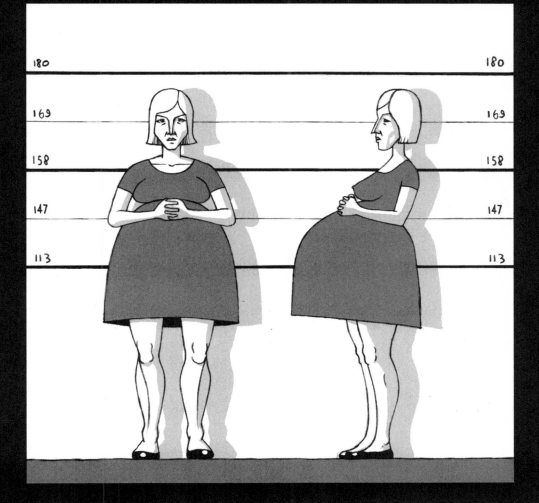

AS FOR THE OLD WOMAN HERSELF, RASKOLNIKOV WAS FILLED WITH EXTREME LOATHING FROM THE FIRST MOMENT HE SET EYES ON HER.

ONE COULD WELL IMAGINE ELIMINATING HER FROM THIS WORLD, TAKING HER MONEY AND USING IT TO SAVE NEEDY PEOPLE FROM POVERTY AND DEPRAVITY. WOULDN'T THOUSANDS OF GOOD WORKS MAKE UP FOR ONE LITTLE CRIME?

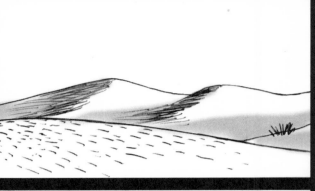

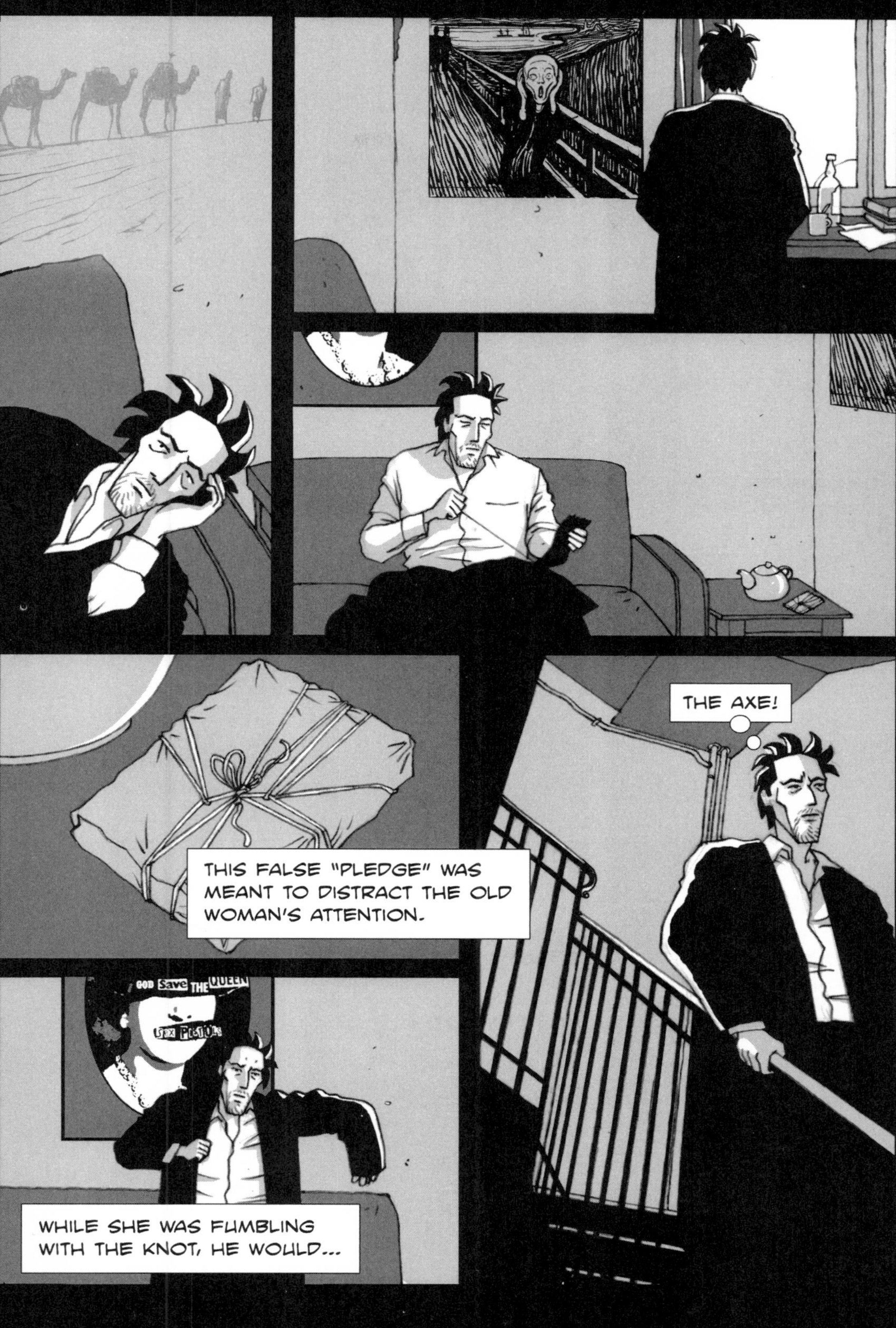
THIS FALSE "PLEDGE" WAS MEANT TO DISTRACT THE OLD WOMAN'S ATTENTION.
GOD Save THE QUEEN
SEX PISTOLS
WHILE SHE WAS FUMBLING WITH THE KNOT, HE WOULD...
THE AXE!

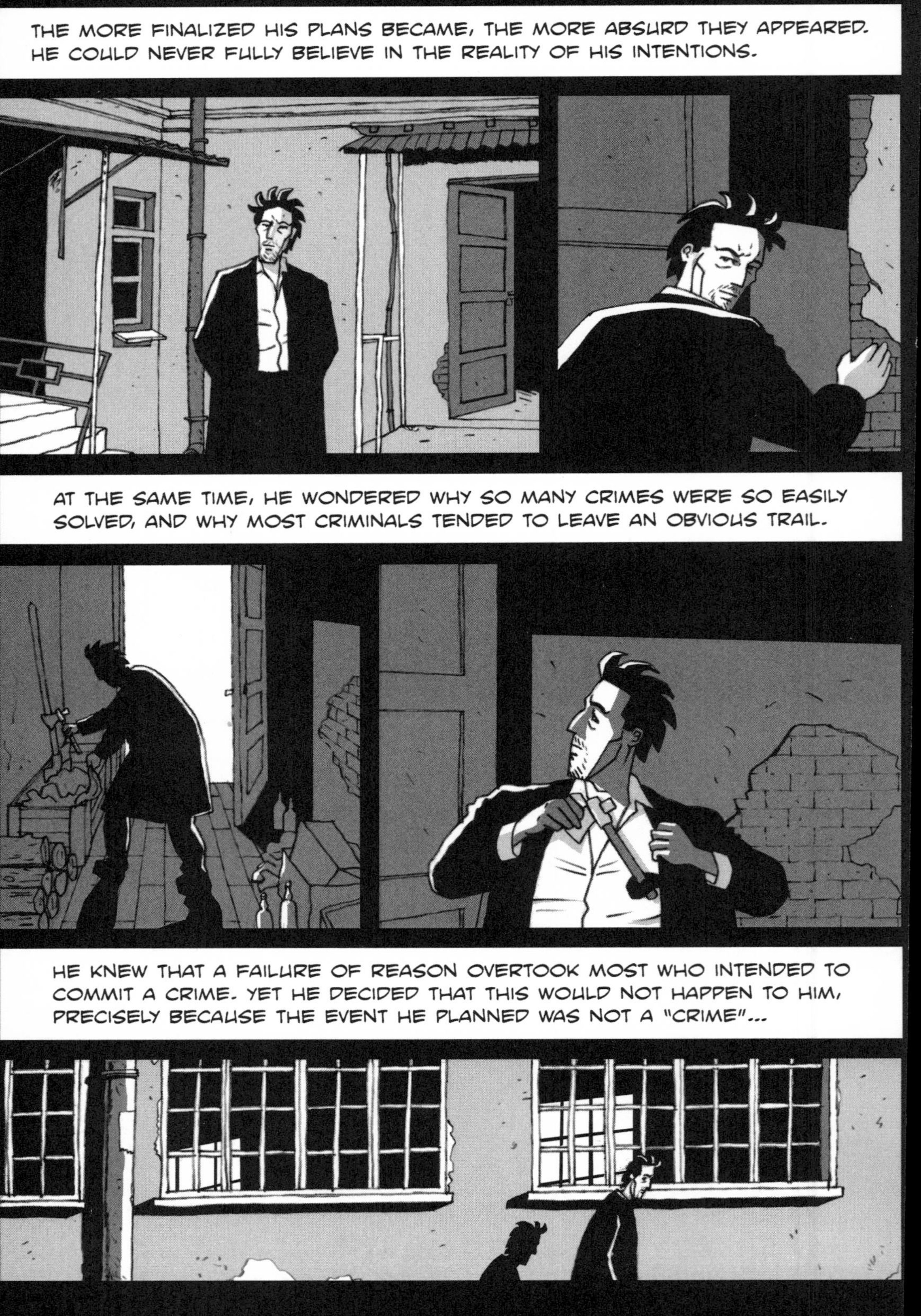
THE MORE FINALIZED HIS PLANS BECAME, THE MORE ABSURD THEY APPEARED. HE COULD NEVER FULLY BELIEVE IN THE REALITY OF HIS INTENTIONS.
AT THE SAME TIME, HE WONDERED WHY SO MANY CRIMES WERE SO EASILY SOLVED, AND WHY MOST CRIMINALS TENDED TO LEAVE AN OBVIOUS TRAIL.
HE KNEW THAT A FAILURE OF REASON OVERTOOK MOST WHO INTENDED TO COMMIT A CRIME. YET HE DECIDED THAT THIS WOULD NOT HAPPEN TO HIM, PRECISELY BECAUSE THE EVENT HE PLANNED WAS NOT A "CRIME"...

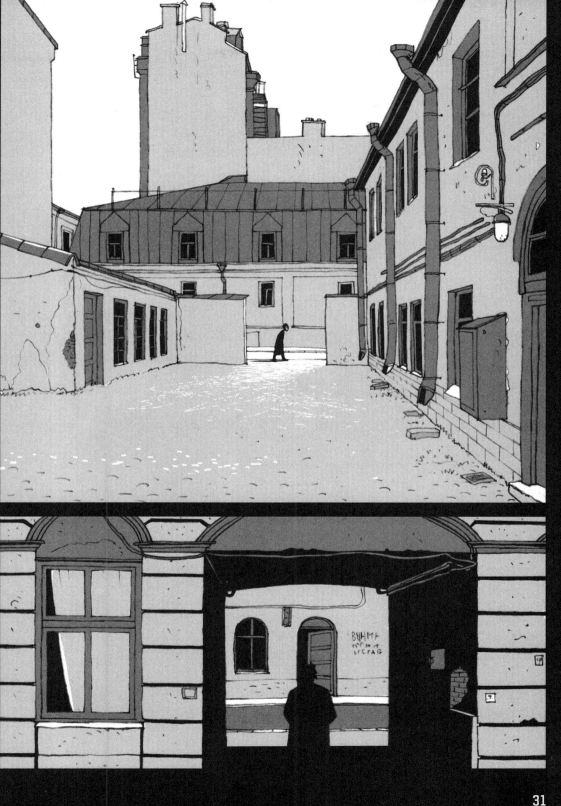

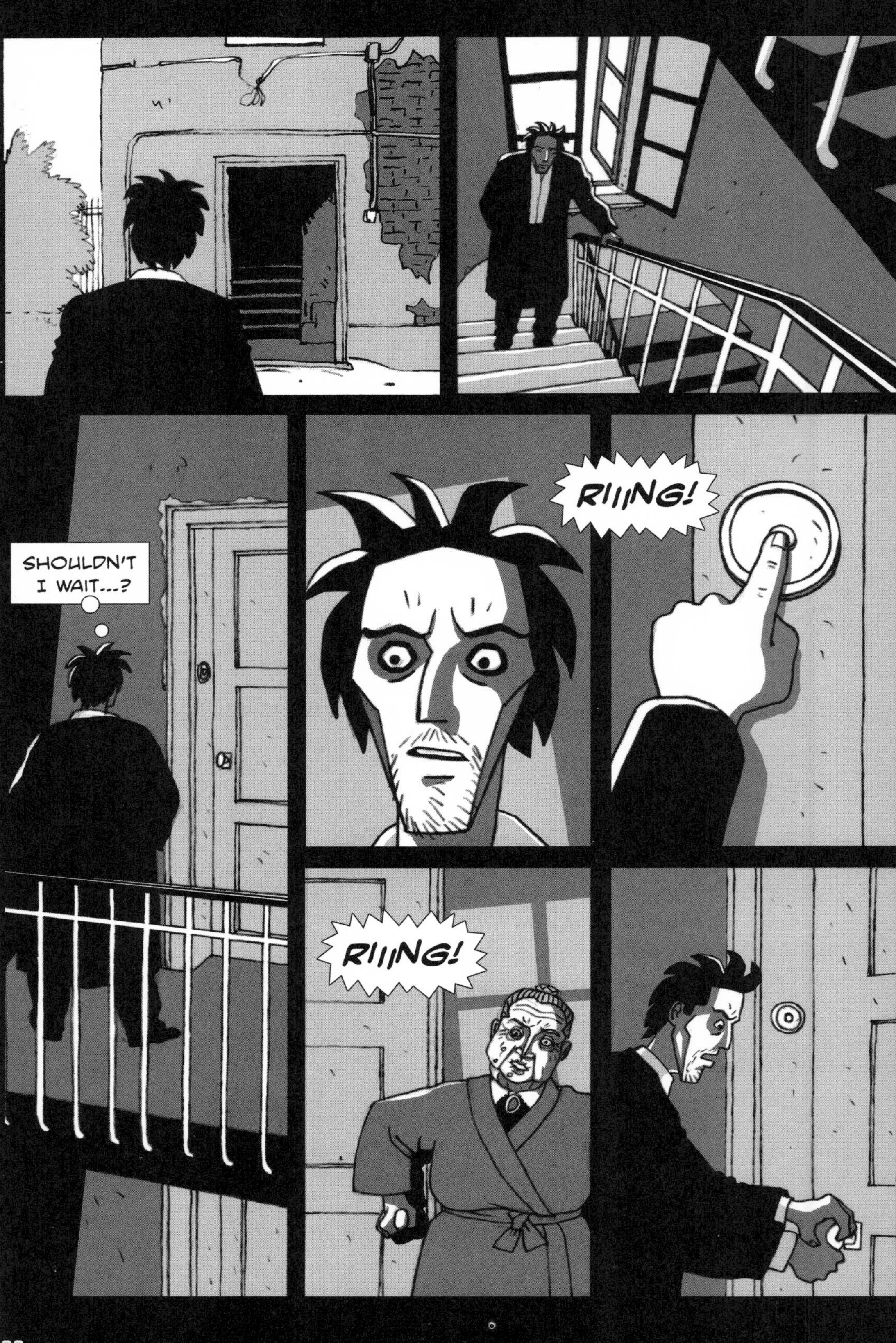
SHOULDN'T I WAIT...?
RIIING!
RIIING!

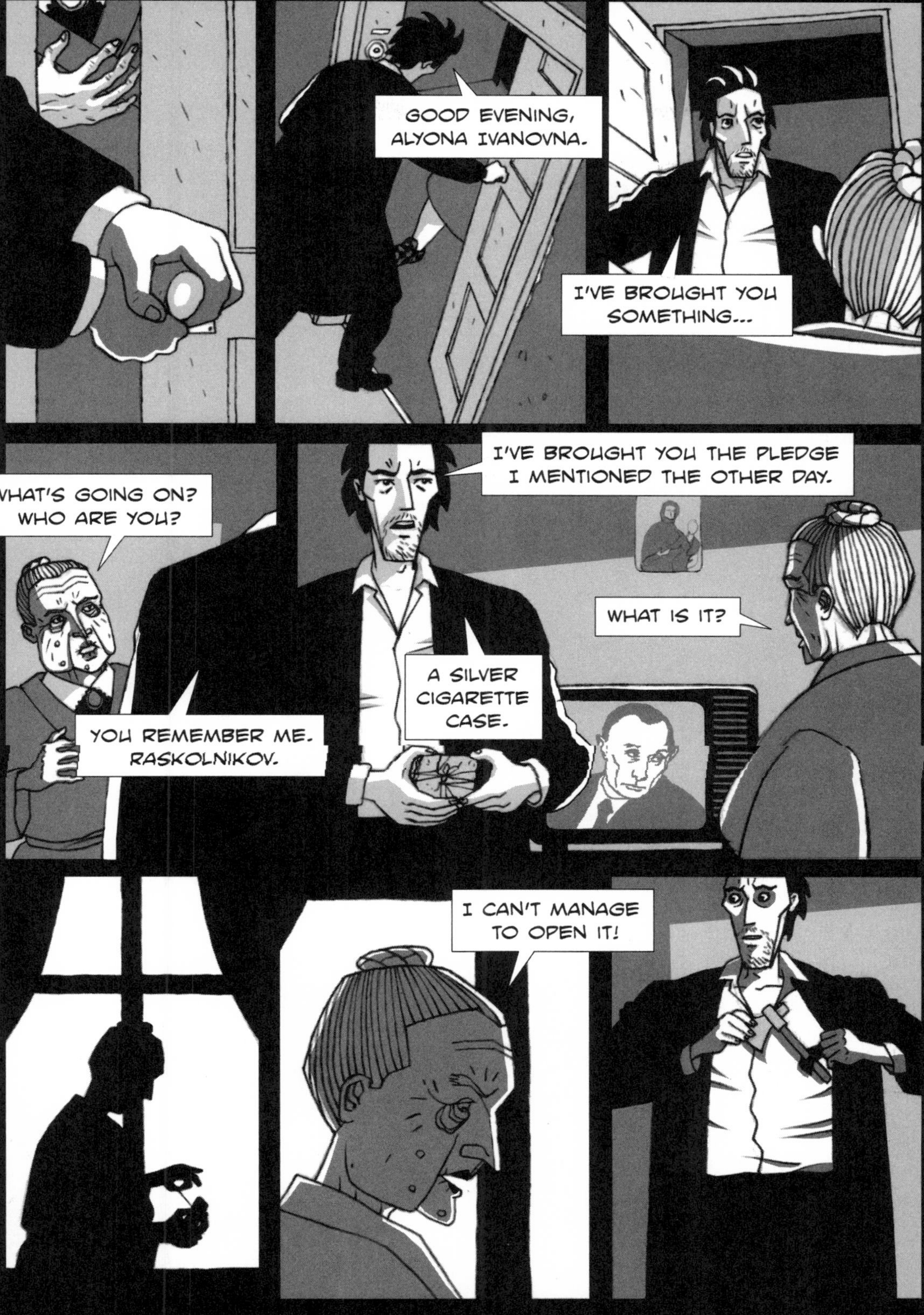
GOOD EVENING, ALYONA IVANOVNA.
I'VE BROUGHT YOU SOMETHING...
WHAT'S GOING ON? WHO ARE YOU?
I'VE BROUGHT YOU THE PLEDGE I MENTIONED THE OTHER DAY.
WHAT IS IT?
A SILVER CIGARETTE CASE.
YOU REMEMBER ME. RASKOLNIKOV.
I CAN'T MANAGE TO OPEN IT!

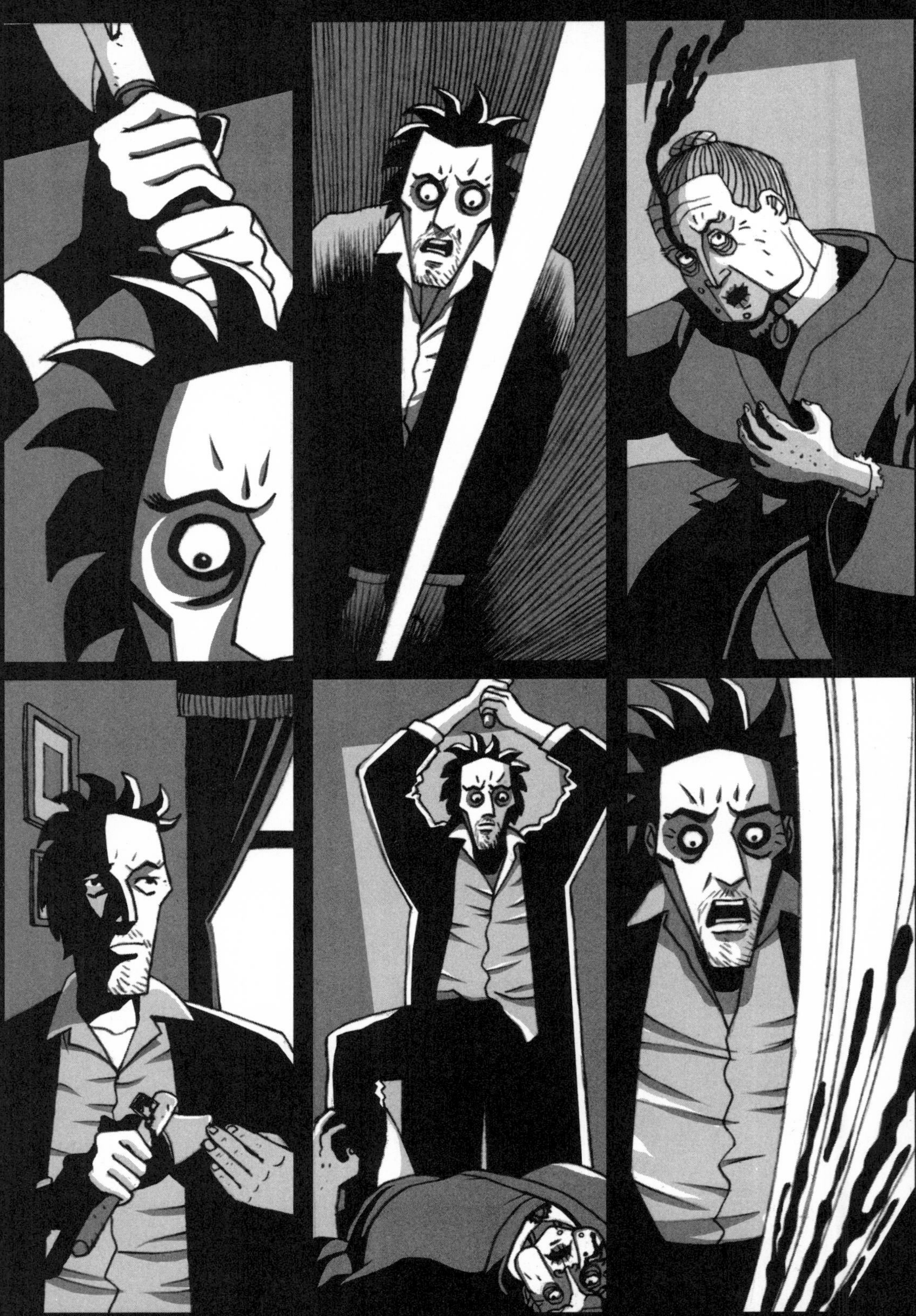

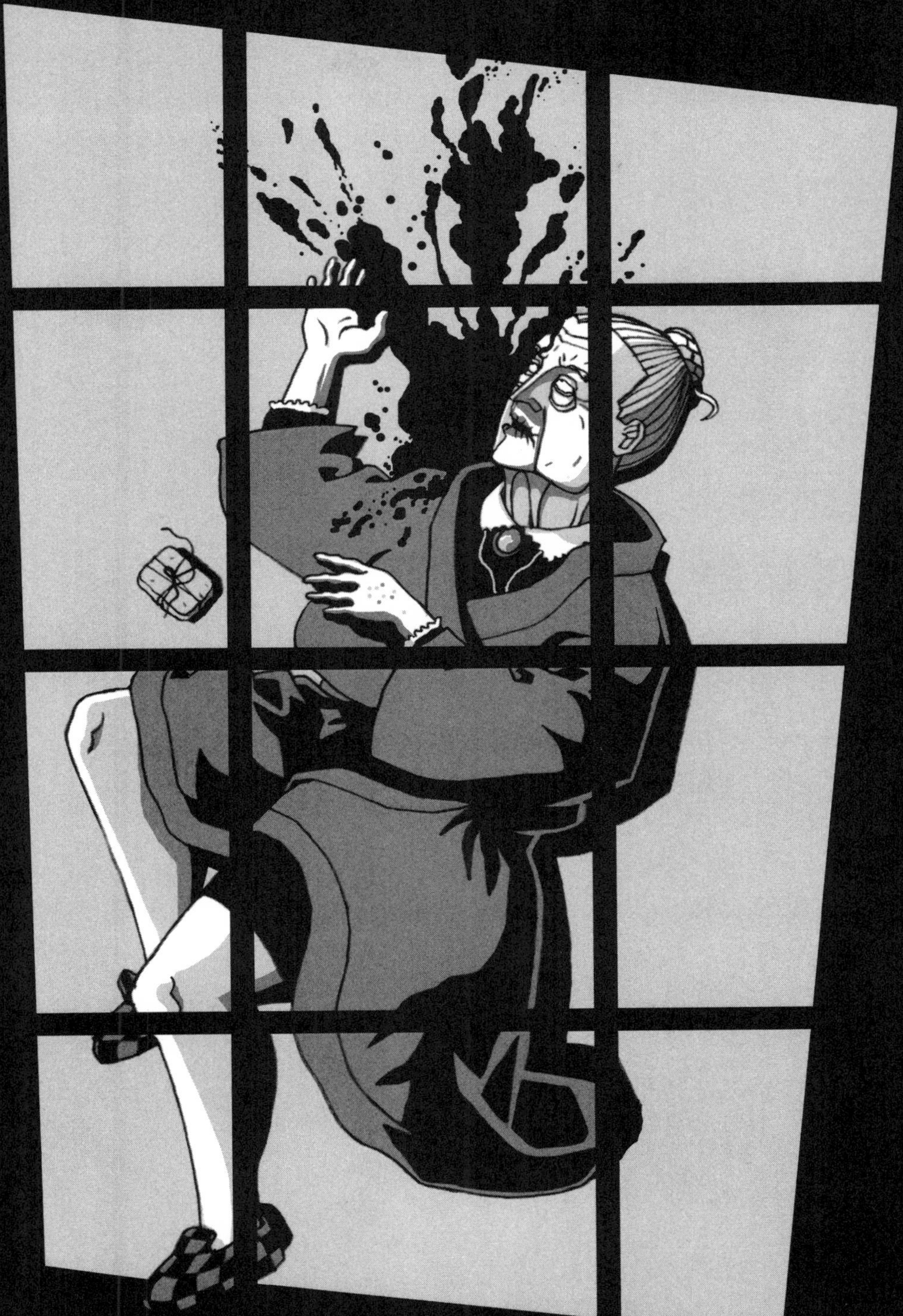

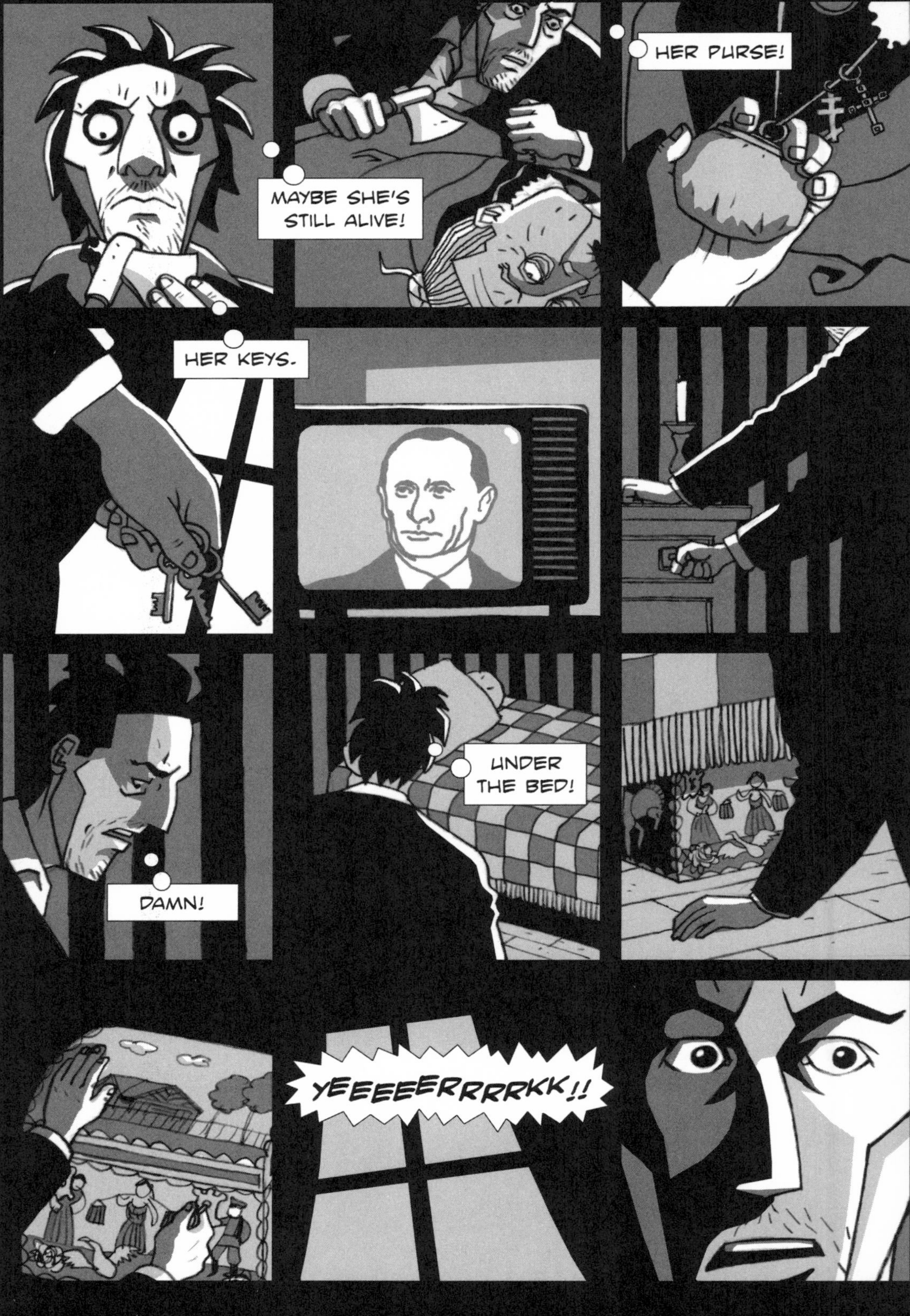
MAYBE SHE'S STILL ALIVE!
HER PURSE!
HER KEYS.
DAMN!
UNDER THE BED!
YEEEEEERRRRKK!!

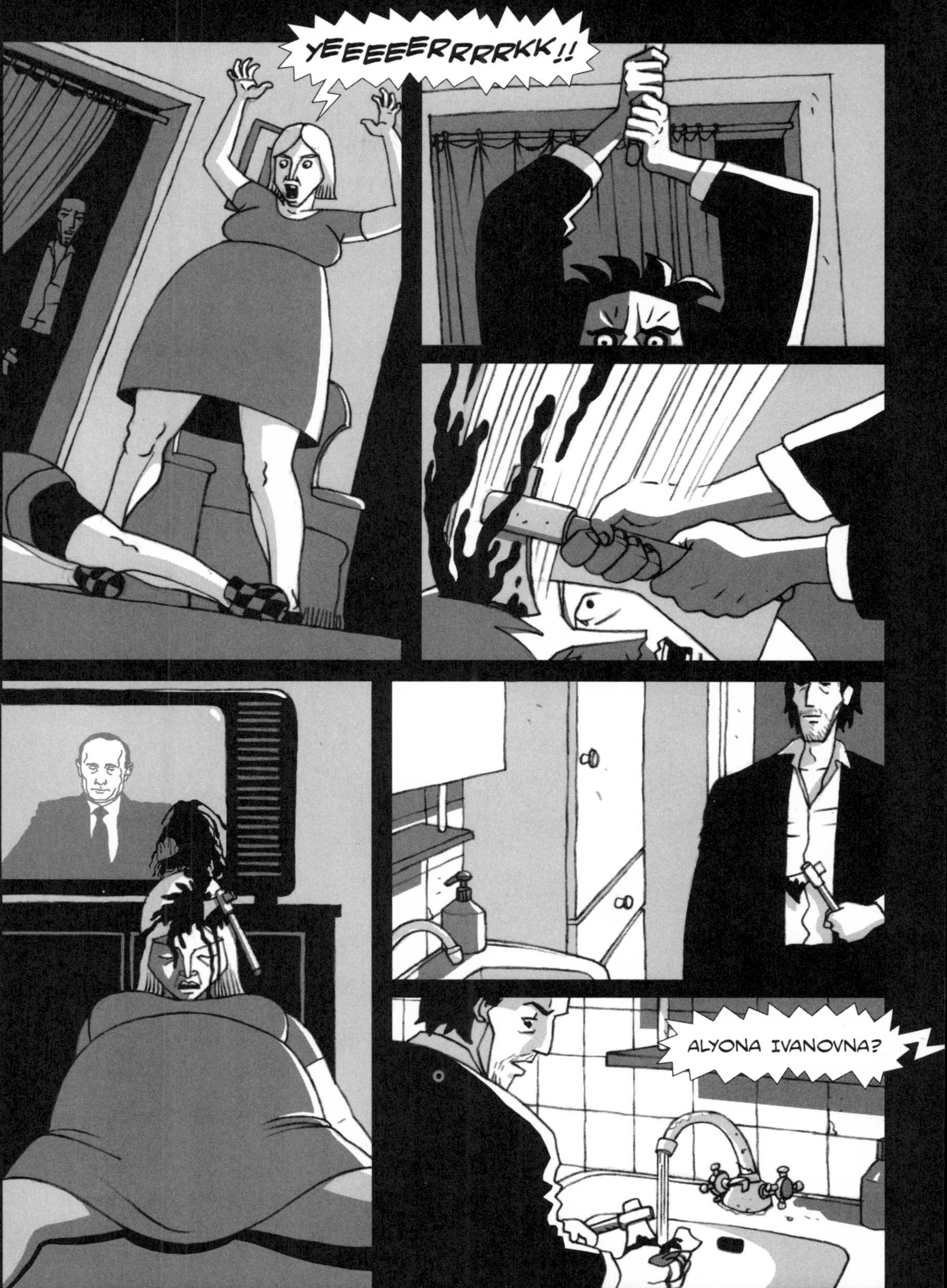
YEEEEERRRRKK!!
ALYONA IVANOVNA?

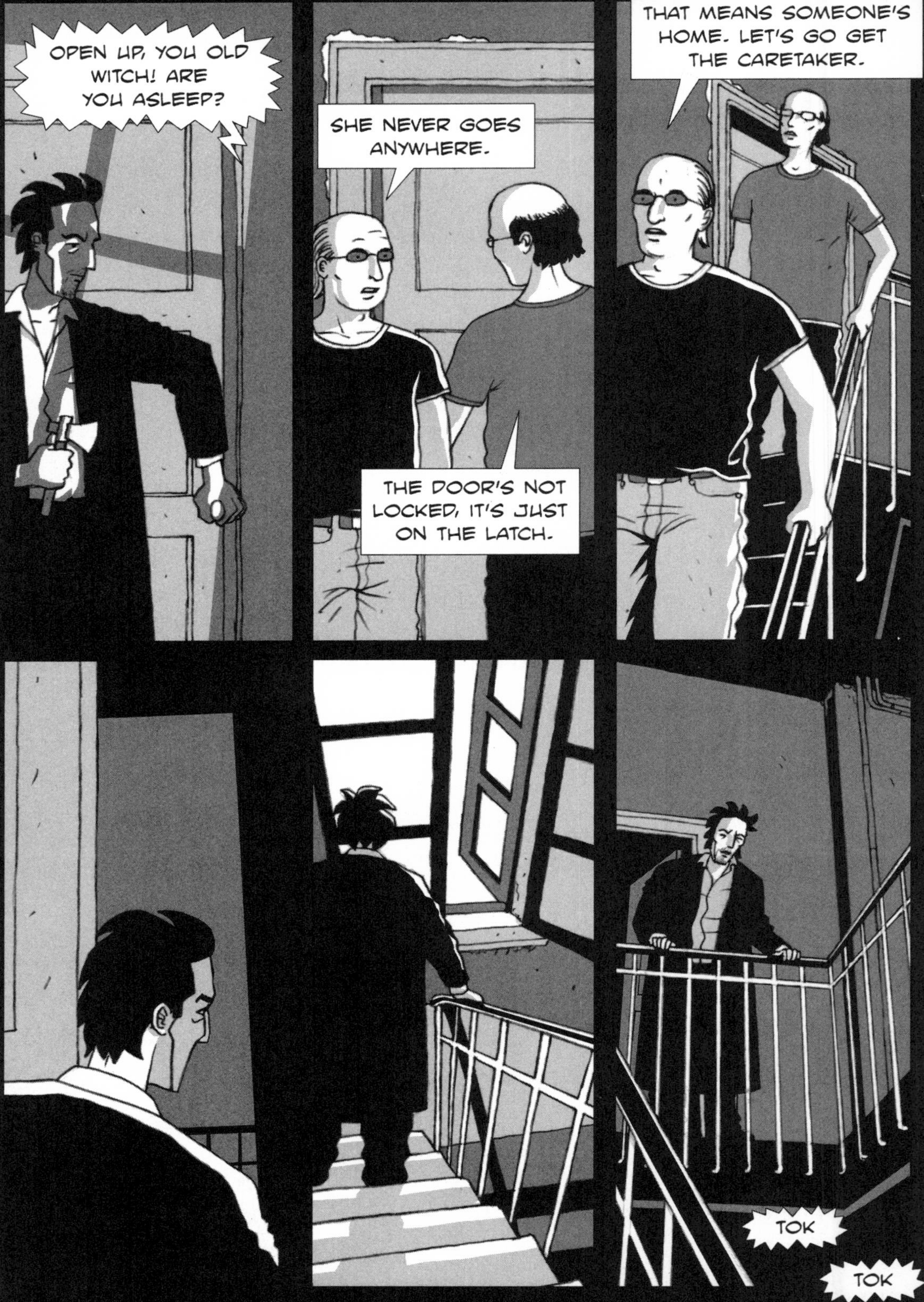
OPEN UP, YOU OLD WITCH! ARE YOU ASLEEP?
SHE NEVER GOES ANYWHERE.
THE DOOR'S NOT LOCKED, IT'S JUST ON THE LATCH.
THAT MEANS SOMEONE'S HOME. LET'S GO GET THE CARETAKER.
TOK
TOK

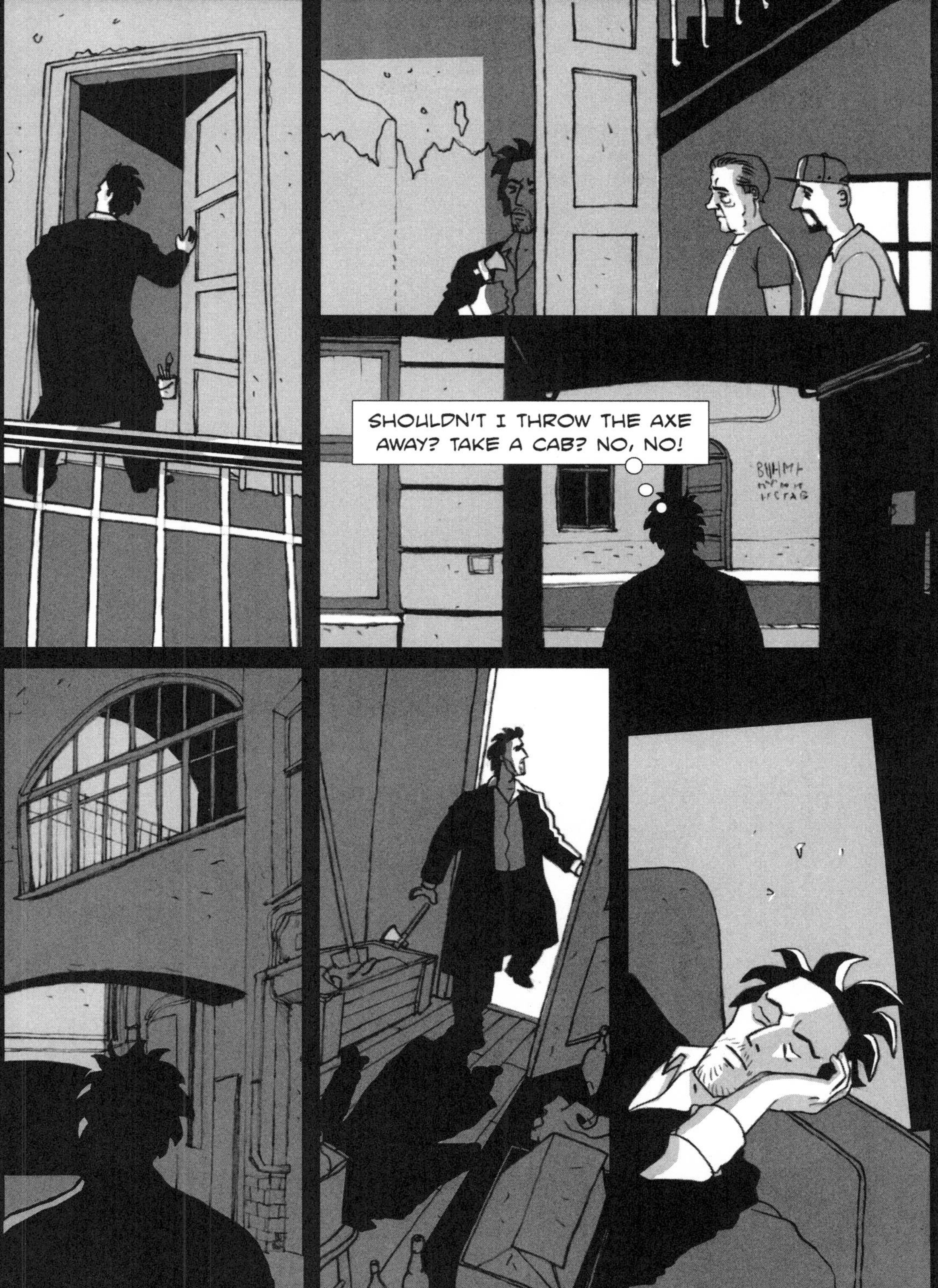
SHOULDN'T I THROW THE AXE AWAY? TAKE A CAB? NO, NO!

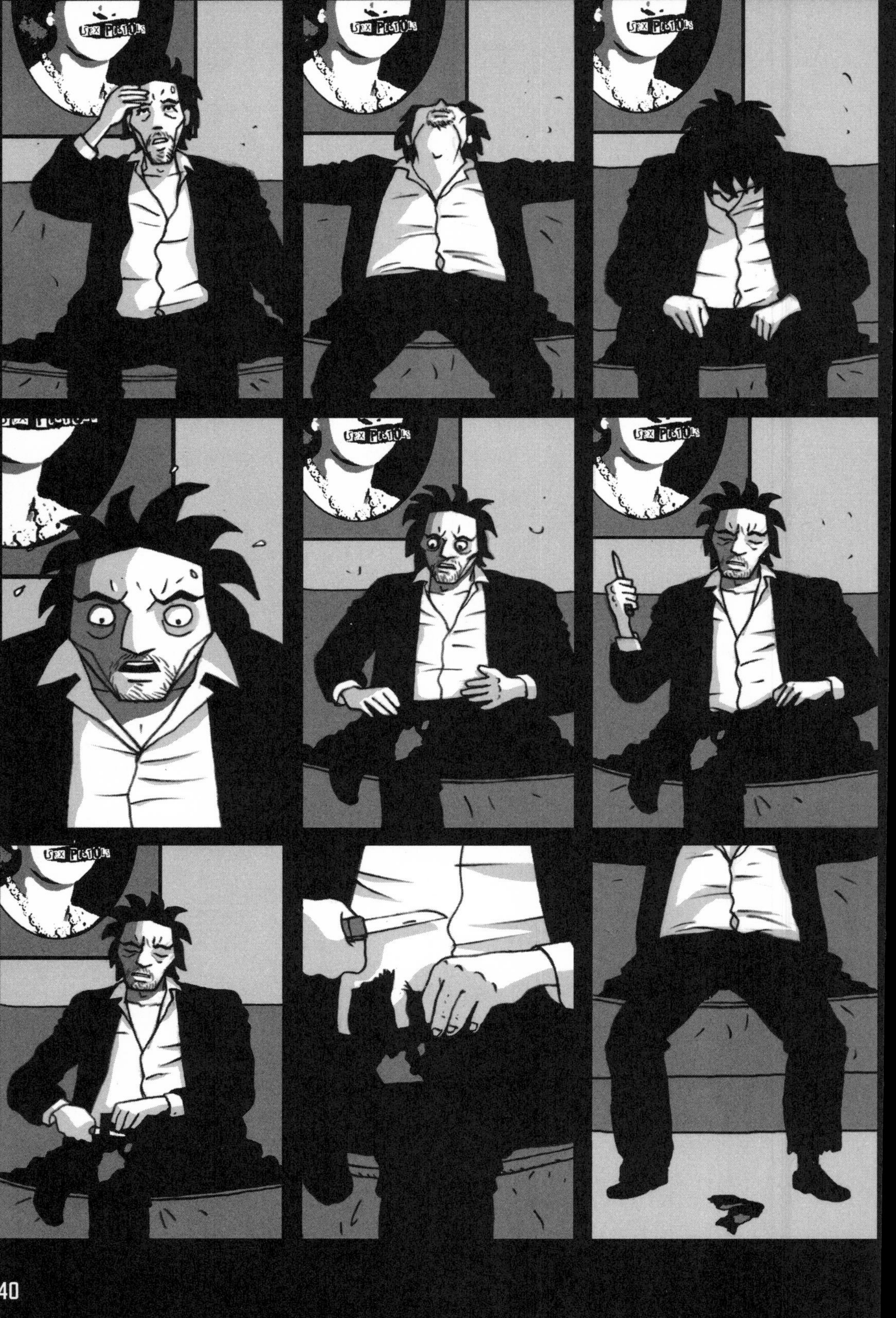
SEX PISTOLS

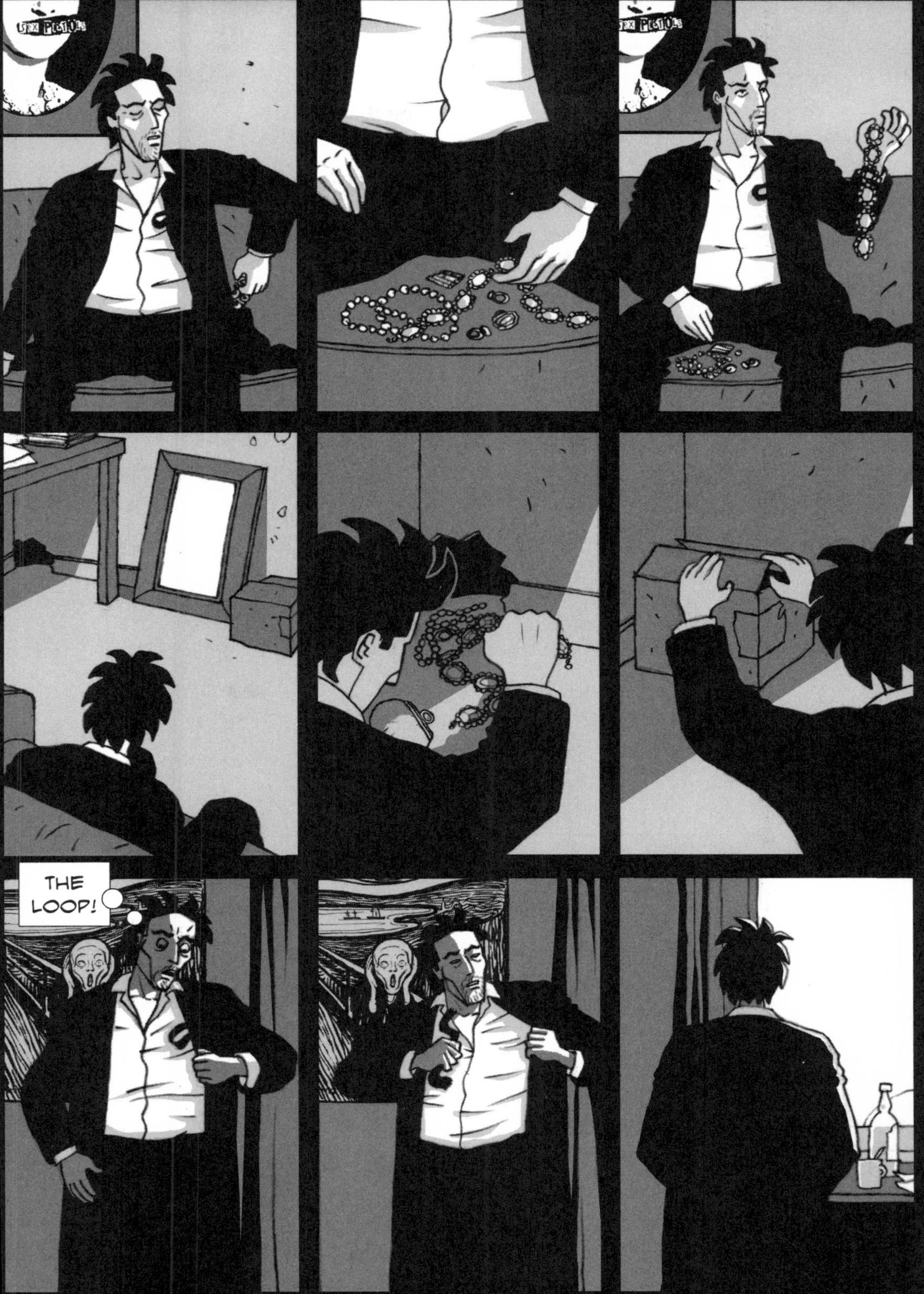
SEX PISTOLS
SEX PISTOLS
THE LOOP!

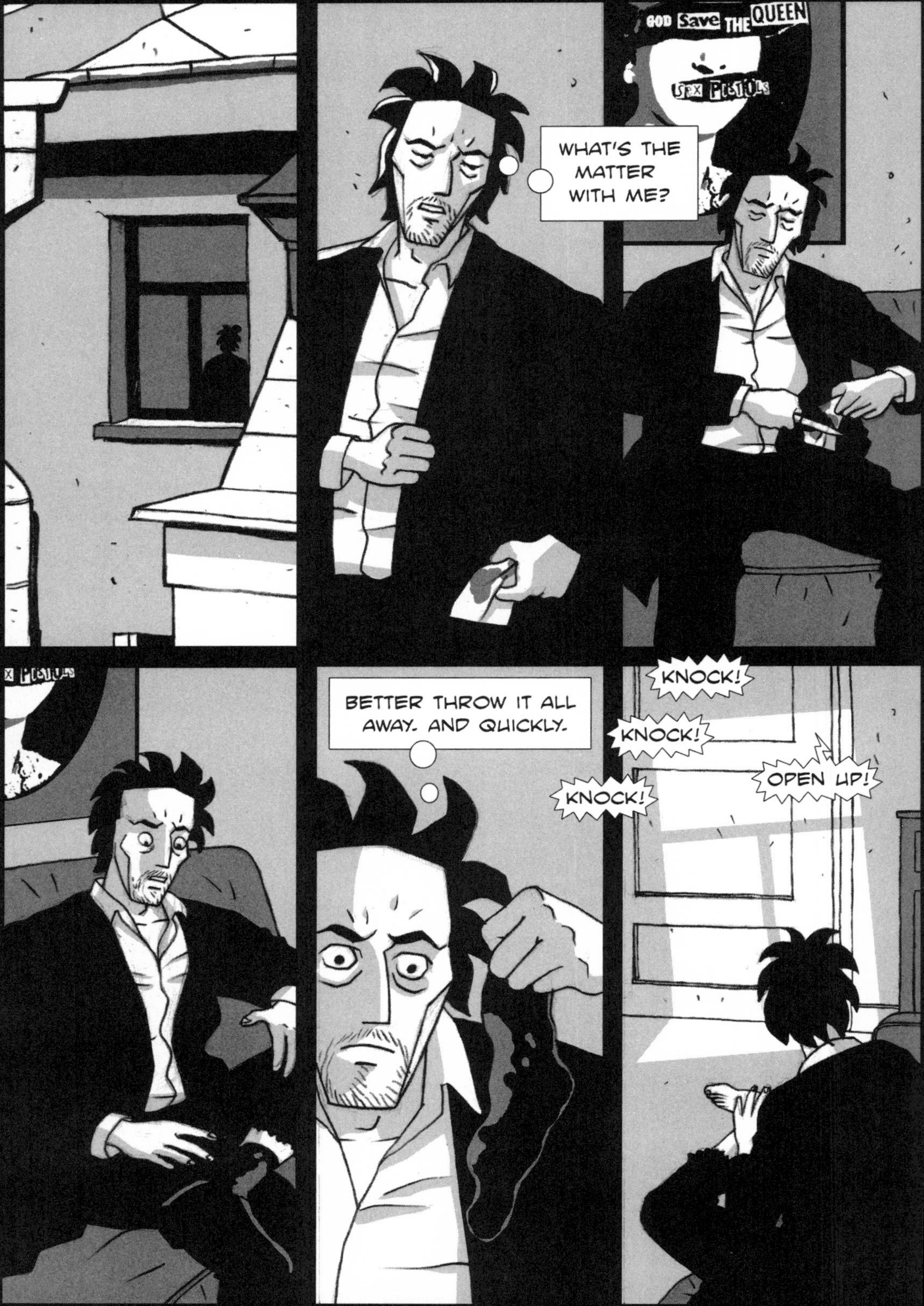
GOD Save THE QUEEN
SEX PISTOLS
WHAT'S THE MATTER WITH ME?
BETTER THROW IT ALL AWAY. AND QUICKLY.
KNOCK!
KNOCK!
KNOCK!
OPEN UP!

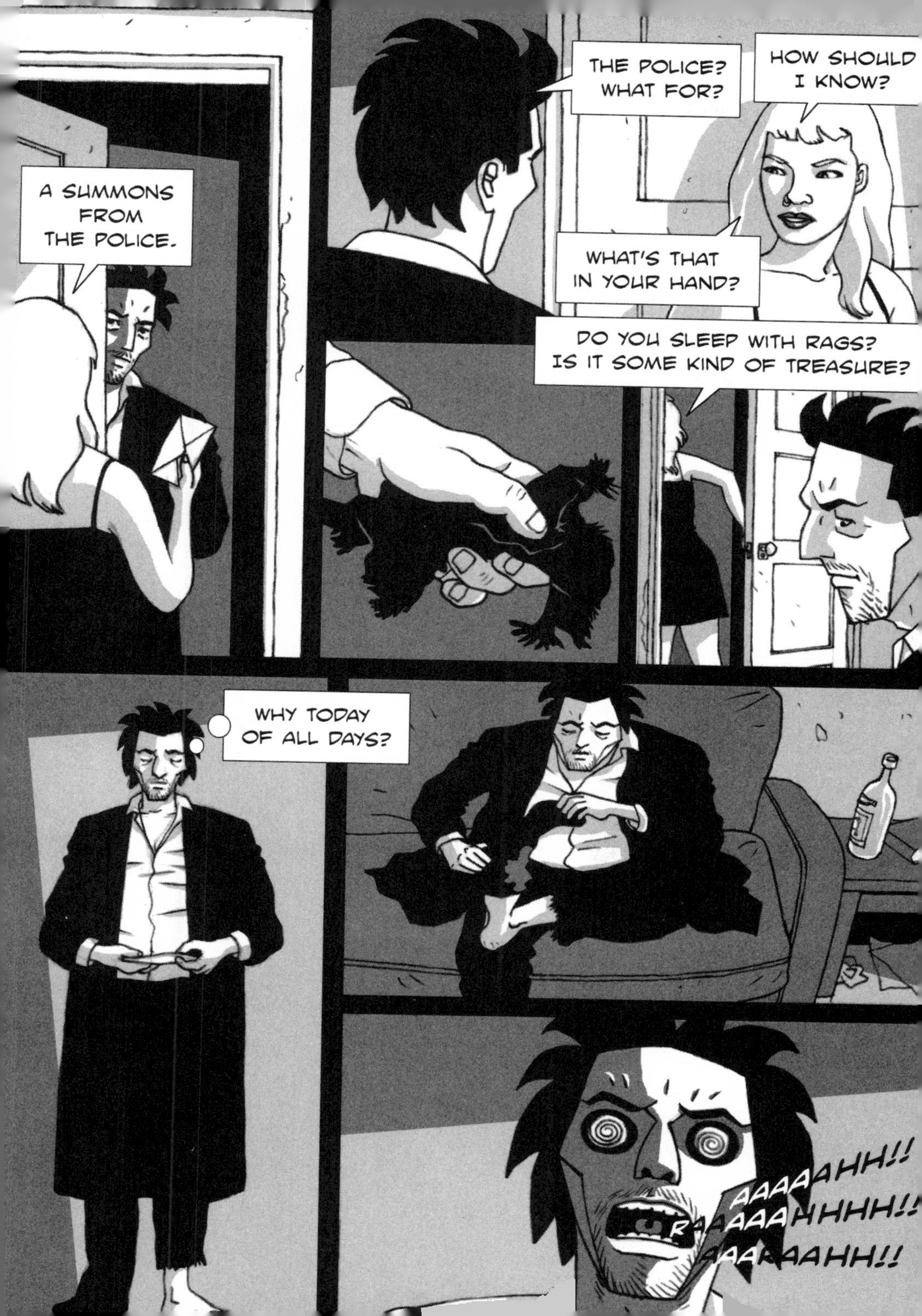
A SUMMONS FROM THE POLICE.
THE POLICE? WHAT FOR?
HOW SHOULD I KNOW?
WHAT'S THAT IN YOUR HAND?
DO YOU SLEEP WITH RAGS? IS IT SOME KIND OF TREASURE?
WHY TODAY OF ALL DAYS?
AAAAAHH!!
RAAAAAHHHH!!
AAAAAAHH!!

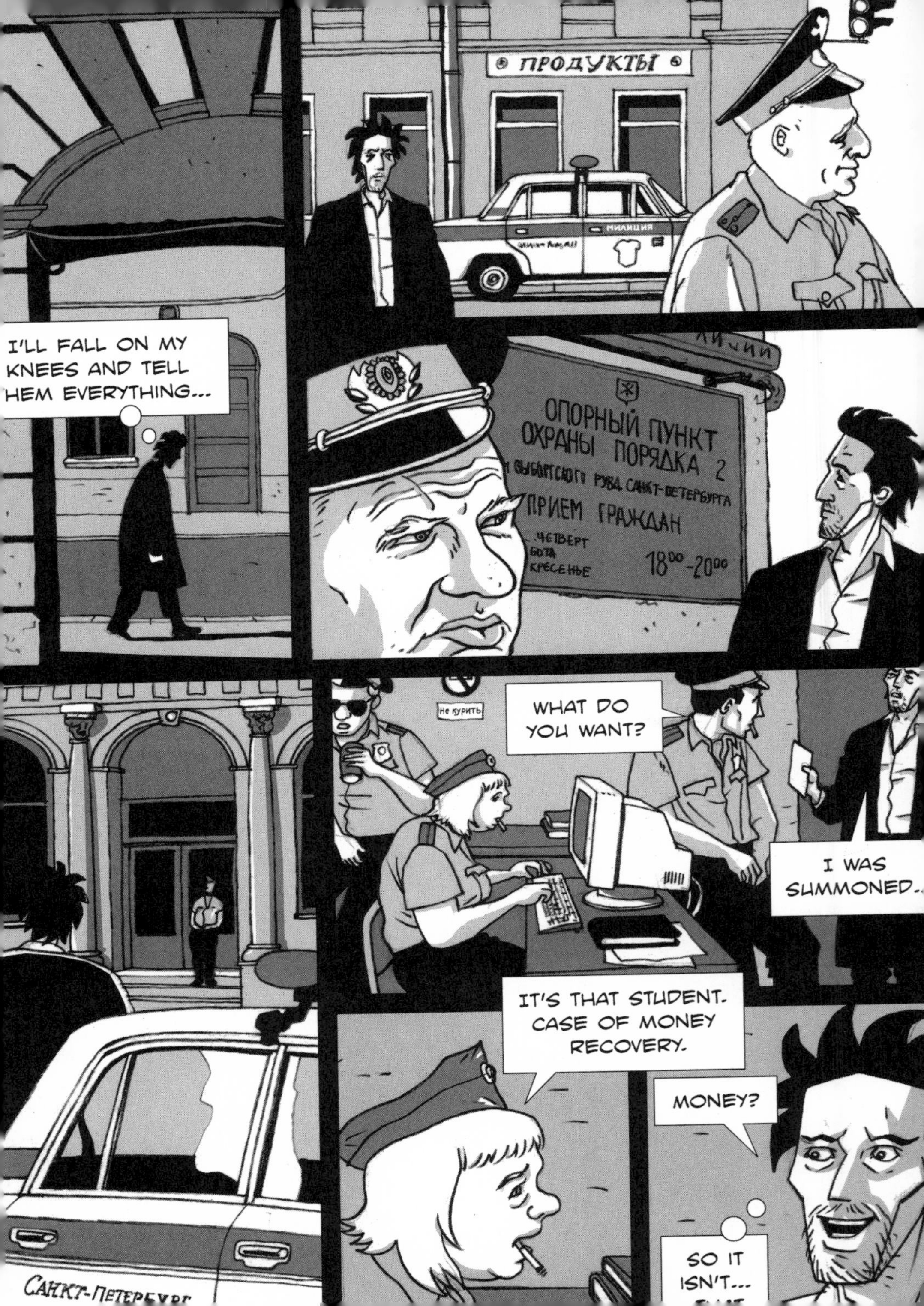
ПРОДУКТЫ
МИЛИЦИЯ
I'LL FALL ON MY KNEES AND TELL HEM EVERYTHING...
ОПОРНЫЙ ПУНКТ
ОХРАНЫ ПОРЯДКА 2
ПРИЕМ ГРАЖДАН
18⁰⁰-20⁰⁰
Не курить
WHAT DO YOU WANT?
I WAS SUMMONED...
IT'S THAT STUDENT. CASE OF MONEY RECOVERY.
MONEY?
SO IT ISN'T...

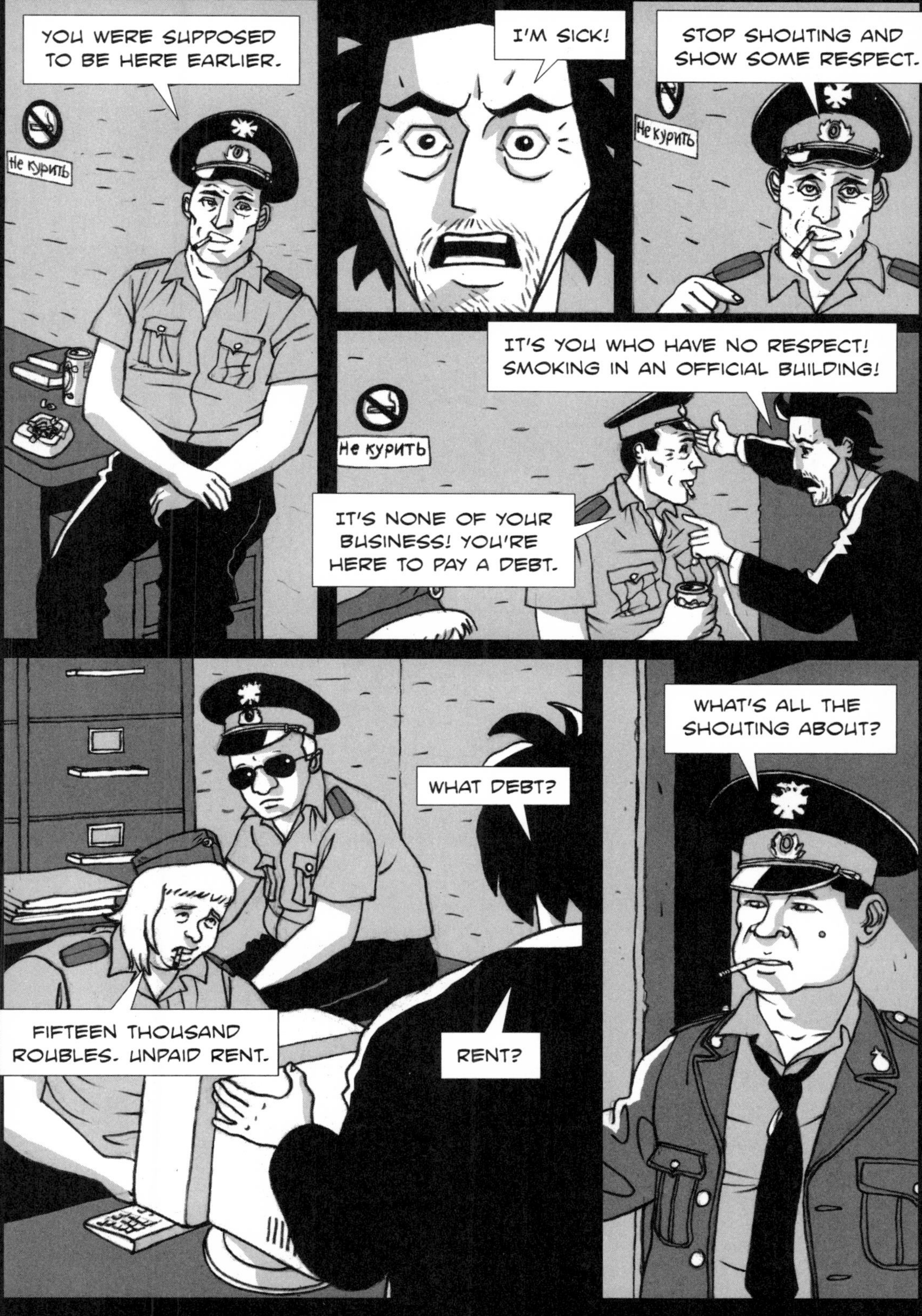
YOU WERE SUPPOSED TO BE HERE EARLIER.
Не курить
I'M SICK!
STOP SHOUTING AND SHOW SOME RESPECT.
Не курить
IT'S YOU WHO HAVE NO RESPECT! SMOKING IN AN OFFICIAL BUILDING!
Не курить
IT'S NONE OF YOUR BUSINESS! YOU'RE HERE TO PAY A DEBT.
WHAT DEBT?
FIFTEEN THOUSAND ROUBLES. UNPAID RENT.
RENT?
WHAT'S ALL THE SHOUTING ABOUT?

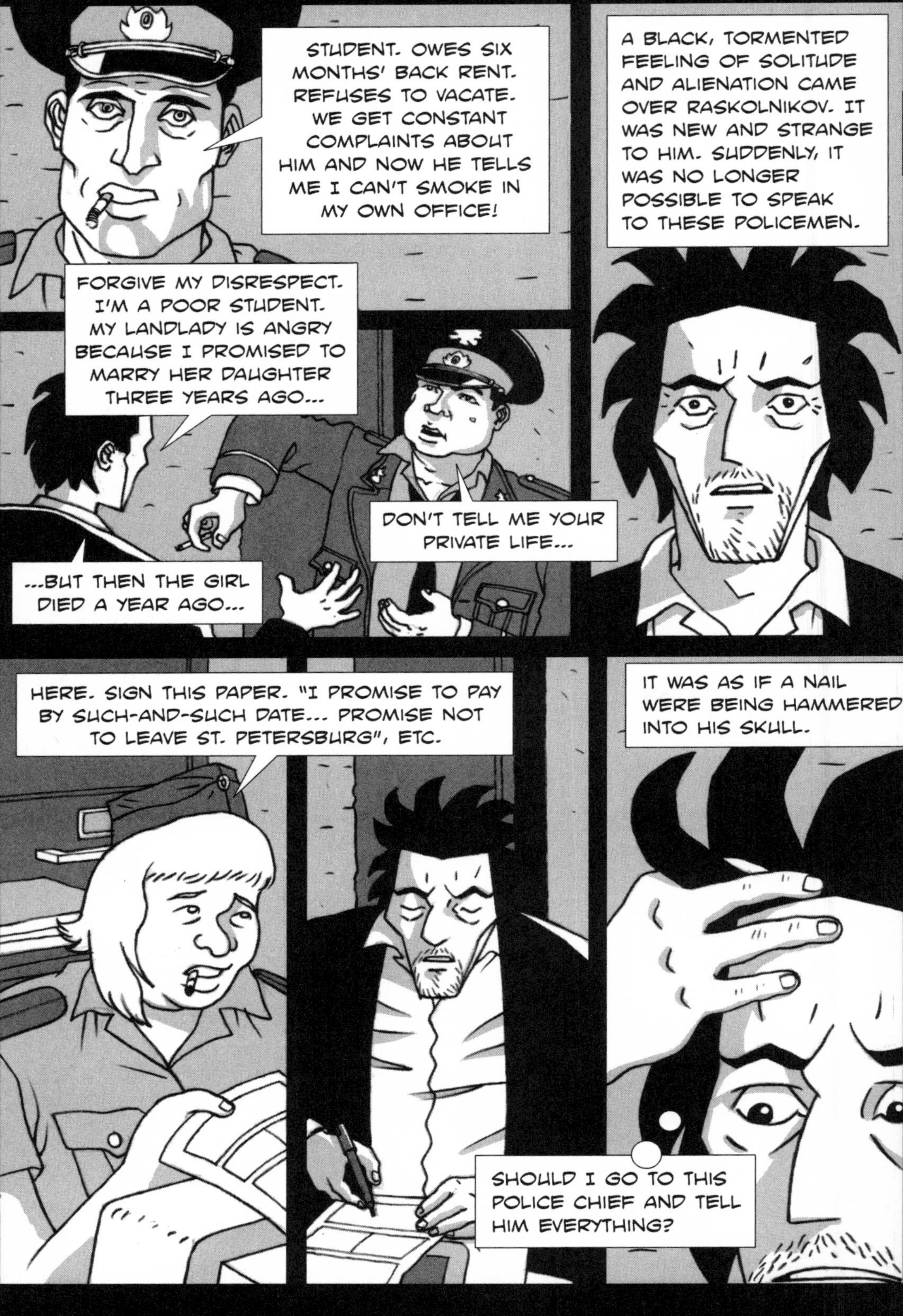
STUDENT. OWES SIX MONTHS' BACK RENT. REFUSES TO VACATE. WE GET CONSTANT COMPLAINTS ABOUT HIM AND NOW HE TELLS ME I CAN'T SMOKE IN MY OWN OFFICE!
FORGIVE MY DISRESPECT. I'M A POOR STUDENT. MY LANDLADY IS ANGRY BECAUSE I PROMISED TO MARRY HER DAUGHTER THREE YEARS AGO...
DON'T TELL ME YOUR PRIVATE LIFE...
...BUT THEN THE GIRL DIED A YEAR AGO...
A BLACK, TORMENTED FEELING OF SOLITUDE AND ALIENATION CAME OVER RASKOLNIKOV. IT WAS NEW AND STRANGE TO HIM. SUDDENLY, IT WAS NO LONGER POSSIBLE TO SPEAK TO THESE POLICEMEN.
HERE. SIGN THIS PAPER. "I PROMISE TO PAY BY SUCH-AND-SUCH DATE... PROMISE NOT TO LEAVE ST. PETERSBURG", ETC.
IT WAS AS IF A NAIL WERE BEING HAMMERED INTO HIS SKULL.
SHOULD I GO TO THIS POLICE CHIEF AND TELL HIM EVERYTHING?

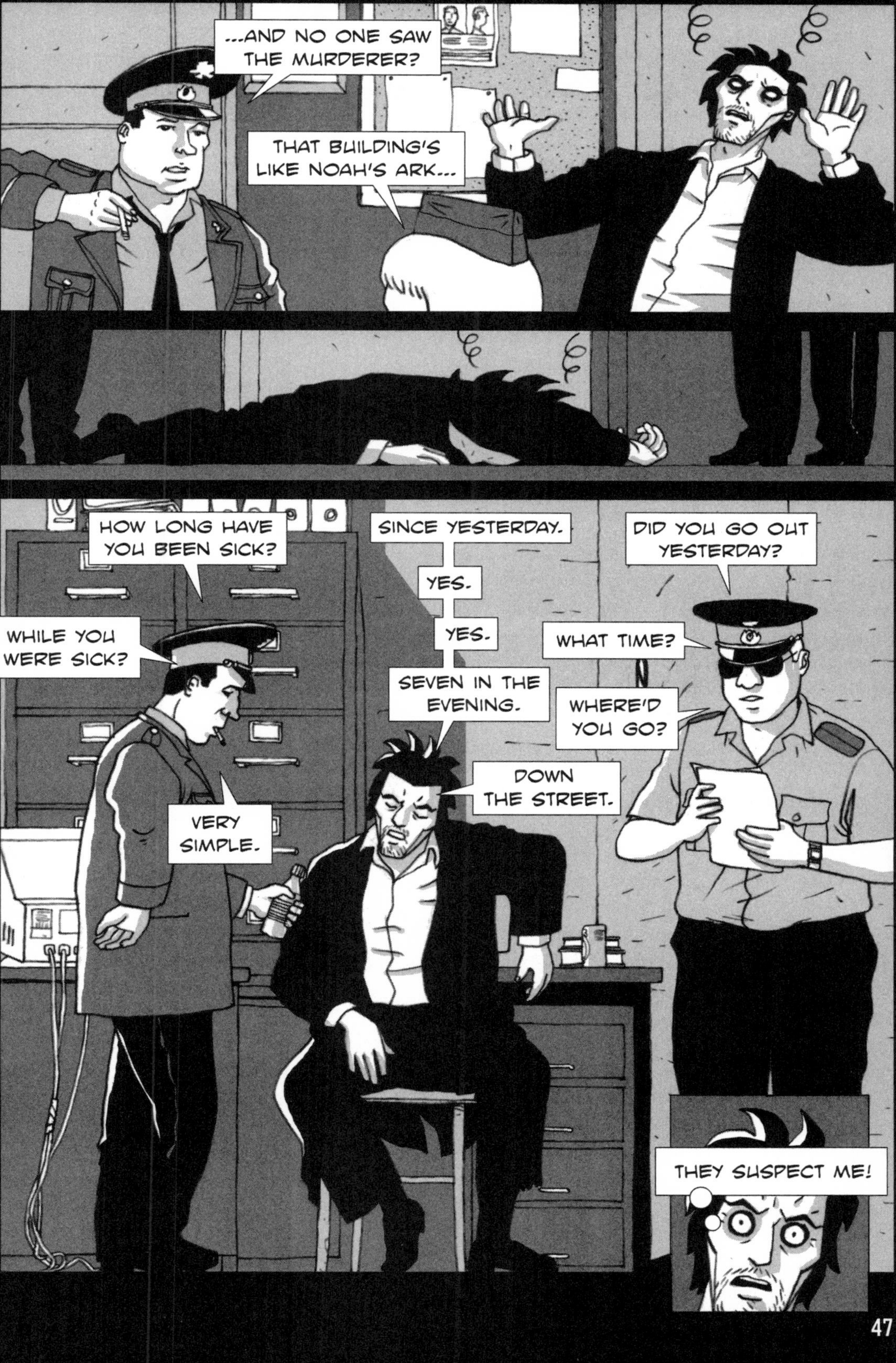
...AND NO ONE SAW THE MURDERER?
THAT BUILDING'S LIKE NOAH'S ARK...
HOW LONG HAVE YOU BEEN SICK?
SINCE YESTERDAY.
DID YOU GO OUT YESTERDAY?
YES.
WHILE YOU WERE SICK?
YES.
WHAT TIME?
SEVEN IN THE EVENING.
WHERE'D YOU GO?
DOWN THE STREET.
VERY SIMPLE.
THEY SUSPECT ME!

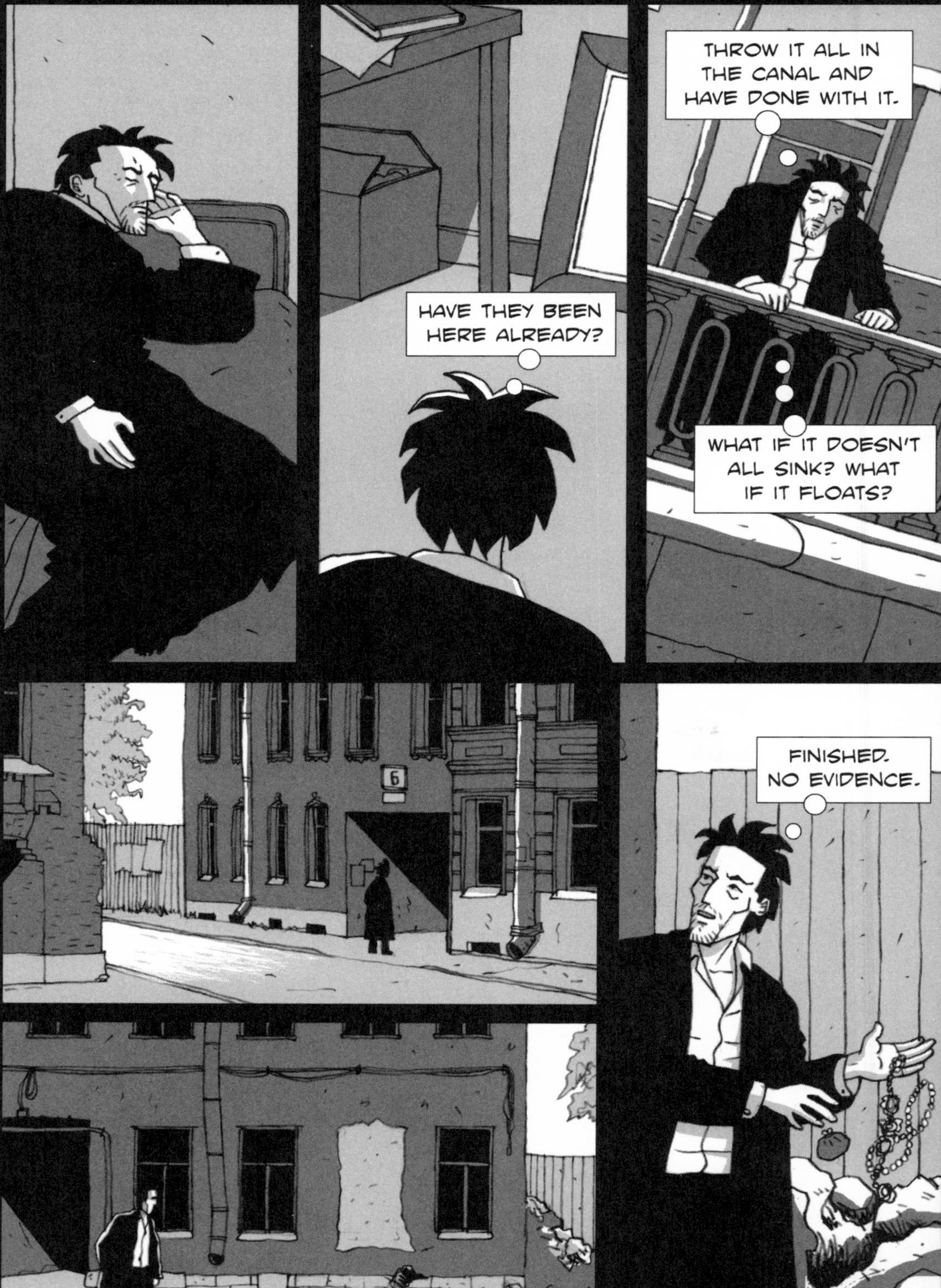
HAVE THEY BEEN HERE ALREADY?
THROW IT ALL IN THE CANAL AND HAVE DONE WITH IT.
WHAT IF IT DOESN'T ALL SINK? WHAT IF IT FLOATS?
FINISHED. NO EVIDENCE.

A NEW FEELING WAS OVERTAKING HIM MINUTE BY MINUTE: A PHYSICAL REVULSION FOR EVERYTHING HE SAW, A LOATHING FOR EVERY PERSON HE MET.

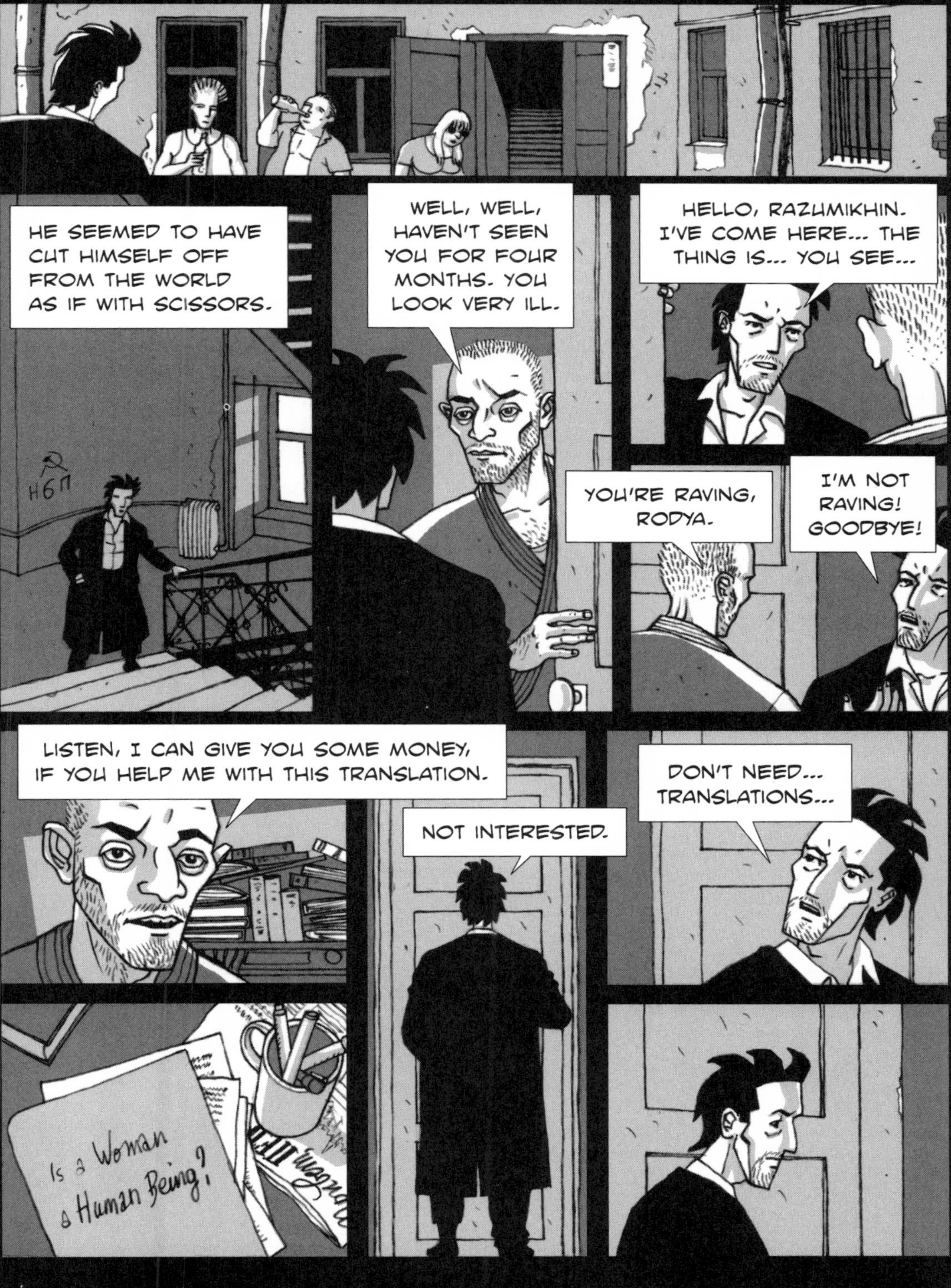
HE SEEMED TO HAVE CUT HIMSELF OFF FROM THE WORLD AS IF WITH SCISSORS.
НБП
WELL, WELL, HAVEN'T SEEN YOU FOR FOUR MONTHS. YOU LOOK VERY ILL.
HELLO, RAZUMIKHIN. I'VE COME HERE... THE THING IS... YOU SEE...
YOU'RE RAVING, RODYA.
I'M NOT RAVING! GOODBYE!
LISTEN, I CAN GIVE YOU SOME MONEY, IF YOU HELP ME WITH THIS TRANSLATION.
Is a Woman a Human Being?
NOT INTERESTED.
DON'T NEED... TRANSLATIONS...

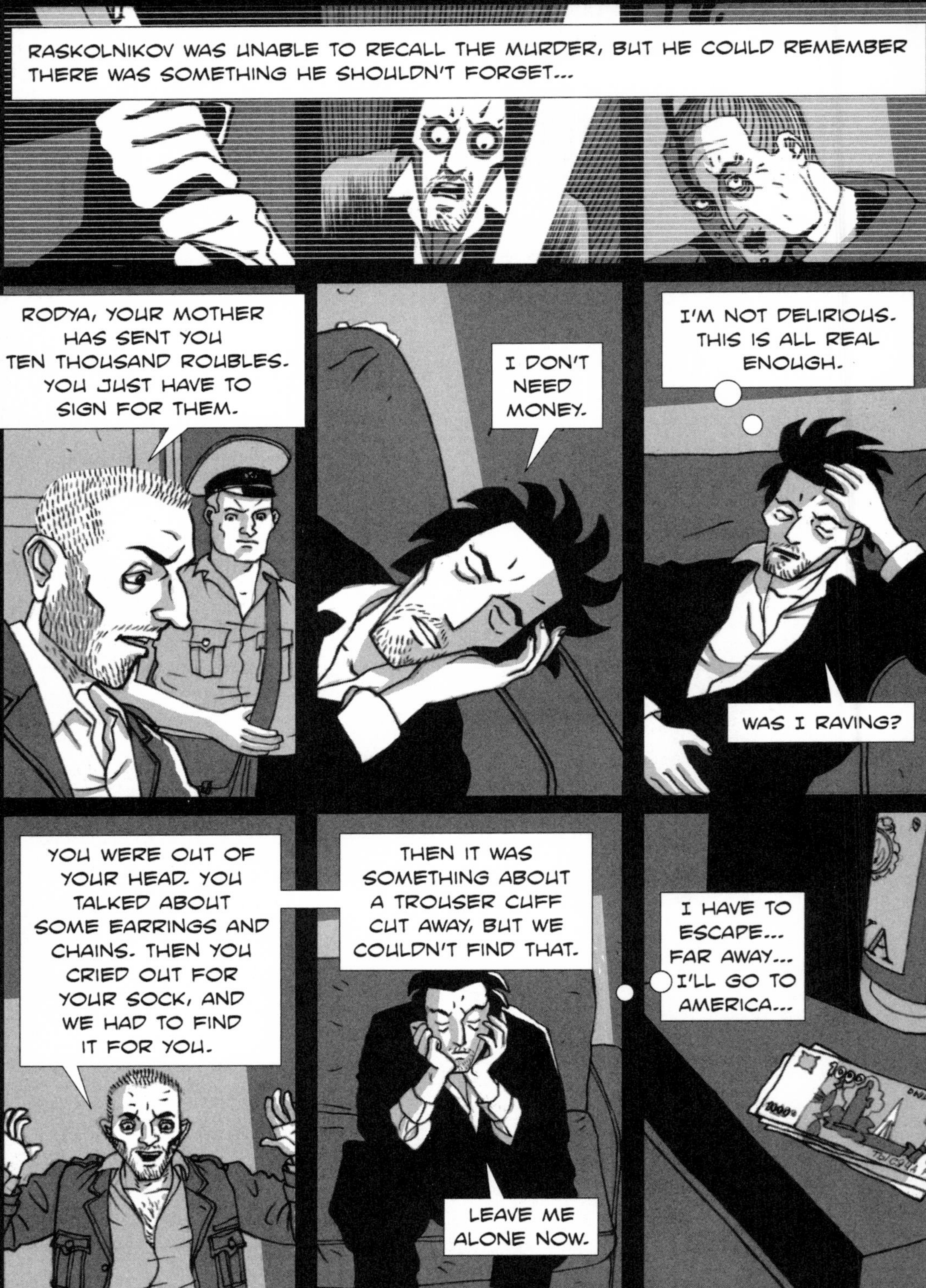
RASKOLNIKOV WAS UNABLE TO RECALL THE MURDER, BUT HE COULD REMEMBER THERE WAS SOMETHING HE SHOULDN'T FORGET...
RODYA, YOUR MOTHER HAS SENT YOU TEN THOUSAND ROUBLES. YOU JUST HAVE TO SIGN FOR THEM.
I DON'T NEED MONEY.
I'M NOT DELIRIOUS. THIS IS ALL REAL ENOUGH.
WAS I RAVING?
YOU WERE OUT OF YOUR HEAD. YOU TALKED ABOUT SOME EARRINGS AND CHAINS. THEN YOU CRIED OUT FOR YOUR SOCK, AND WE HAD TO FIND IT FOR YOU.
THEN IT WAS SOMETHING ABOUT A TROUSER CUFF CUT AWAY, BUT WE COULDN'T FIND THAT.
LEAVE ME ALONE NOW.
I HAVE TO ESCAPE... FAR AWAY... I'LL GO TO AMERICA...

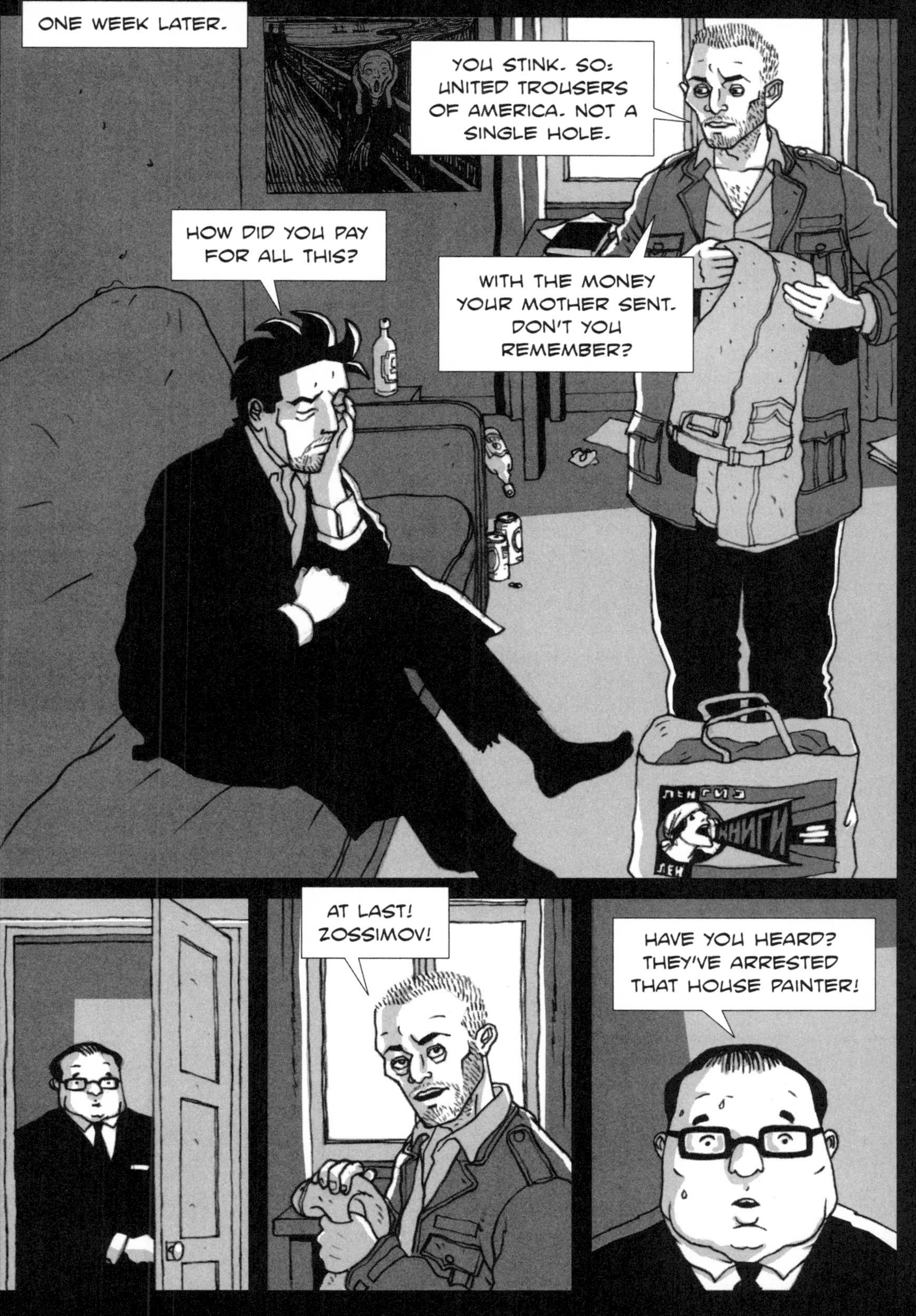
ONE WEEK LATER.
YOU STINK. SO: UNITED TROUSERS OF AMERICA. NOT A SINGLE HOLE.
HOW DID YOU PAY FOR ALL THIS?
WITH THE MONEY YOUR MOTHER SENT. DON'T YOU REMEMBER?
AT LAST! ZOSSIMOV!
HAVE YOU HEARD? THEY'VE ARRESTED THAT HOUSE PAINTER!

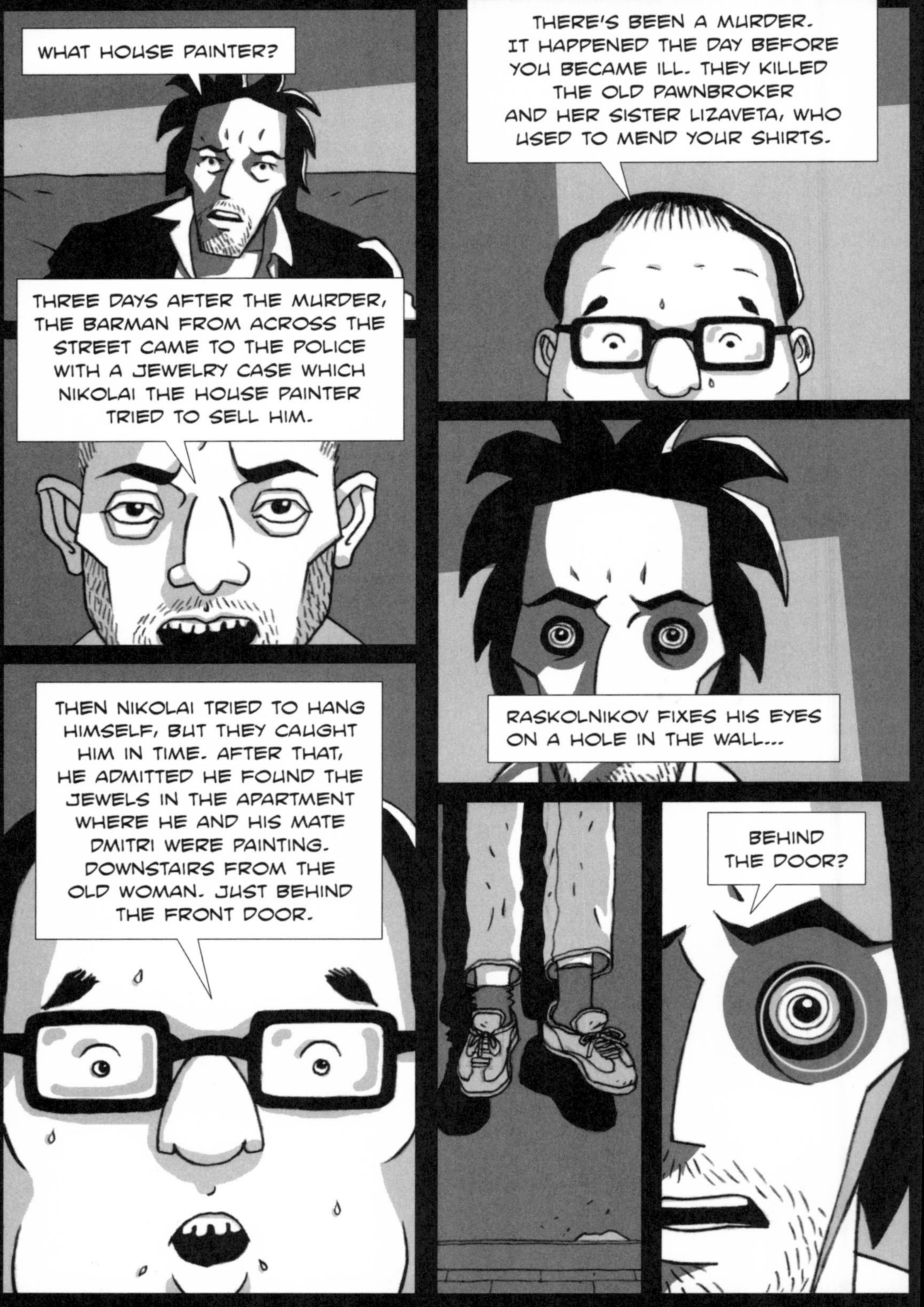

WHAT HOUSE PAINTER?
THERE'S BEEN A MURDER. IT HAPPENED THE DAY BEFORE YOU BECAME ILL. THEY KILLED THE OLD PAWNBROKER AND HER SISTER LIZAVETA, WHO USED TO MEND YOUR SHIRTS.
THREE DAYS AFTER THE MURDER, THE BARMAN FROM ACROSS THE STREET CAME TO THE POLICE WITH A JEWELRY CASE WHICH NIKOLAI THE HOUSE PAINTER TRIED TO SELL HIM.
RASKOLNIKOV FIXES HIS EYES ON A HOLE IN THE WALL...
THEN NIKOLAI TRIED TO HANG HIMSELF, BUT THEY CAUGHT HIM IN TIME. AFTER THAT, HE ADMITTED HE FOUND THE JEWELS IN THE APARTMENT WHERE HE AND HIS MATE DMITRI WERE PAINTING. DOWNSTAIRS FROM THE OLD WOMAN. JUST BEHIND THE FRONT DOOR.
BEHIND THE DOOR?

THEN HOW DO YOU EXPLAIN HIM HAVING THE OLD WOMAN'S JEWELRY BOX?

BUT I DON'T BELIEVE HE'S GUILTY.

THE MURDERER MUST HAVE RUN DOWNSTAIRS, HEARD SOMEBODY COMING UP, AND HIDDEN IN THE EMPTY APARTMENT. AND HE DROPPED THE BOX WHILE STANDING BEHIND THE DOOR.

HE COULD HAVE BEEN ONE OF HER CLIENTS. AND VERY SMART.

NO, VERY DUMB. OBVIOUSLY AN AMATEUR. HE TAKES SOME WORTHLESS TRINKETS, STUFFS HIS POCKETS, RUMMAGES IN HER TRUNK. BUT SHE HAD A SAFE, AND THE POLICE FOUND 300,000 ROUBLES IN IT IN CASH. HE DIDN'T EVEN LOOK THERE. ALL HE COULD DO WAS KILL, AND THEN HE LOST HIS HEAD. HE WAS LUCKY TO GET AWAY.

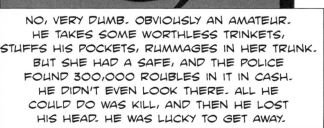

IT ALL COMES TOGETHER NICELY: LIKE A CRIME NOVEL.

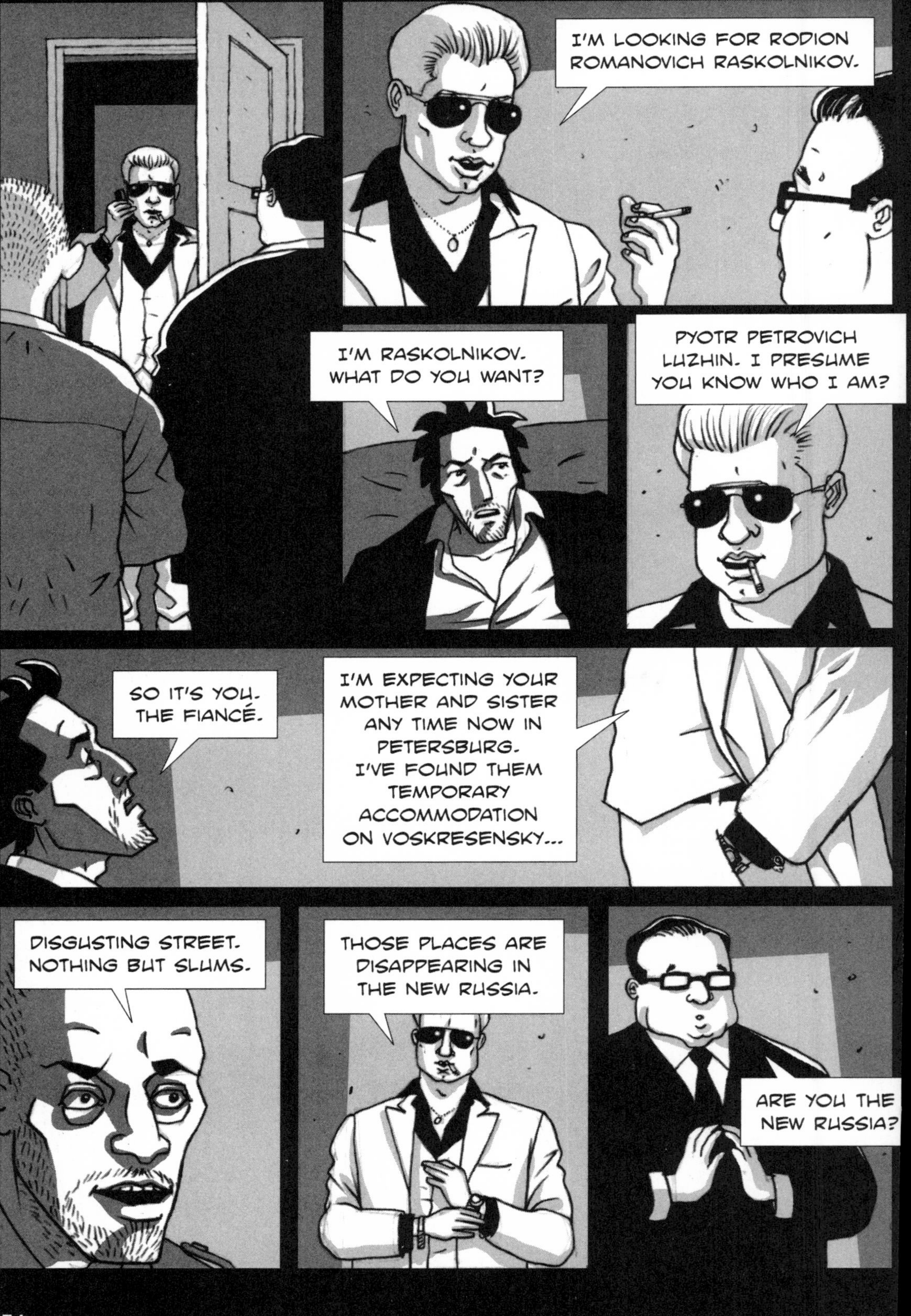
I'M LOOKING FOR RODION ROMANOVICH RASKOLNIKOV.
I'M RASKOLNIKOV. WHAT DO YOU WANT?
PYOTR PETROVICH LUZHIN. I PRESUME YOU KNOW WHO I AM?
SO IT'S YOU. THE FIANCÉ.
I'M EXPECTING YOUR MOTHER AND SISTER ANY TIME NOW IN PETERSBURG. I'VE FOUND THEM TEMPORARY ACCOMMODATION ON VOSKRESENSKY...
DISGUSTING STREET. NOTHING BUT SLUMS.
THOSE PLACES ARE DISAPPEARING IN THE NEW RUSSIA.
ARE YOU THE NEW RUSSIA?

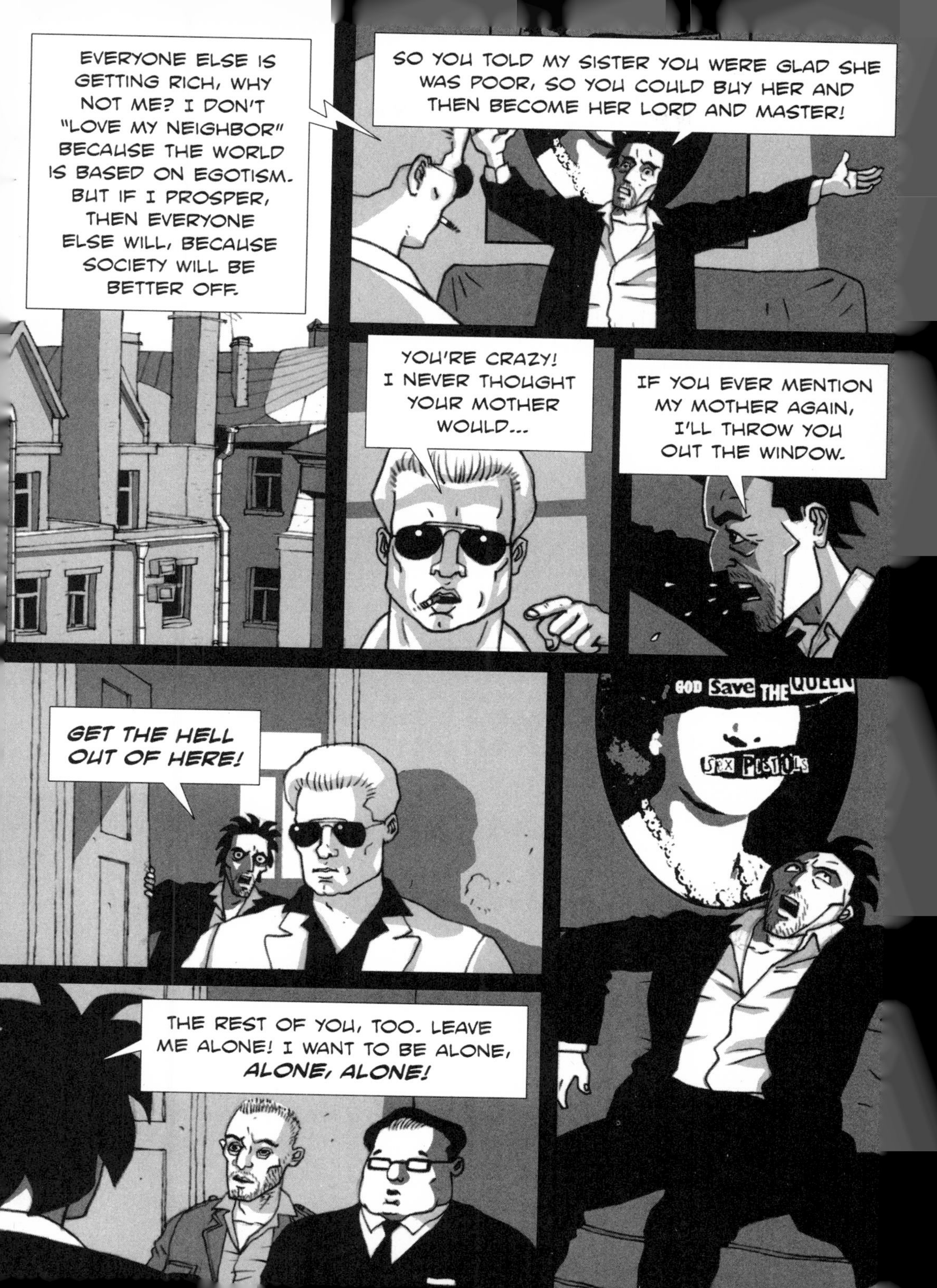
EVERYONE ELSE IS GETTING RICH, WHY NOT ME? I DON'T "LOVE MY NEIGHBOR" BECAUSE THE WORLD IS BASED ON EGOTISM. BUT IF I PROSPER, THEN EVERYONE ELSE WILL, BECAUSE SOCIETY WILL BE BETTER OFF.
SO YOU TOLD MY SISTER YOU WERE GLAD SHE WAS POOR, SO YOU COULD BUY HER AND THEN BECOME HER LORD AND MASTER!
YOU'RE CRAZY! I NEVER THOUGHT YOUR MOTHER WOULD...
IF YOU EVER MENTION MY MOTHER AGAIN, I'LL THROW YOU OUT THE WINDOW.
GET THE HELL OUT OF HERE!
GOD Save THE QUEEN
SEX PISTOLS
THE REST OF YOU, TOO. LEAVE ME ALONE! I WANT TO BE ALONE, ALONE, ALONE!

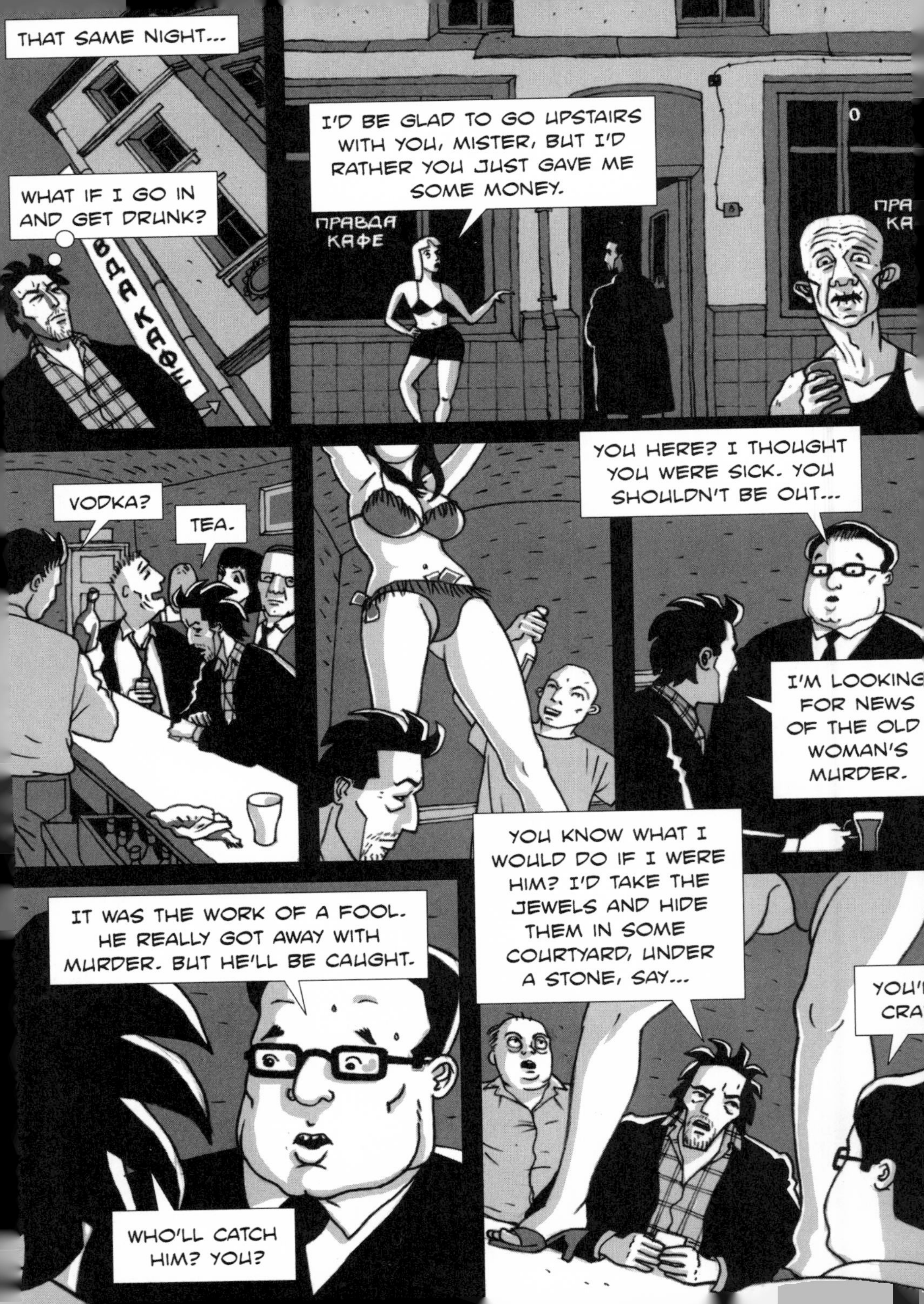

THAT SAME NIGHT...
WHAT IF I GO IN AND GET DRUNK?
ВДА КАФЕ
I'D BE GLAD TO GO UPSTAIRS WITH YOU, MISTER, BUT I'D RATHER YOU JUST GAVE ME SOME MONEY.
ПРАВДА КАФЕ
VODKA?
TEA.
YOU HERE? I THOUGHT YOU WERE SICK. YOU SHOULDN'T BE OUT...
I'M LOOKING FOR NEWS OF THE OLD WOMAN'S MURDER.
IT WAS THE WORK OF A FOOL. HE REALLY GOT AWAY WITH MURDER. BUT HE'LL BE CAUGHT.
WHO'LL CATCH HIM? YOU?
YOU KNOW WHAT I WOULD DO IF I WERE HIM? I'D TAKE THE JEWELS AND HIDE THEM IN SOME COURTYARD, UNDER A STONE, SAY...

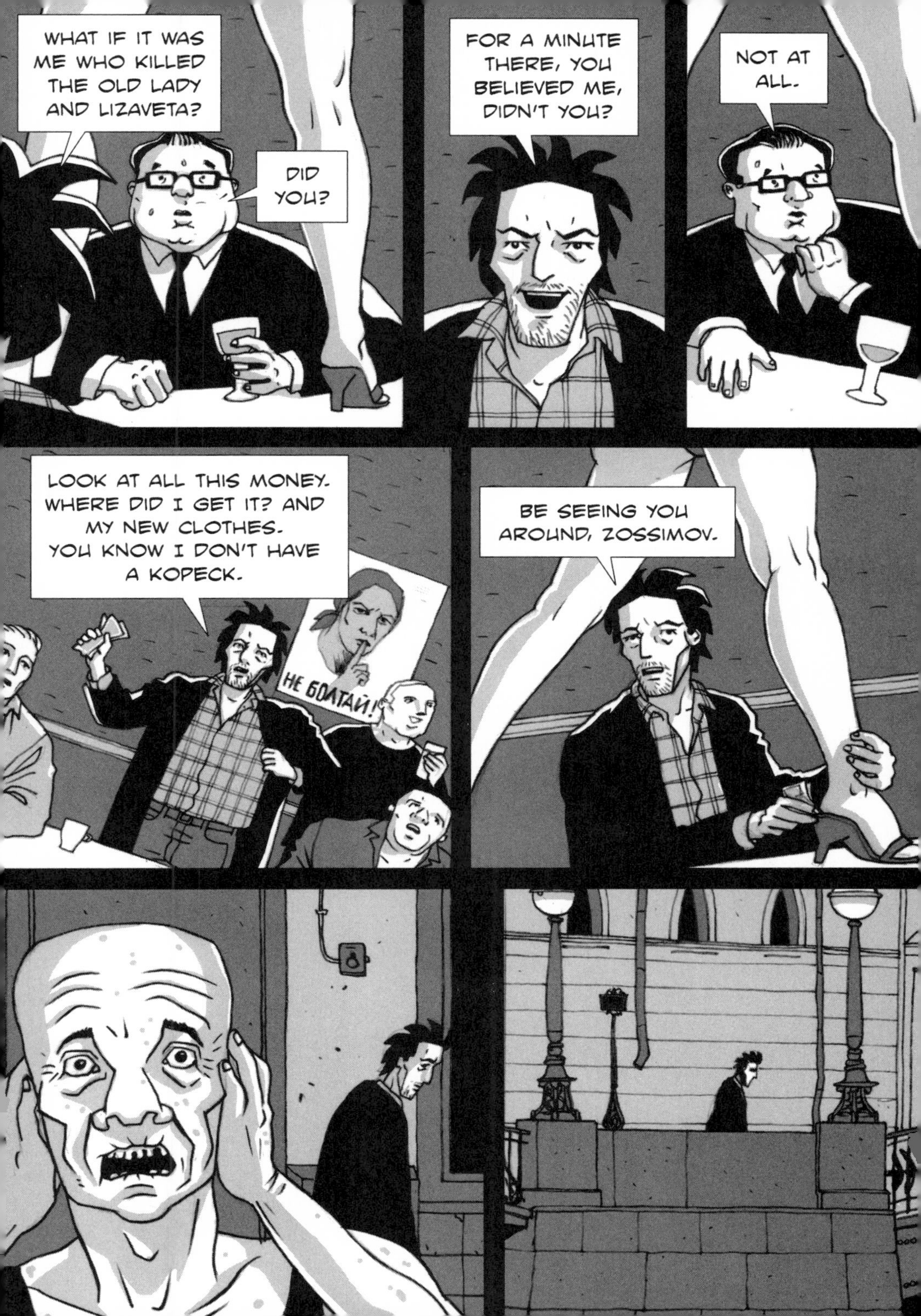
WHAT IF IT WAS ME WHO KILLED THE OLD LADY AND LIZAVETA?
DID YOU?
FOR A MINUTE THERE, YOU BELIEVED ME, DIDN'T YOU?
NOT AT ALL.
LOOK AT ALL THIS MONEY. WHERE DID I GET IT? AND MY NEW CLOTHES. YOU KNOW I DON'T HAVE A KOPECK.
НЕ БОЛТАЙ!
BE SEEING YOU AROUND, ZOSSIMOV.

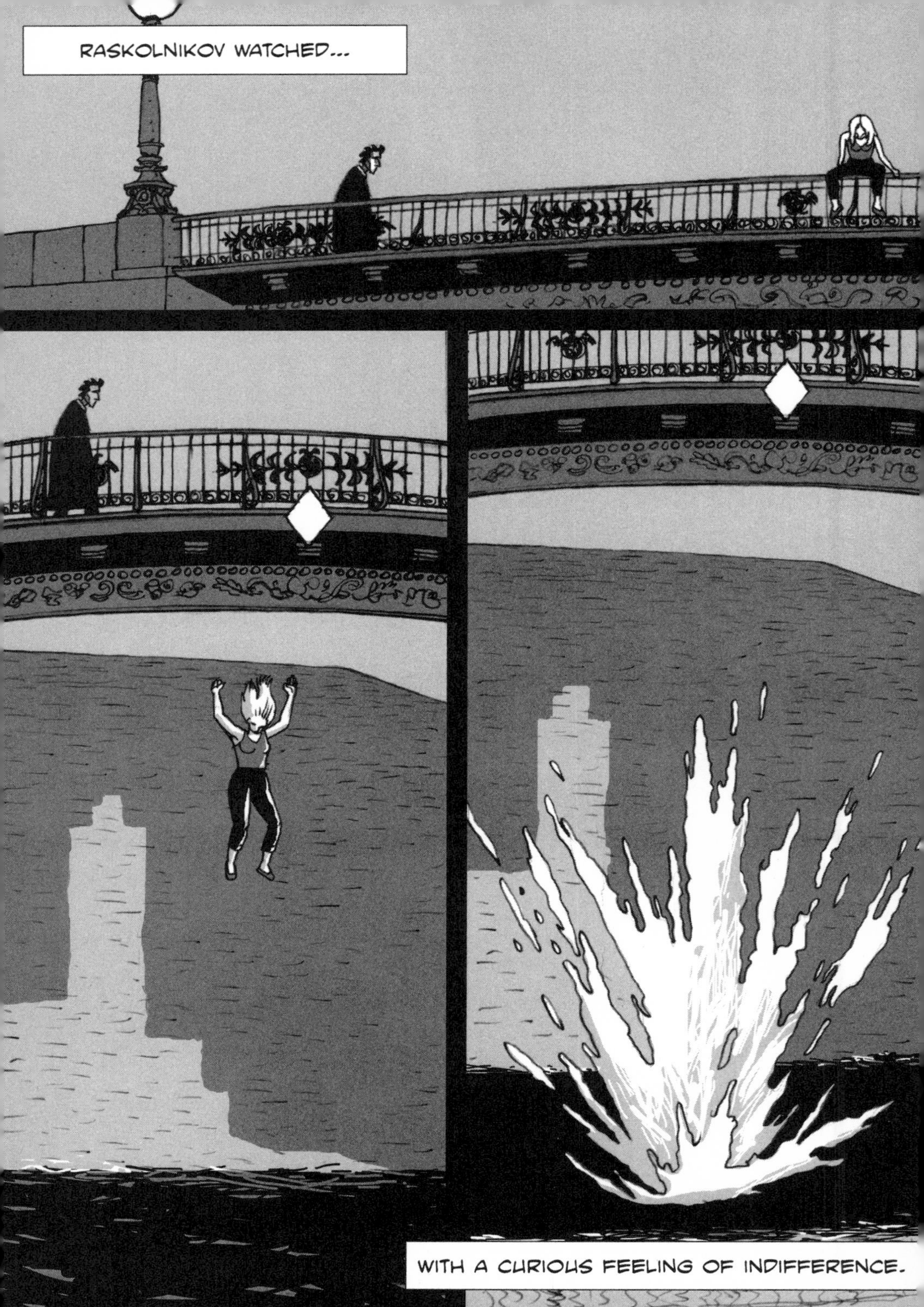
RASKOLNIKOV WATCHED...
WITH A CURIOUS FEELING OF INDIFFERENCE.

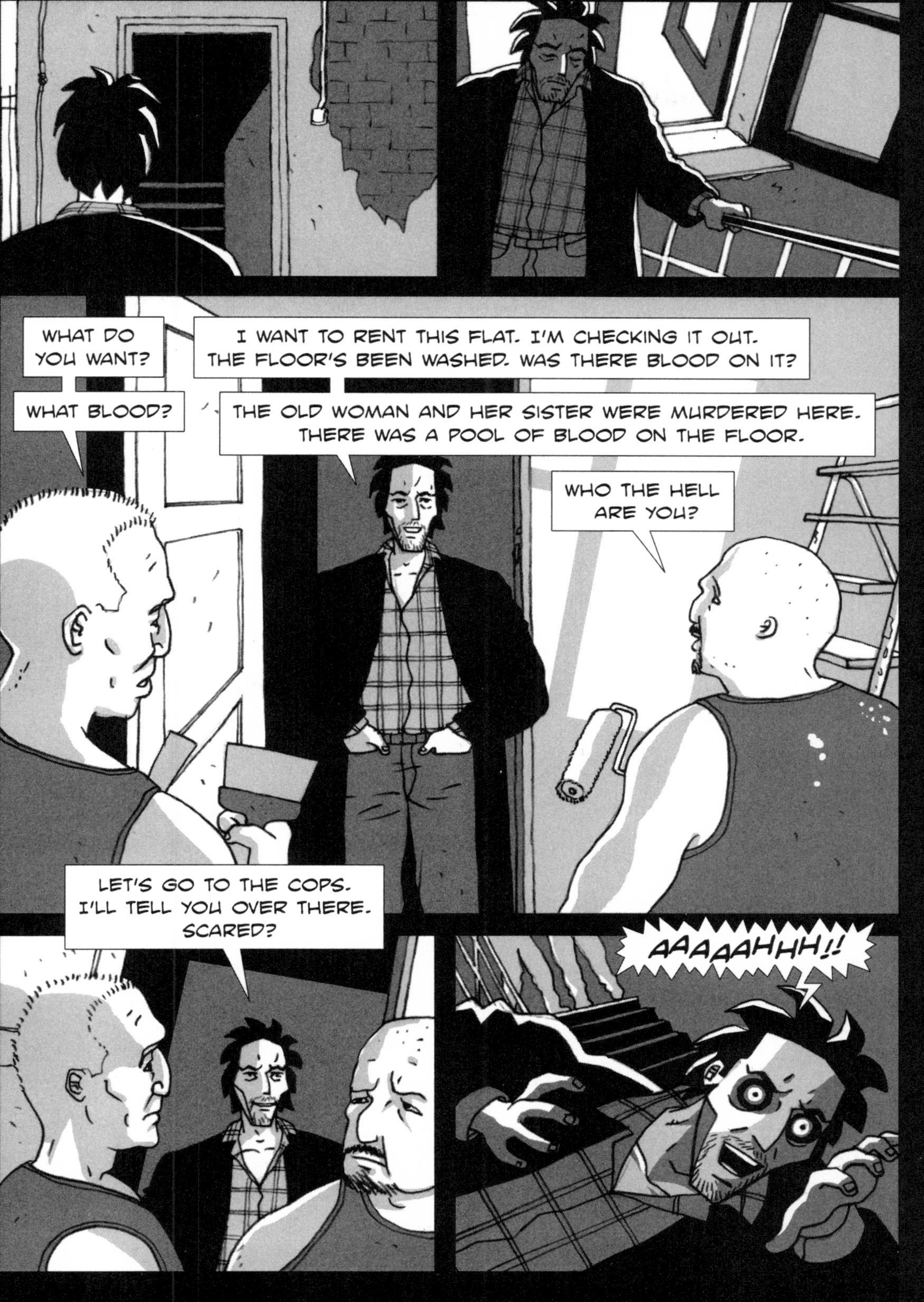

WHAT DO YOU WANT?
I WANT TO RENT THIS FLAT. I'M CHECKING IT OUT. THE FLOOR'S BEEN WASHED. WAS THERE BLOOD ON IT?
WHAT BLOOD?
THE OLD WOMAN AND HER SISTER WERE MURDERED HERE. THERE WAS A POOL OF BLOOD ON THE FLOOR.
WHO THE HELL ARE YOU?
LET'S GO TO THE COPS. I'LL TELL YOU OVER THERE. SCARED?
AAAAAHHH!!

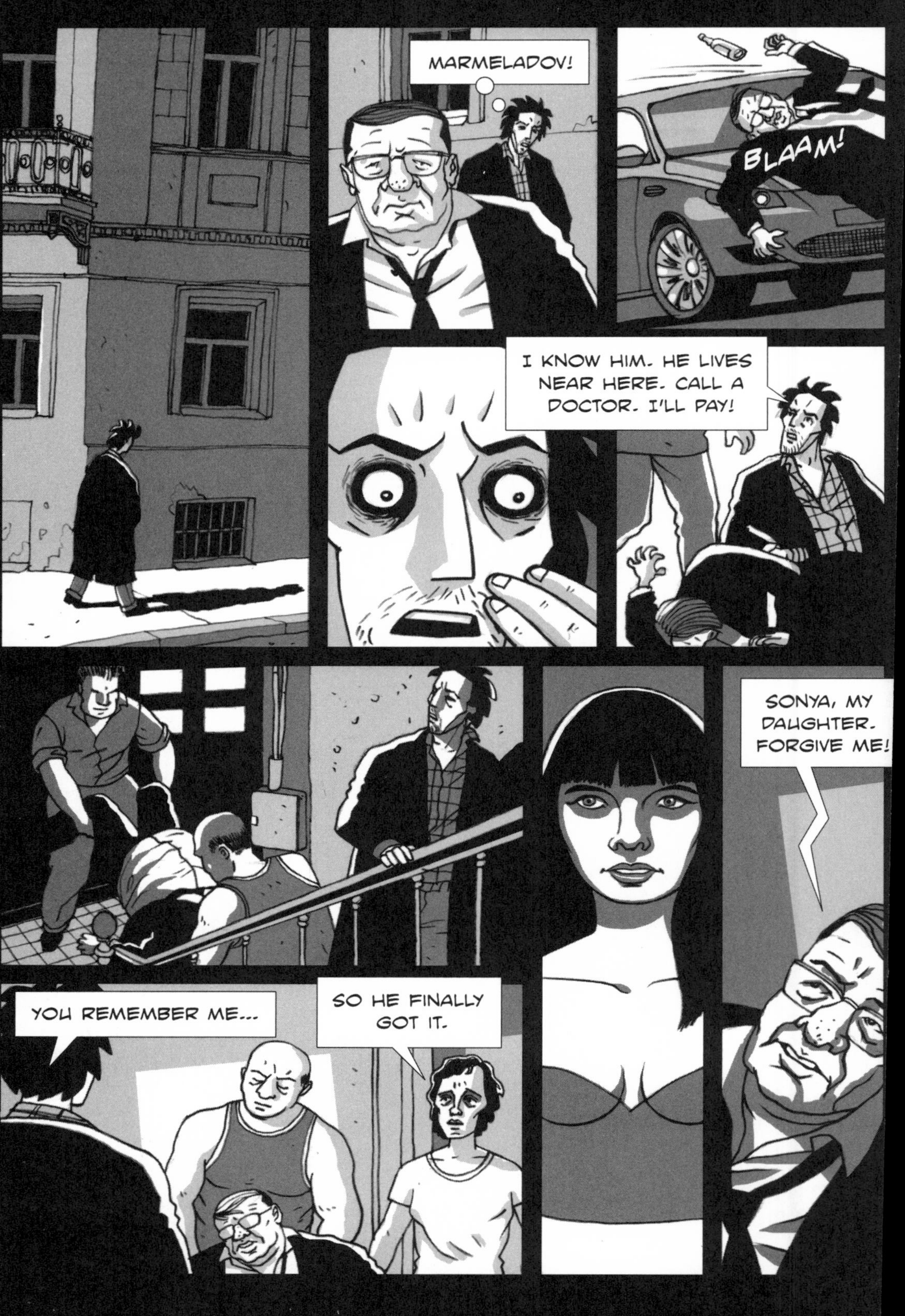
MARMELADOV!
BLAAM!
I KNOW HIM. HE LIVES NEAR HERE. CALL A DOCTOR. I'LL PAY!
YOU REMEMBER ME...
SO HE FINALLY GOT IT.
SONYA, MY DAUGHTER. FORGIVE ME!

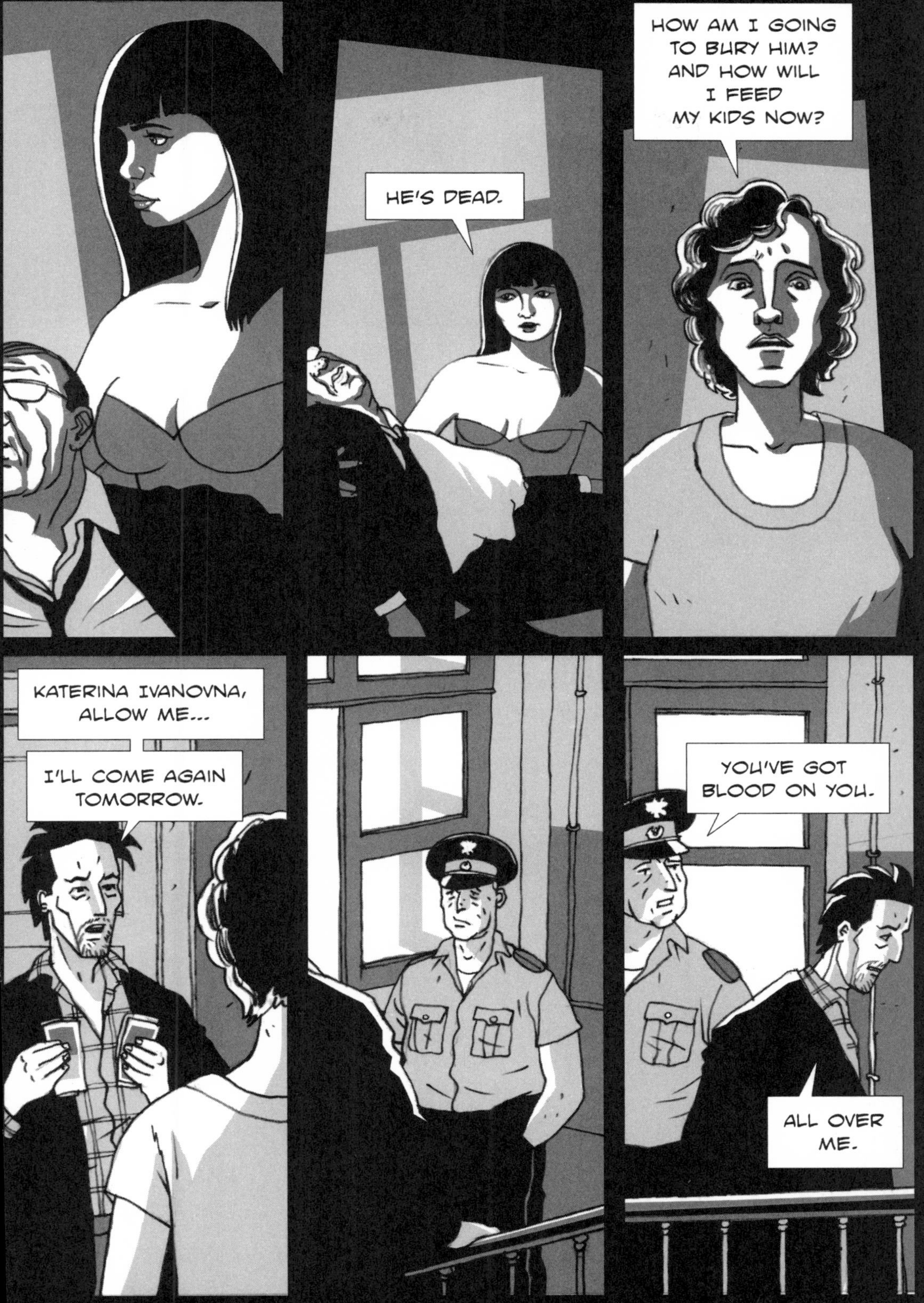
HE'S DEAD.
HOW AM I GOING TO BURY HIM? AND HOW WILL I FEED MY KIDS NOW?
KATERINA IVANOVNA, ALLOW ME...
I'LL COME AGAIN TOMORROW.
YOU'VE GOT BLOOD ON YOU.
ALL OVER ME.

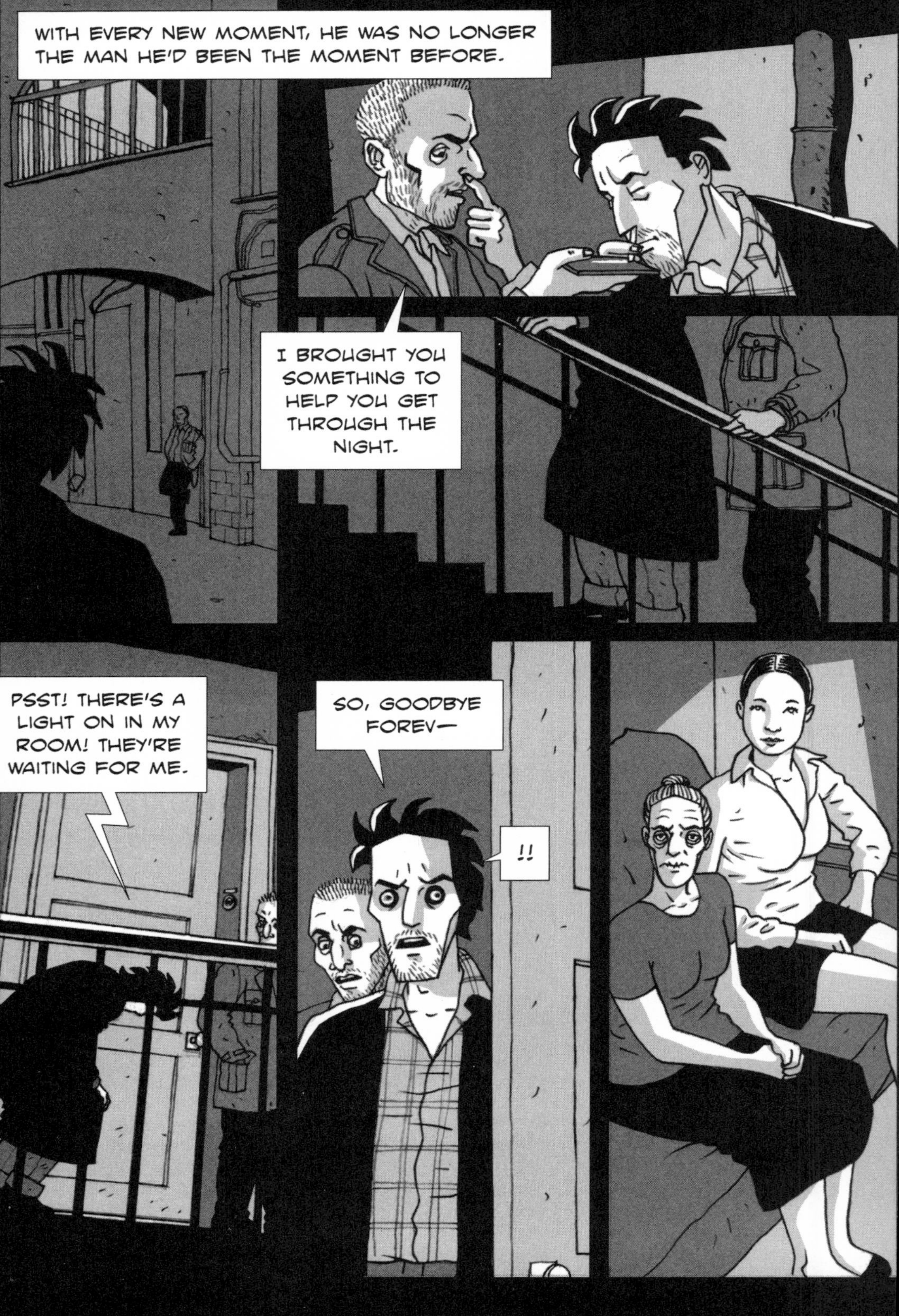
WITH EVERY NEW MOMENT, HE WAS NO LONGER THE MAN HE'D BEEN THE MOMENT BEFORE.
I BROUGHT YOU SOMETHING TO HELP YOU GET THROUGH THE NIGHT.
PSST! THERE'S A LIGHT ON IN MY ROOM! THEY'RE WAITING FOR ME.
SO, GOODBYE FOREV—
!!

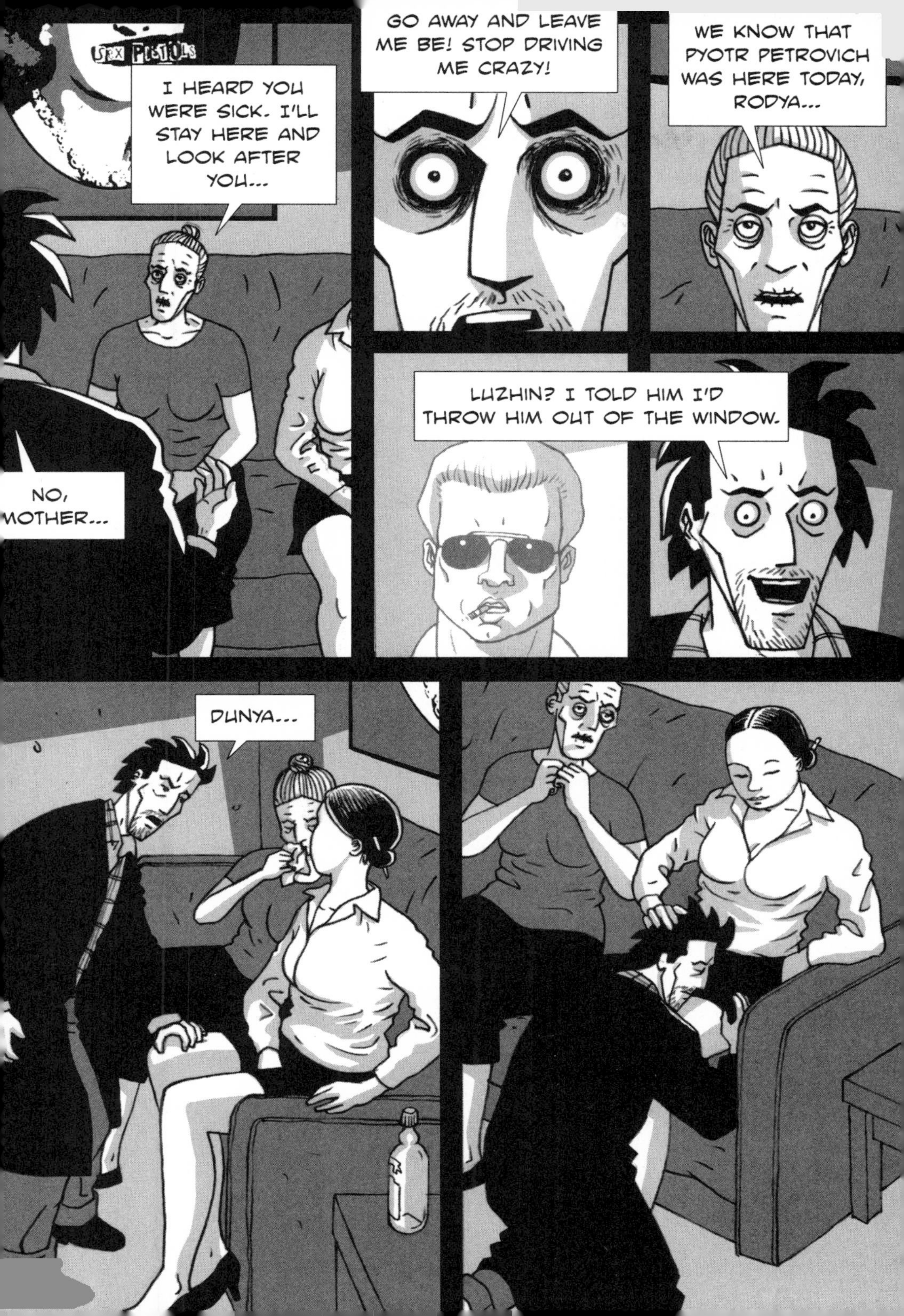
SEX PISTOLS
I HEARD YOU WERE SICK. I'LL STAY HERE AND LOOK AFTER YOU...
NO, MOTHER...
GO AWAY AND LEAVE ME BE! STOP DRIVING ME CRAZY!
WE KNOW THAT PYOTR PETROVICH WAS HERE TODAY, RODYA...
LUZHIN? I TOLD HIM I'D THROW HIM OUT OF THE WINDOW.
DUNYA...

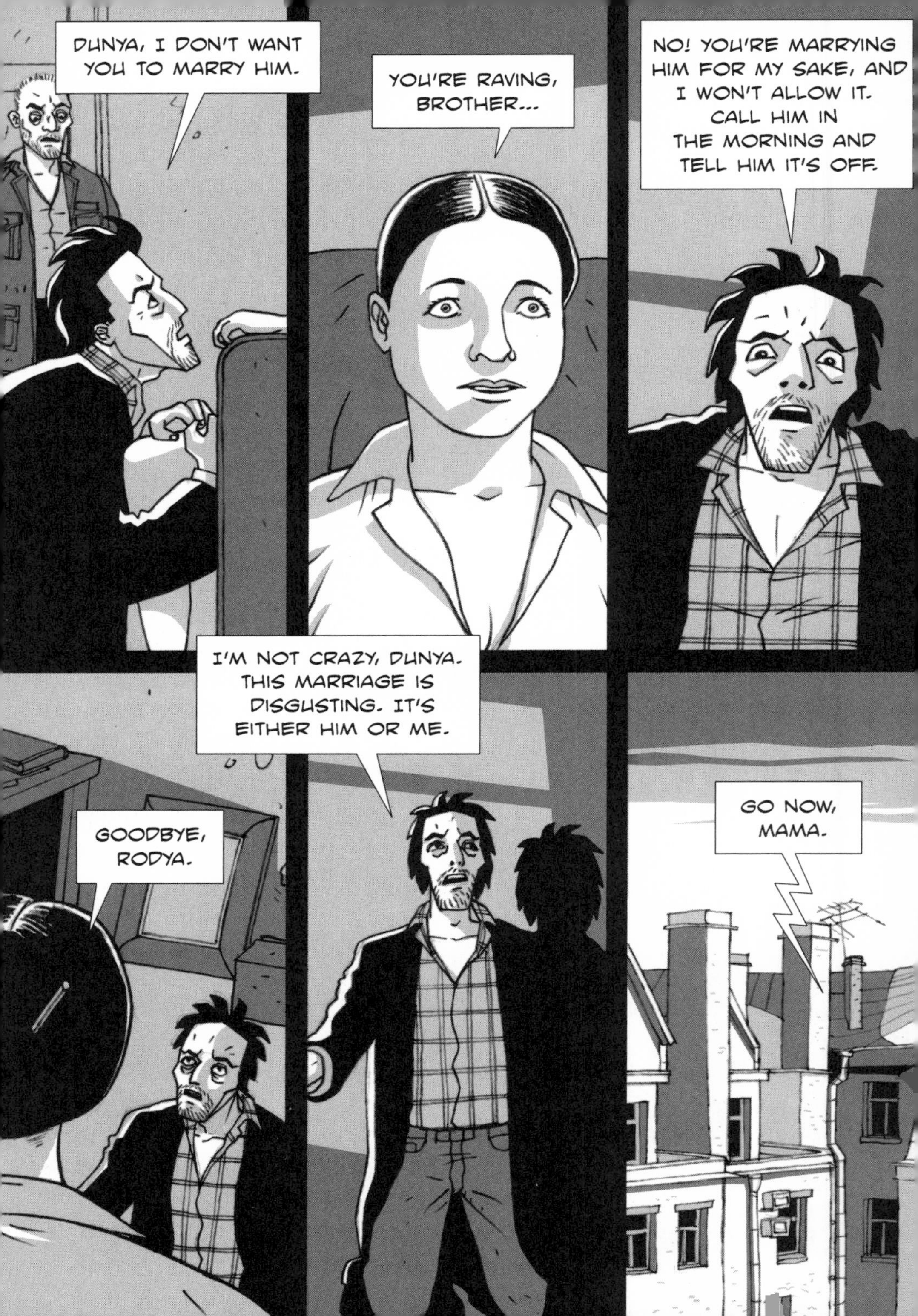
DUNYA, I DON'T WANT YOU TO MARRY HIM.
YOU'RE RAVING, BROTHER...
NO! YOU'RE MARRYING HIM FOR MY SAKE, AND I WON'T ALLOW IT. CALL HIM IN THE MORNING AND TELL HIM IT'S OFF.
I'M NOT CRAZY, DUNYA. THIS MARRIAGE IS DISGUSTING. IT'S EITHER HIM OR ME.
GOODBYE, RODYA.
GO NOW, MAMA.

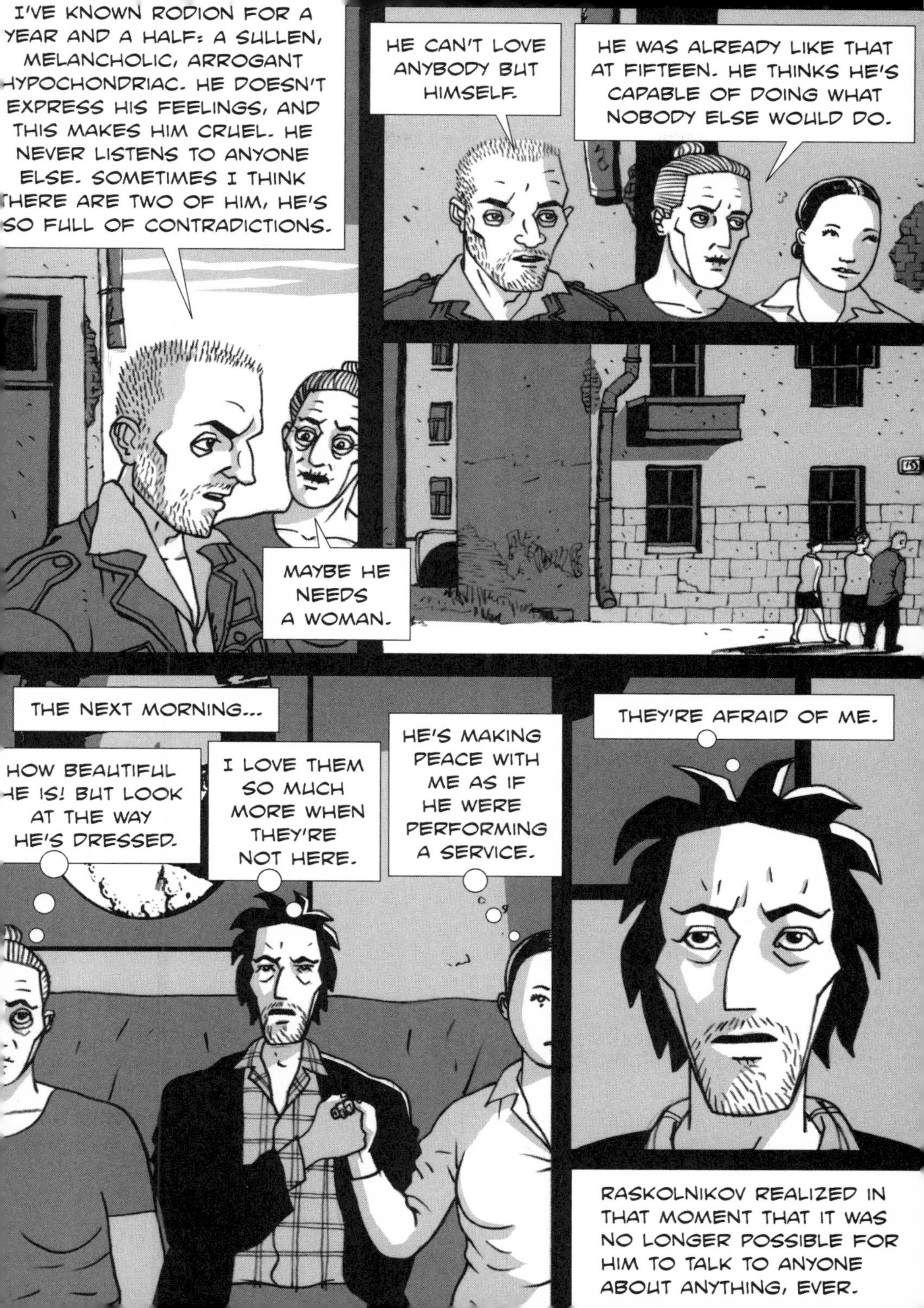

I'VE KNOWN RODION FOR A YEAR AND A HALF: A SULLEN, MELANCHOLIC, ARROGANT HYPOCHONDRIAC. HE DOESN'T EXPRESS HIS FEELINGS, AND THIS MAKES HIM CRUEL. HE NEVER LISTENS TO ANYONE ELSE. SOMETIMES I THINK THERE ARE TWO OF HIM, HE'S SO FULL OF CONTRADICTIONS.
MAYBE HE NEEDS A WOMAN.
HE CAN'T LOVE ANYBODY BUT HIMSELF.
HE WAS ALREADY LIKE THAT AT FIFTEEN. HE THINKS HE'S CAPABLE OF DOING WHAT NOBODY ELSE WOULD DO.
THE NEXT MORNING...
HOW BEAUTIFUL HE IS! BUT LOOK AT THE WAY HE'S DRESSED.
I LOVE THEM SO MUCH MORE WHEN THEY'RE NOT HERE.
HE'S MAKING PEACE WITH ME AS IF HE WERE PERFORMING A SERVICE.
THEY'RE AFRAID OF ME.
RASKOLNIKOV REALIZED IN THAT MOMENT THAT IT WAS NO LONGER POSSIBLE FOR HIM TO TALK TO ANYONE ABOUT ANYTHING, EVER.

WHAT A TERRIBLE FLAT YOU HAVE, RODYA. IT'S LIKE A COFFIN.

LISTEN, DUNYA, I MEANT WHAT I SAID LAST NIGHT: IF YOU MARRY LUZHIN, YOU'RE NO LONGER MY SISTER.

YOU'RE LYING! YOU'RE SELLING YOURSELF FOR HIS MONEY.

I'M MARRYING HIM FOR MY OWN SAKE, NOT FOR YOURS.

DON'T ASK ME TO BE A HEROINE. IF I DESTROY ANYONE, IT WILL ONLY BE MYSELF.

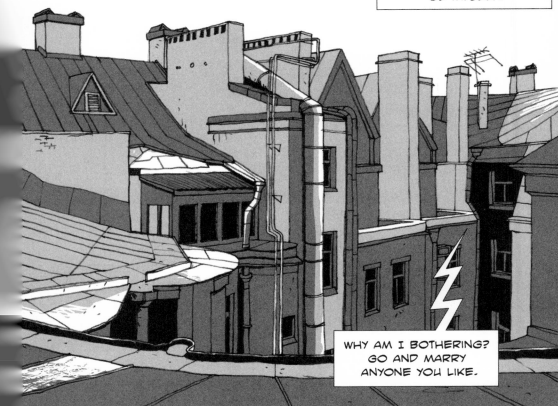

WHY AM I BOTHERING? GO AND MARRY ANYONE YOU LIKE.

SOON THEIR PRESENCE WOULD BECOME UNBEARABLE TO HIM.

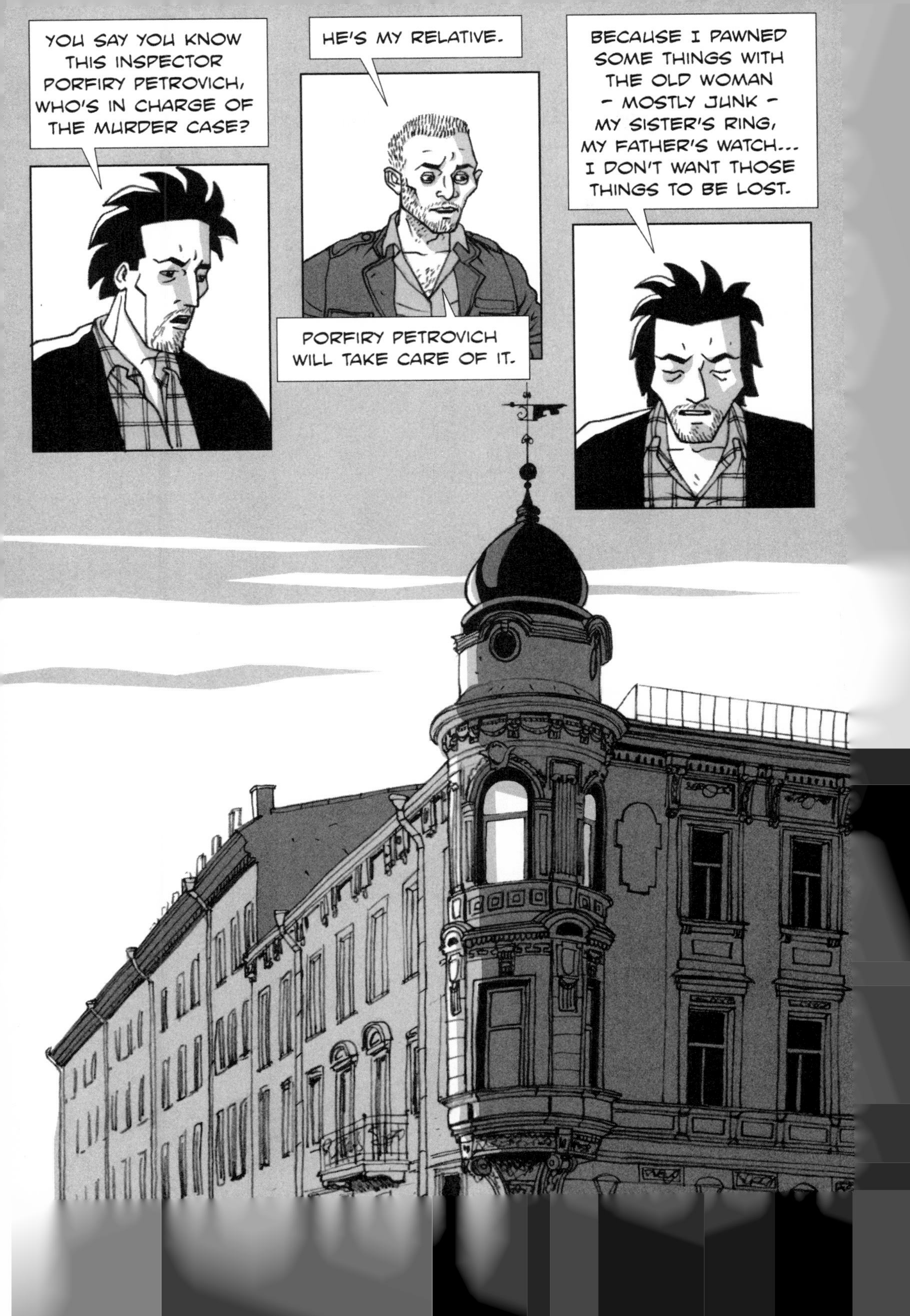
YOU SAY YOU KNOW THIS INSPECTOR PORFIRY PETROVICH, WHO'S IN CHARGE OF THE MURDER CASE?
HE'S MY RELATIVE.
PORFIRY PETROVICH WILL TAKE CARE OF IT.
BECAUSE I PAWNED SOME THINGS WITH THE OLD WOMAN - MOSTLY JUNK - MY SISTER'S RING, MY FATHER'S WATCH... I DON'T WANT THOSE THINGS TO BE LOST.

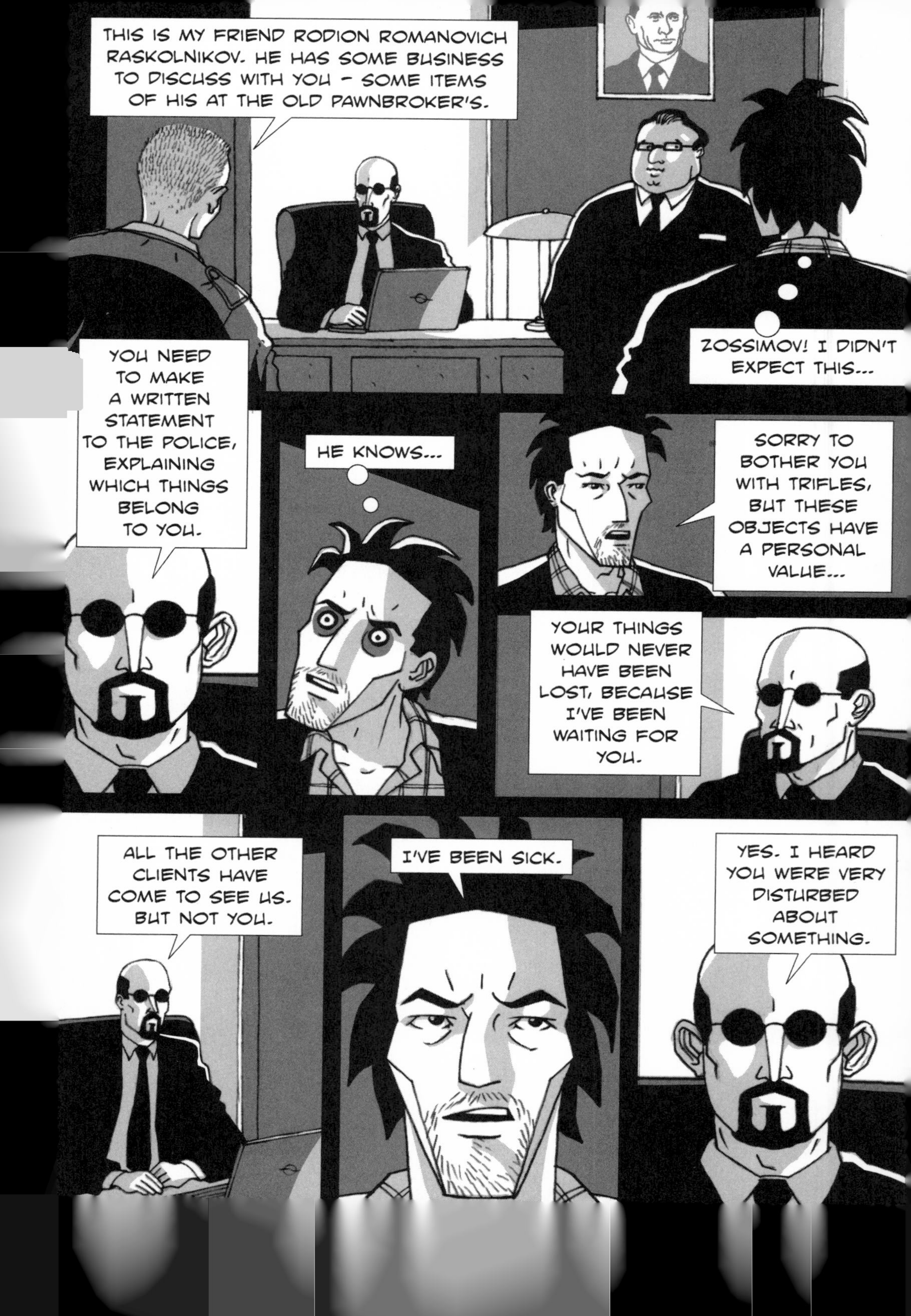
THIS IS MY FRIEND RODION ROMANOVICH RASKOLNIKOV. HE HAS SOME BUSINESS TO DISCUSS WITH YOU - SOME ITEMS OF HIS AT THE OLD PAWNBROKER'S.
ZOSSIMOV! I DIDN'T EXPECT THIS...
YOU NEED TO MAKE A WRITTEN STATEMENT TO THE POLICE, EXPLAINING WHICH THINGS BELONG TO YOU.
HE KNOWS...
SORRY TO BOTHER YOU WITH TRIFLES, BUT THESE OBJECTS HAVE A PERSONAL VALUE...
YOUR THINGS WOULD NEVER HAVE BEEN LOST, BECAUSE I'VE BEEN WAITING FOR YOU.
ALL THE OTHER CLIENTS HAVE COME TO SEE US. BUT NOT YOU.
I'VE BEEN SICK.
YES. I HEARD YOU WERE VERY DISTURBED ABOUT SOMETHING.

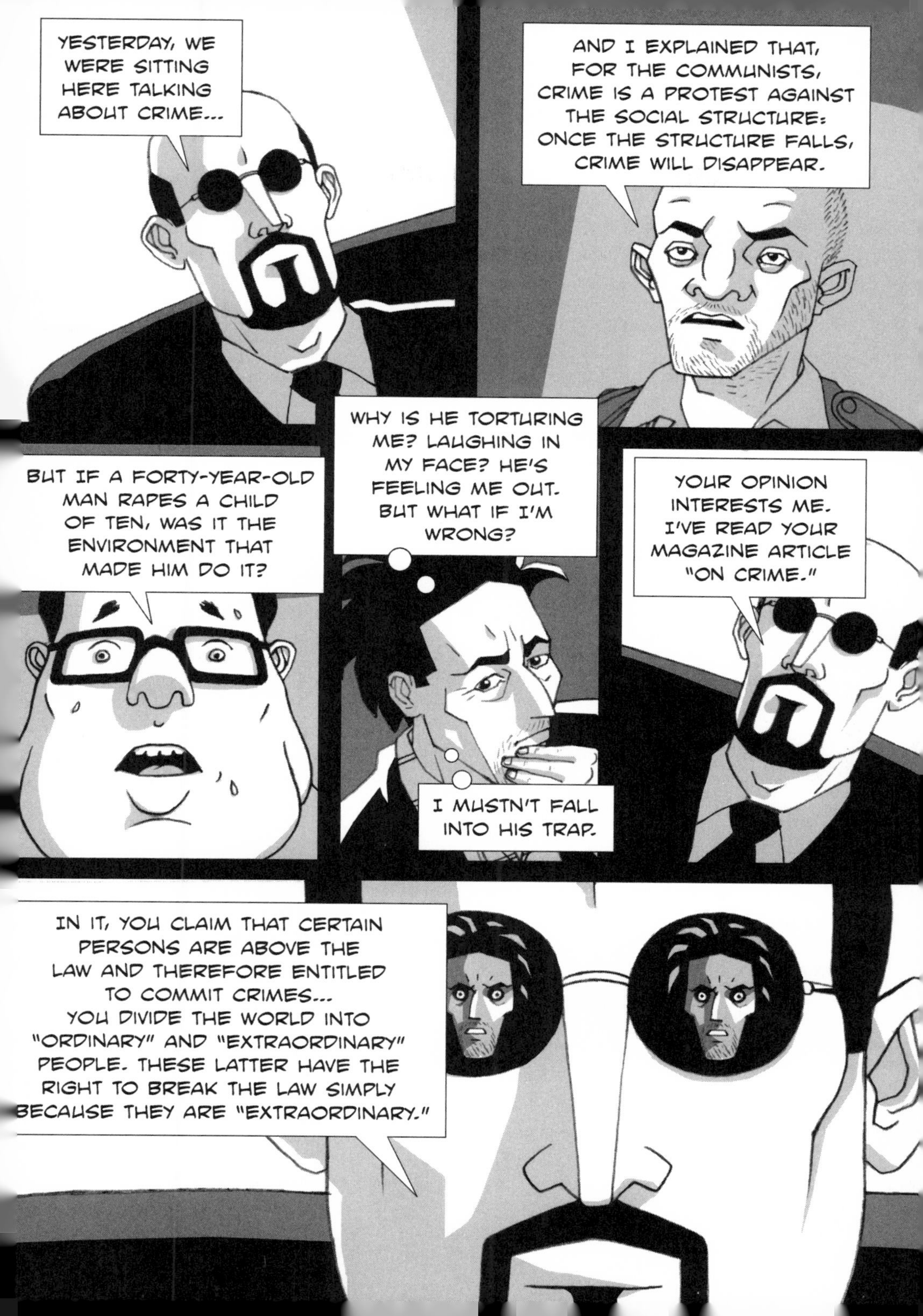
YESTERDAY, WE WERE SITTING HERE TALKING ABOUT CRIME...
AND I EXPLAINED THAT, FOR THE COMMUNISTS, CRIME IS A PROTEST AGAINST THE SOCIAL STRUCTURE: ONCE THE STRUCTURE FALLS, CRIME WILL DISAPPEAR.
BUT IF A FORTY-YEAR-OLD MAN RAPES A CHILD OF TEN, WAS IT THE ENVIRONMENT THAT MADE HIM DO IT?
WHY IS HE TORTURING ME? LAUGHING IN MY FACE? HE'S FEELING ME OUT. BUT WHAT IF I'M WRONG?
I MUSTN'T FALL INTO HIS TRAP.
YOUR OPINION INTERESTS ME. I'VE READ YOUR MAGAZINE ARTICLE "ON CRIME."
IN IT, YOU CLAIM THAT CERTAIN PERSONS ARE ABOVE THE LAW AND THEREFORE ENTITLED TO COMMIT CRIMES... YOU DIVIDE THE WORLD INTO "ORDINARY" AND "EXTRAORDINARY" PEOPLE. THESE LATTER HAVE THE RIGHT TO BREAK THE LAW SIMPLY BECAUSE THEY ARE "EXTRAORDINARY."

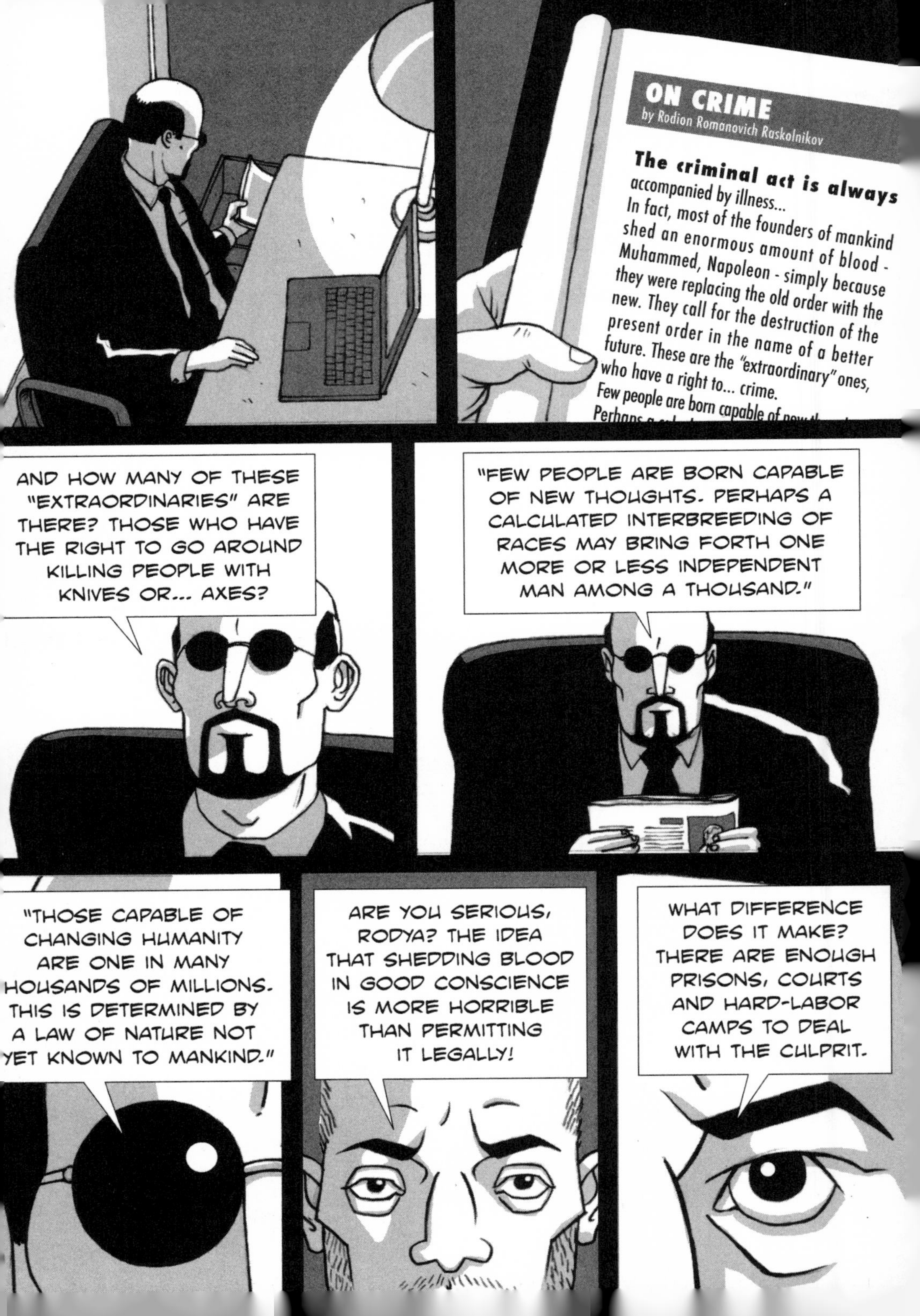
ON CRIME
by Rodion Romanovich Raskolnikov
The criminal act is always accompanied by illness...
In fact, most of the founders of mankind shed an enormous amount of blood - Muhammed, Napoleon - simply because they were replacing the old order with the new. They call for the destruction of the present order in the name of a better future. These are the "extraordinary" ones, who have a right to... crime.
Few people are born capable of
AND HOW MANY OF THESE "EXTRAORDINARIES" ARE THERE? THOSE WHO HAVE THE RIGHT TO GO AROUND KILLING PEOPLE WITH KNIVES OR... AXES?
"FEW PEOPLE ARE BORN CAPABLE OF NEW THOUGHTS. PERHAPS A CALCULATED INTERBREEDING OF RACES MAY BRING FORTH ONE MORE OR LESS INDEPENDENT MAN AMONG A THOUSAND."
"THOSE CAPABLE OF CHANGING HUMANITY ARE ONE IN MANY HOUSANDS OF MILLIONS. THIS IS DETERMINED BY A LAW OF NATURE NOT YET KNOWN TO MANKIND."
ARE YOU SERIOUS, RODYA? THE IDEA THAT SHEDDING BLOOD IN GOOD CONSCIENCE IS MORE HORRIBLE THAN PERMITTING IT LEGALLY!
WHAT DIFFERENCE DOES IT MAKE? THERE ARE ENOUGH PRISONS, COURTS AND HARD-LABOR CAMPS TO DEAL WITH THE CULPRIT.

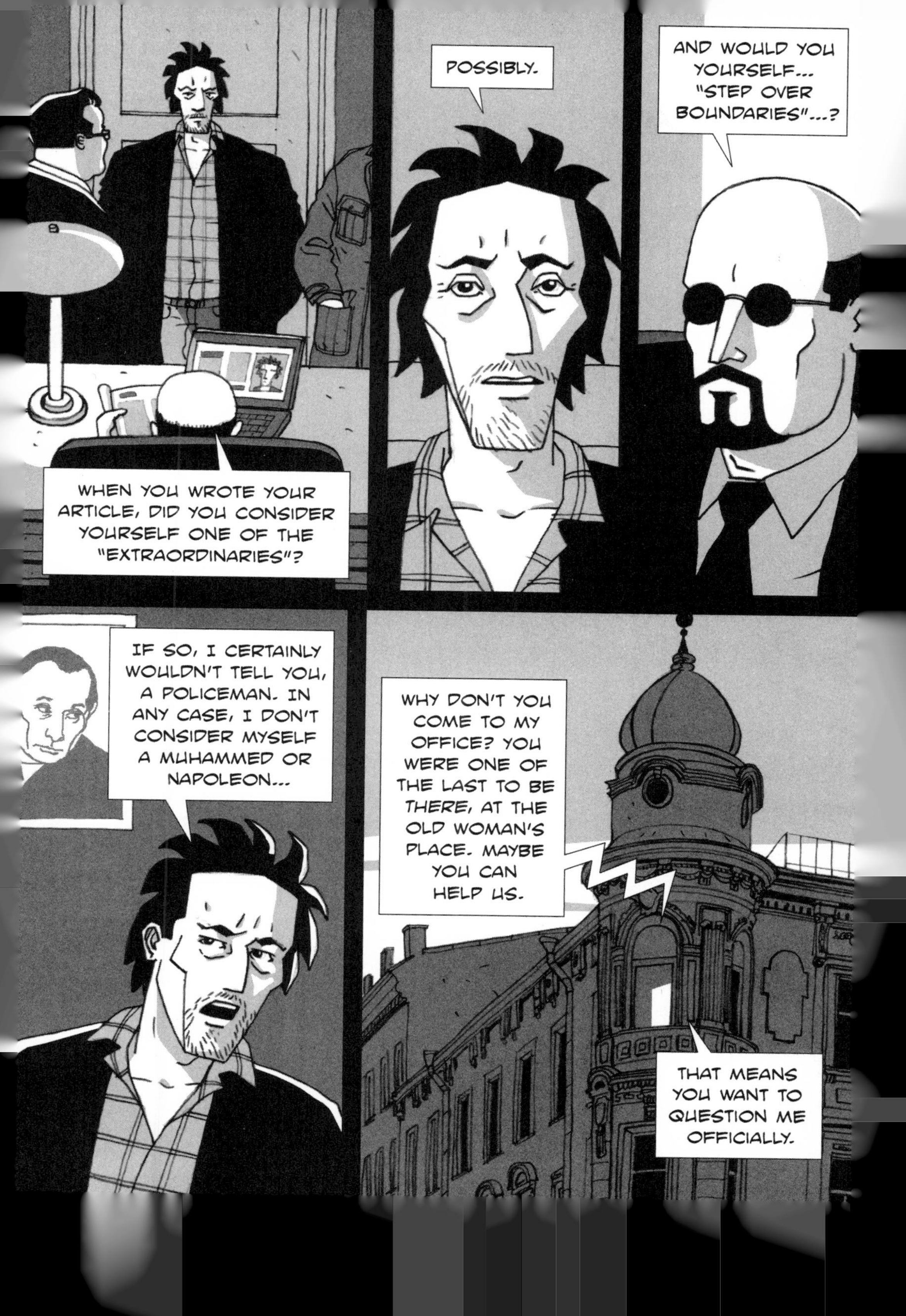
WHEN YOU WROTE YOUR ARTICLE, DID YOU CONSIDER YOURSELF ONE OF THE "EXTRAORDINARIES"?
POSSIBLY.
AND WOULD YOU YOURSELF... "STEP OVER BOUNDARIES"...?
IF SO, I CERTAINLY WOULDN'T TELL YOU, A POLICEMAN. IN ANY CASE, I DON'T CONSIDER MYSELF A MUHAMMED OR NAPOLEON...
WHY DON'T YOU COME TO MY OFFICE? YOU WERE ONE OF THE LAST TO BE *THERE*, AT THE OLD WOMAN'S PLACE. MAYBE YOU CAN HELP US.
THAT MEANS YOU WANT TO QUESTION ME OFFICIALLY.

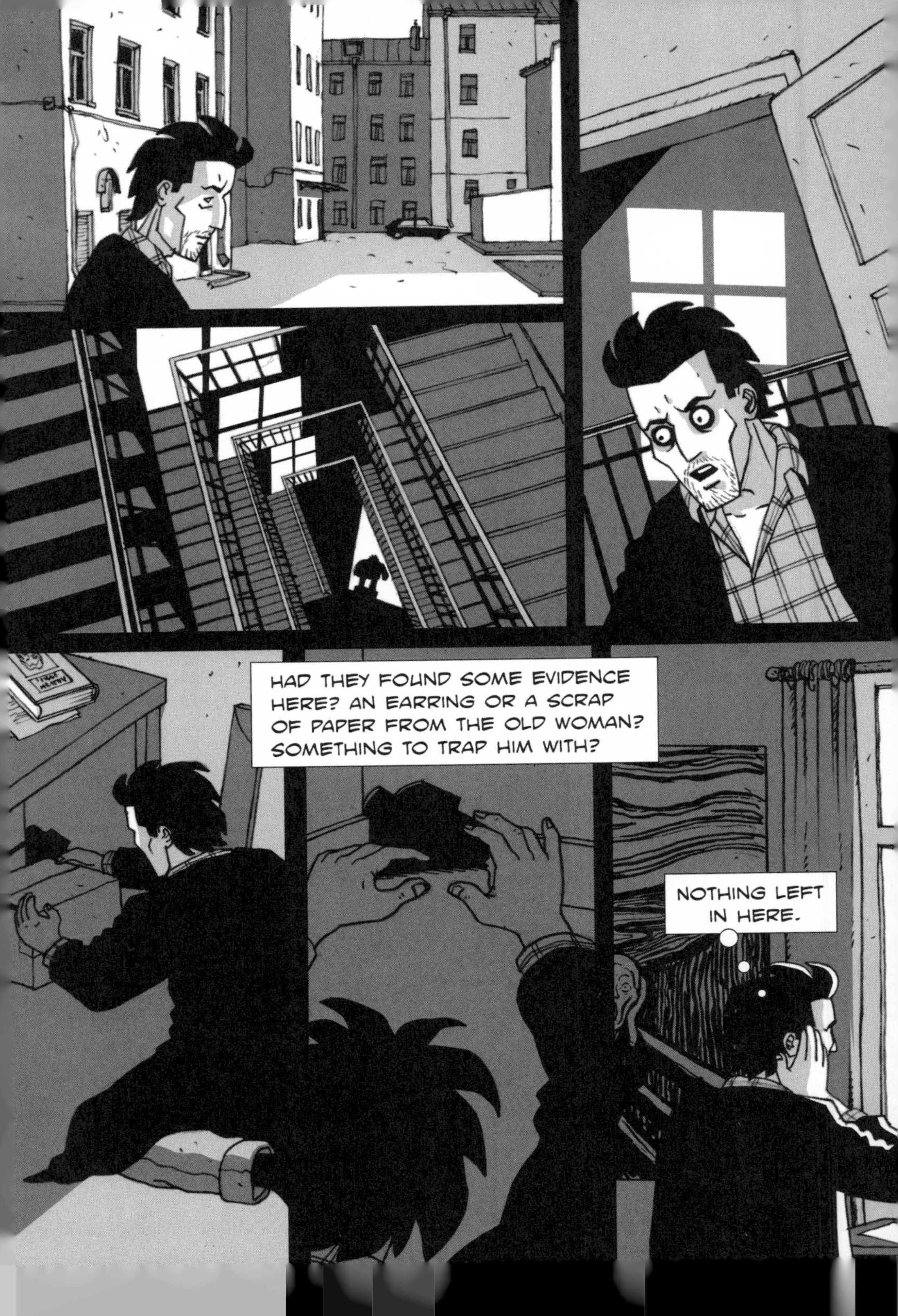
HAD THEY FOUND SOME EVIDENCE HERE? AN EARRING OR A SCRAP OF PAPER FROM THE OLD WOMAN? SOMETHING TO TRAP HIM WITH?
NOTHING LEFT IN HERE.

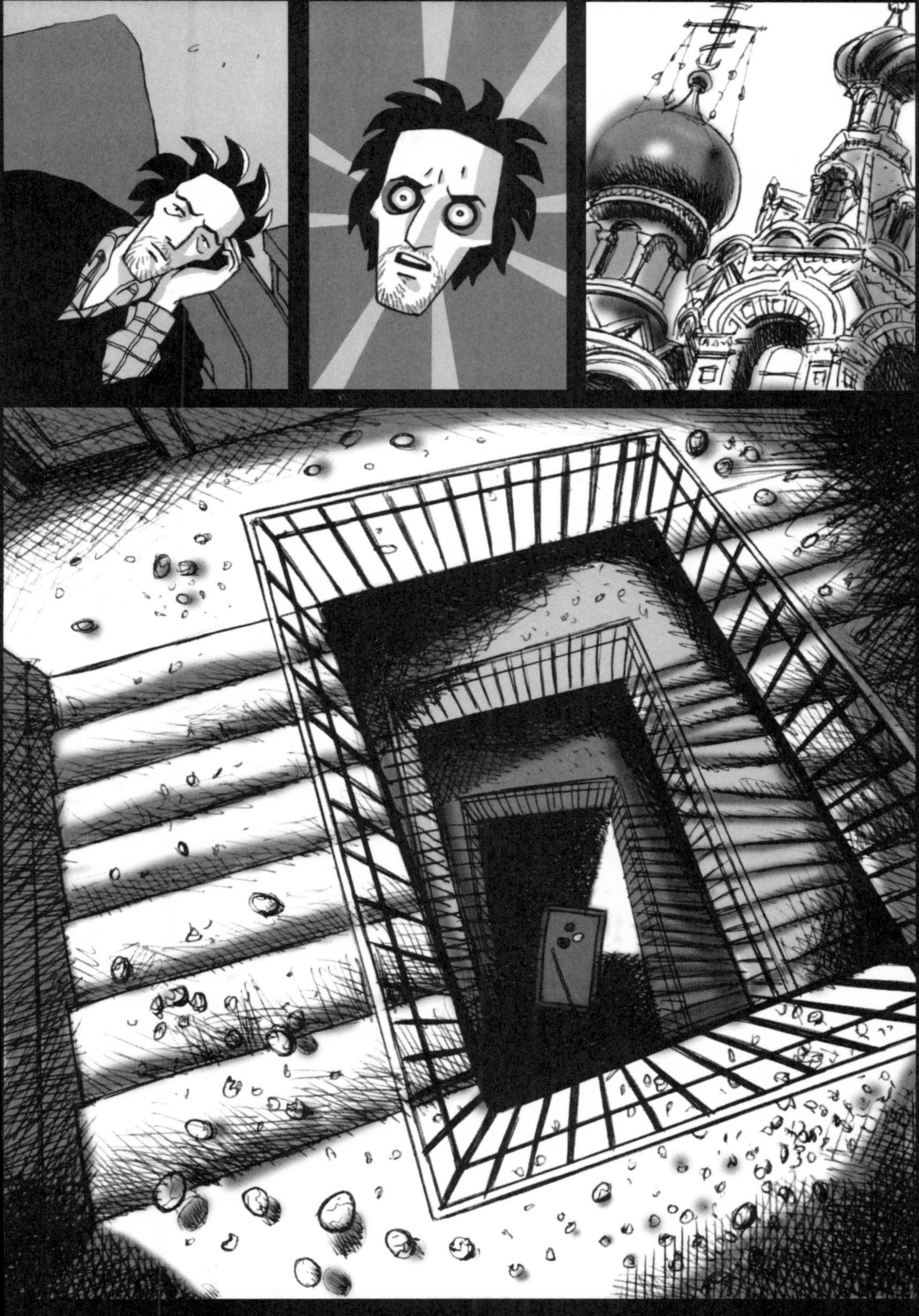

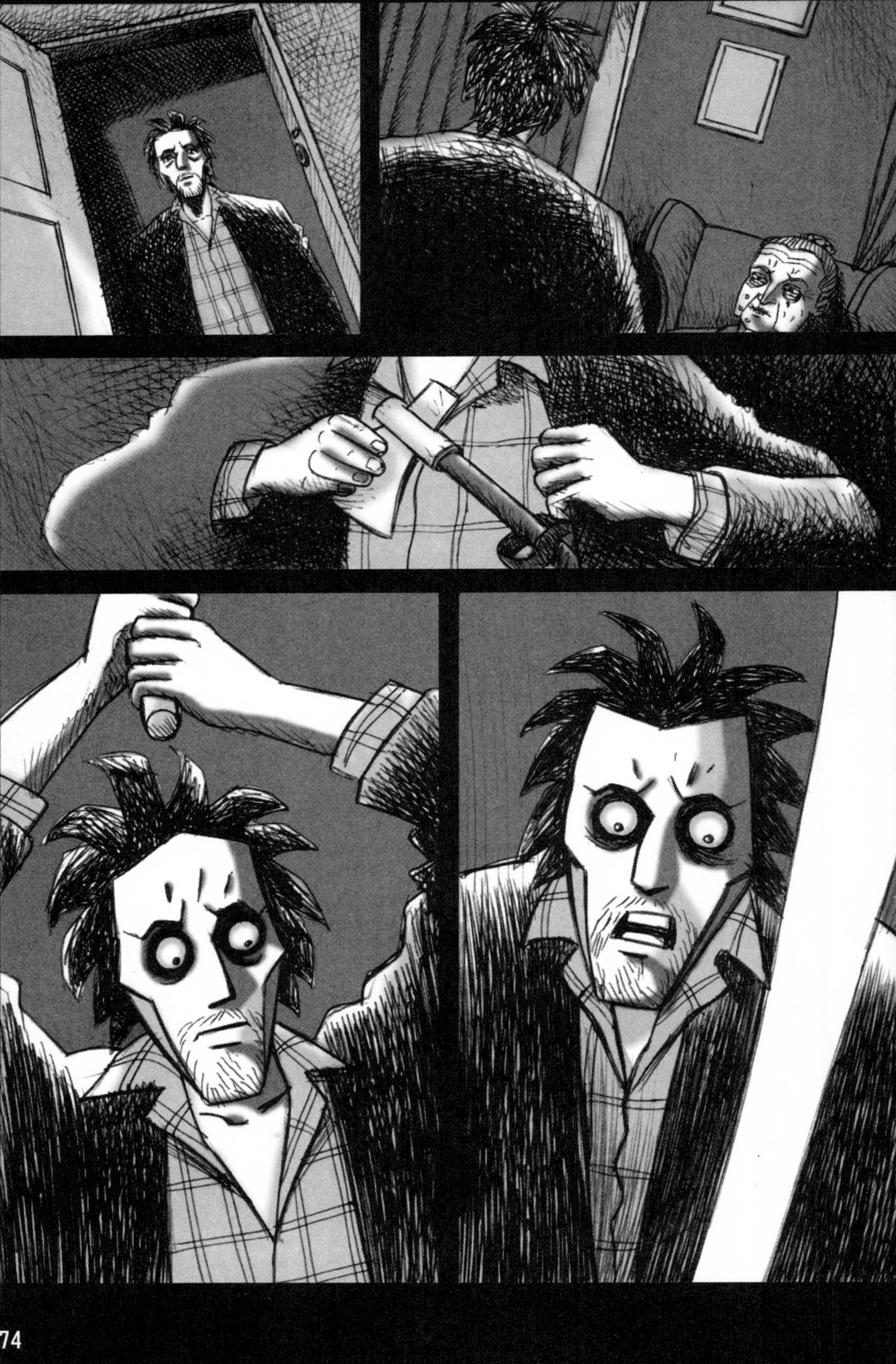

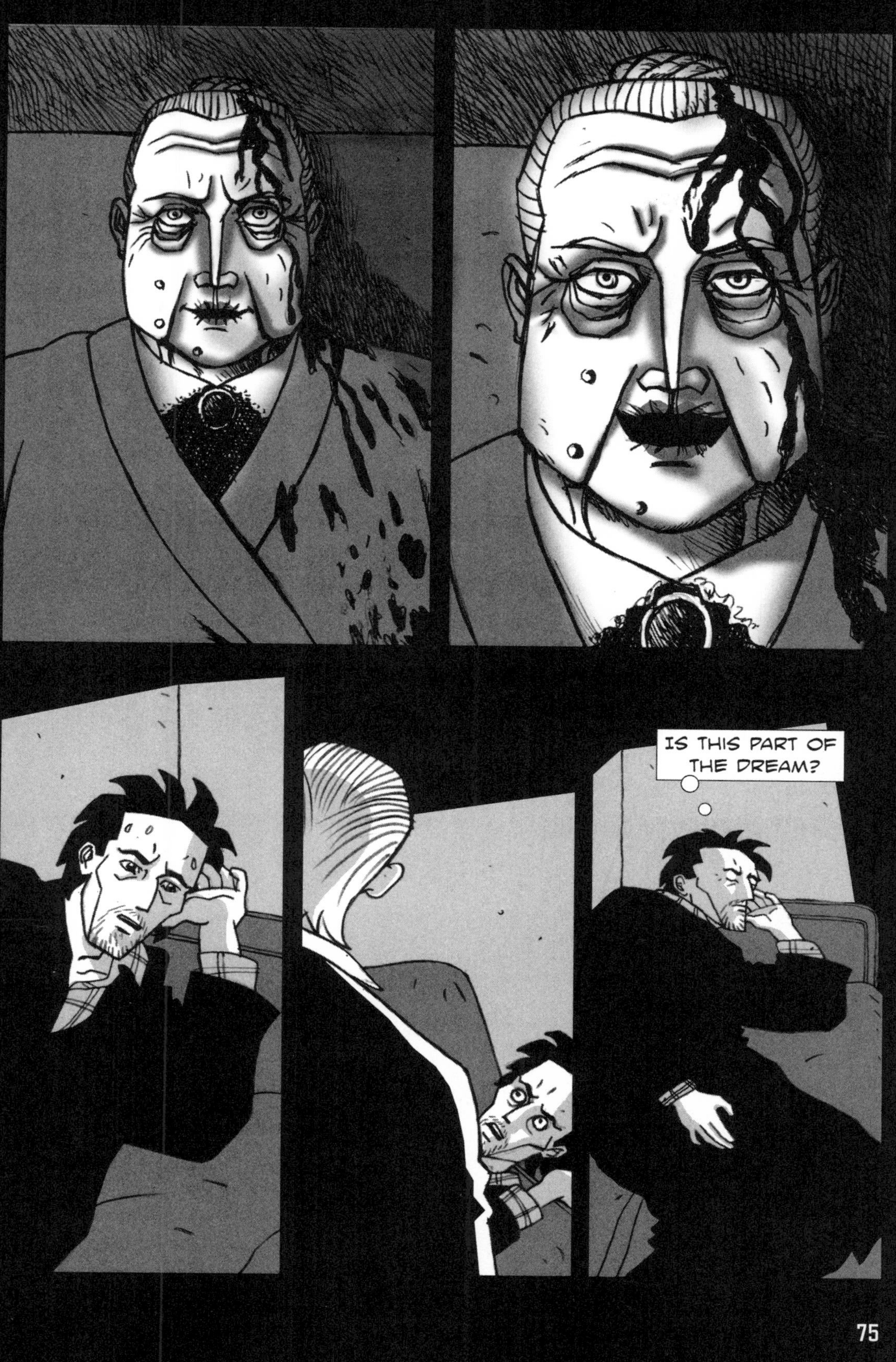
IS THIS PART OF THE DREAM?

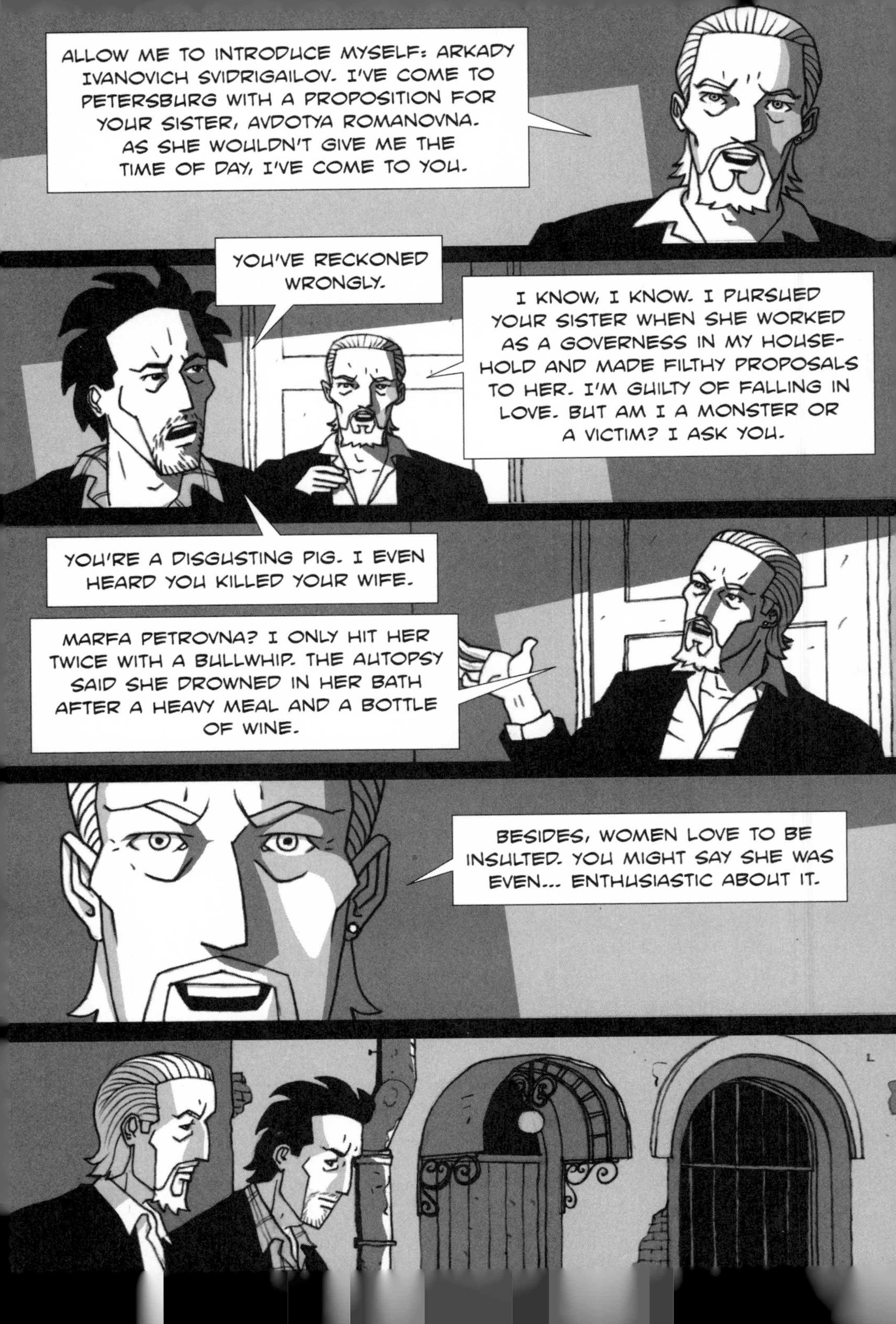
ALLOW ME TO INTRODUCE MYSELF: ARKADY IVANOVICH SVIDRIGAILOV. I'VE COME TO PETERSBURG WITH A PROPOSITION FOR YOUR SISTER, AVDOTYA ROMANOVNA. AS SHE WOULDN'T GIVE ME THE TIME OF DAY, I'VE COME TO YOU.
YOU'VE RECKONED WRONGLY.
I KNOW, I KNOW. I PURSUED YOUR SISTER WHEN SHE WORKED AS A GOVERNESS IN MY HOUSEHOLD AND MADE FILTHY PROPOSALS TO HER. I'M GUILTY OF FALLING IN LOVE. BUT AM I A MONSTER OR A VICTIM? I ASK YOU.
YOU'RE A DISGUSTING PIG. I EVEN HEARD YOU KILLED YOUR WIFE.
MARFA PETROVNA? I ONLY HIT HER TWICE WITH A BULLWHIP. THE AUTOPSY SAID SHE DROWNED IN HER BATH AFTER A HEAVY MEAL AND A BOTTLE OF WINE.
BESIDES, WOMEN LOVE TO BE INSULTED. YOU MIGHT SAY SHE WAS EVEN... ENTHUSIASTIC ABOUT IT.

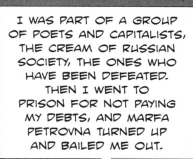

I WAS PART OF A GROUP OF POETS AND CAPITALISTS, THE CREAM OF RUSSIAN SOCIETY, THE ONES WHO HAVE BEEN DEFEATED. THEN I WENT TO PRISON FOR NOT PAYING MY DEBTS, AND MARFA PETROVNA TURNED UP AND BAILED ME OUT.

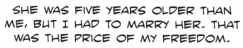

SHE WAS FIVE YEARS OLDER THAN ME, BUT I HAD TO MARRY HER. THAT WAS THE PRICE OF MY FREEDOM.

SHE STILL COMES TO SEE ME FROM TIME TO TIME.

I THOUGHT SHE WAS DEAD.

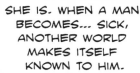

SHE IS. WHEN A MAN BECOMES... SICK, ANOTHER WORLD MAKES ITSELF KNOWN TO HIM.

I DON'T BELIEVE IN ANOTHER WORLD.

WE ALWAYS THINK OF ETERNITY AS IMMENSE. BUT WHAT IF IT'S JUST A FILTHY BROOM CLOSET FILLED WITH SPIDERS?

THIS LUZHIN CHARACTER IS NO MATCH FOR YOUR SISTER. SHE'S SACRIFICING HERSELF. I WOULD LIKE TO CONVINCE HER OF THIS, ALTHOUGH I'M NO LONGER IN LOVE WITH HER, AND TO GIVE HER TEN THOUSAND ROUBLES IN CASH TO MAKE IT EASY FOR HER TO BREAK WITH HIM.

I MUST INFORM YOU THAT SVIDRIGAILOV IS HERE IN PETERSBURG.

HE JUST CAME TO SEE ME. HALF AN HOUR AGO. I WAS SLEEPING. HE WANTS ME TO BE HIS FRIEND.

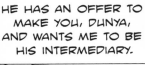

HE HAS AN OFFER TO MAKE YOU, DUNYA, AND WANTS ME TO BE HIS INTERMEDIARY.

THEY SAY HE KILLED HIS WIFE, MARFA PETROVNA.

MY GOD!

THERE IS ALSO A RUMOR ABOUT A FOURTEEN-YEAR-OLD GIRL WHO LIVED HERE IN PETERSBURG. DEAF AND DUMB.

ONE DAY, THEY FOUND HER HANGING IN THE ATTIC. WORD HAS IT SHE WAS... ABUSED BY SVIDRIGAILOV.

THAT'S ENOUGH ABOUT SVIDRIGAILOV. HE MAKES MY FLESH CRAWL... YOU WANTED TO TALK TO US, PYOTR PETROVICH?

NOT IN FRONT OF RODION ROMANOVICH.

HE'S MY BROTHER.

THAT DOESN'T MEAN I HAVE TO TOLERATE HIM.

WHY DON'T YOU DROP YOUR PRIDE? I DON'T WANT TO HAVE TO CHOOSE BETWEEN MY HUSBAND AND MY BROTHER.

HE CAN'T SUPPORT YOU. I CAN.

SO YOU'RE COUNTING ON OUR HELPLESSNESS...

JUST AS I SAID. WELL, SISTER, WHAT DO YOU SAY NOW?

I SAY: GET OUT OF HERE!

IF I WALK OUT THAT DOOR, I'M NEVER COMING BACK.

OUT!

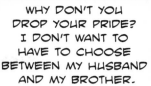

79

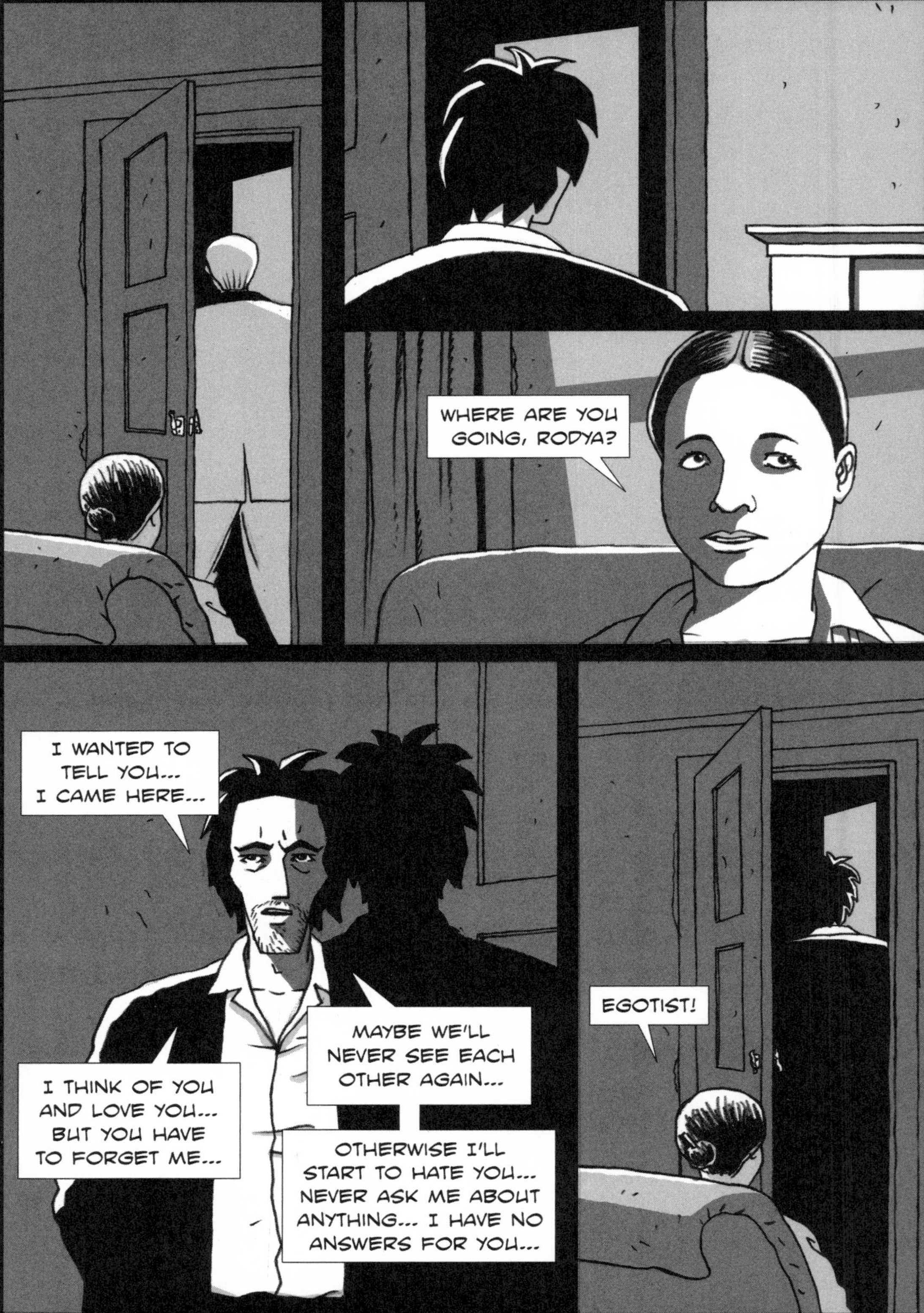
WHERE ARE YOU GOING, RODYA?
I WANTED TO TELL YOU... I CAME HERE...
I THINK OF YOU AND LOVE YOU... BUT YOU HAVE TO FORGET ME...
MAYBE WE'LL NEVER SEE EACH OTHER AGAIN...
OTHERWISE I'LL START TO HATE YOU... NEVER ASK ME ABOUT ANYTHING... I HAVE NO ANSWERS FOR YOU...
EGOTIST!

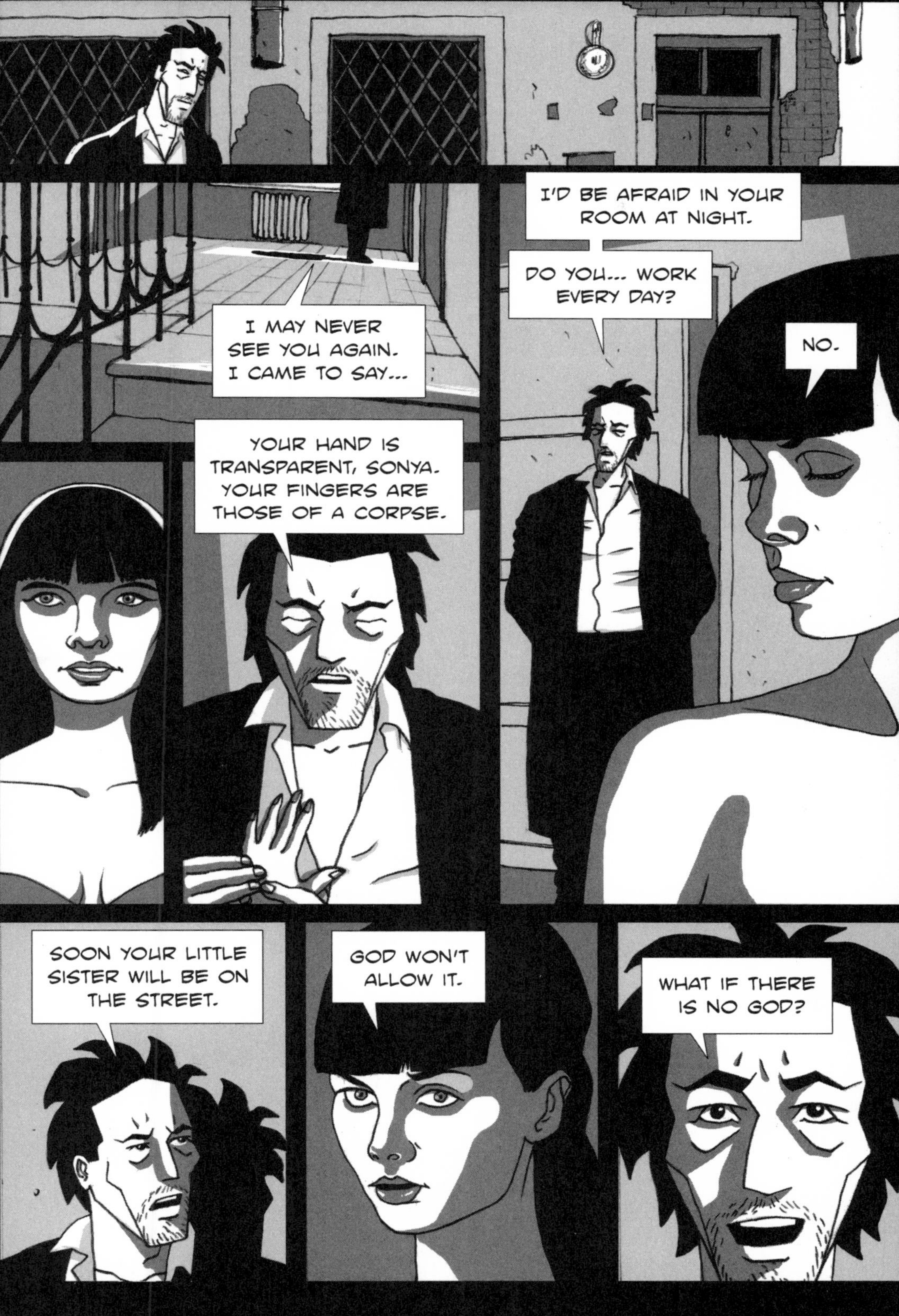
I MAY NEVER SEE YOU AGAIN. I CAME TO SAY...
I'D BE AFRAID IN YOUR ROOM AT NIGHT.
DO YOU... WORK EVERY DAY?
NO.
YOUR HAND IS TRANSPARENT, SONYA. YOUR FINGERS ARE THOSE OF A CORPSE.
SOON YOUR LITTLE SISTER WILL BE ON THE STREET.
GOD WON'T ALLOW IT.
WHAT IF THERE IS NO GOD?

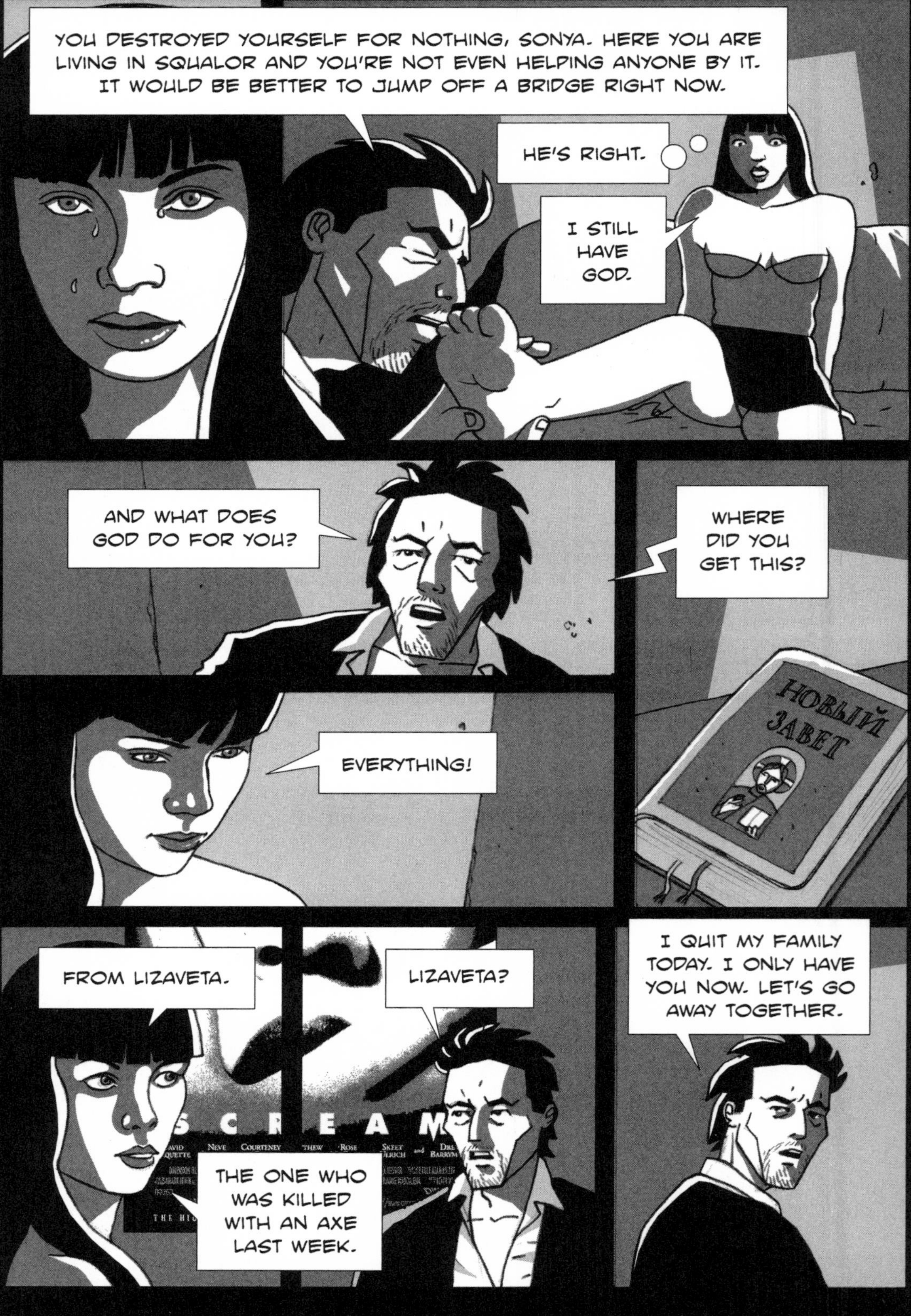
YOU DESTROYED YOURSELF FOR NOTHING, SONYA. HERE YOU ARE LIVING IN SQUALOR AND YOU'RE NOT EVEN HELPING ANYONE BY IT. IT WOULD BE BETTER TO JUMP OFF A BRIDGE RIGHT NOW.
HE'S RIGHT.
I STILL HAVE GOD.
AND WHAT DOES GOD DO FOR YOU?
WHERE DID YOU GET THIS?
EVERYTHING!
НОВЫЙ ЗАВЕТ
FROM LIZAVETA.
LIZAVETA?
THE ONE WHO WAS KILLED WITH AN AXE LAST WEEK.
I QUIT MY FAMILY TODAY. I ONLY HAVE YOU NOW. LET'S GO AWAY TOGETHER.

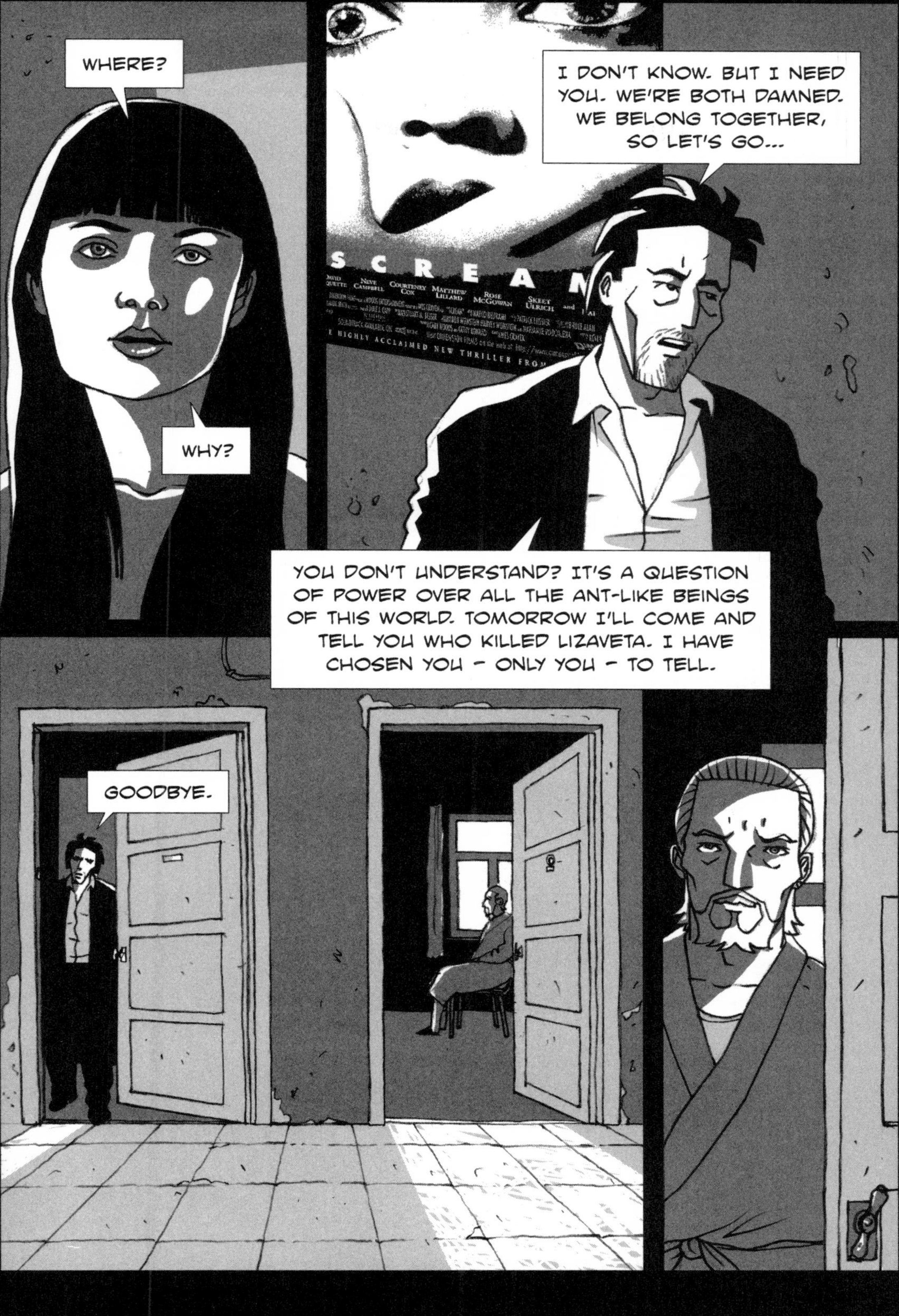
WHERE?
WHY?
I DON'T KNOW. BUT I NEED YOU. WE'RE BOTH DAMNED. WE BELONG TOGETHER, SO LET'S GO...
YOU DON'T UNDERSTAND? IT'S A QUESTION OF POWER OVER ALL THE ANT-LIKE BEINGS OF THIS WORLD. TOMORROW I'LL COME AND TELL YOU WHO KILLED LIZAVETA. I HAVE CHOSEN YOU - ONLY YOU - TO TELL.
GOODBYE.

I'VE BROUGHT YOU THE PAPER YOU ASKED FOR... ABOUT MY FATHER'S WATCH...

THIS WILL DO FINE.

YOU SEEMED TO SAY YESTERDAY YOU WANTED TO SPEAK TO ME... OFFICIALLY, ABOUT THAT MURDERED WOMAN.

WHY DID I SAY "SEEMED"?

YOU KNOW, I'M ON TO YOUR TECHNIQUE. YOU START BY DIVERTING THE SUBJECT'S ATTENTION WITH TRIFLES...

YOU LULL HIM INTO COMPLACENCY, THEN YOU TRAP HIM WITH A FATAL QUESTION. IT MAKES ME SICK. SO: EITHER ASK YOUR QUESTIONS OR LET ME GET OUT OF HERE.

WHAT IS THERE TO ASK?

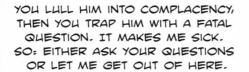

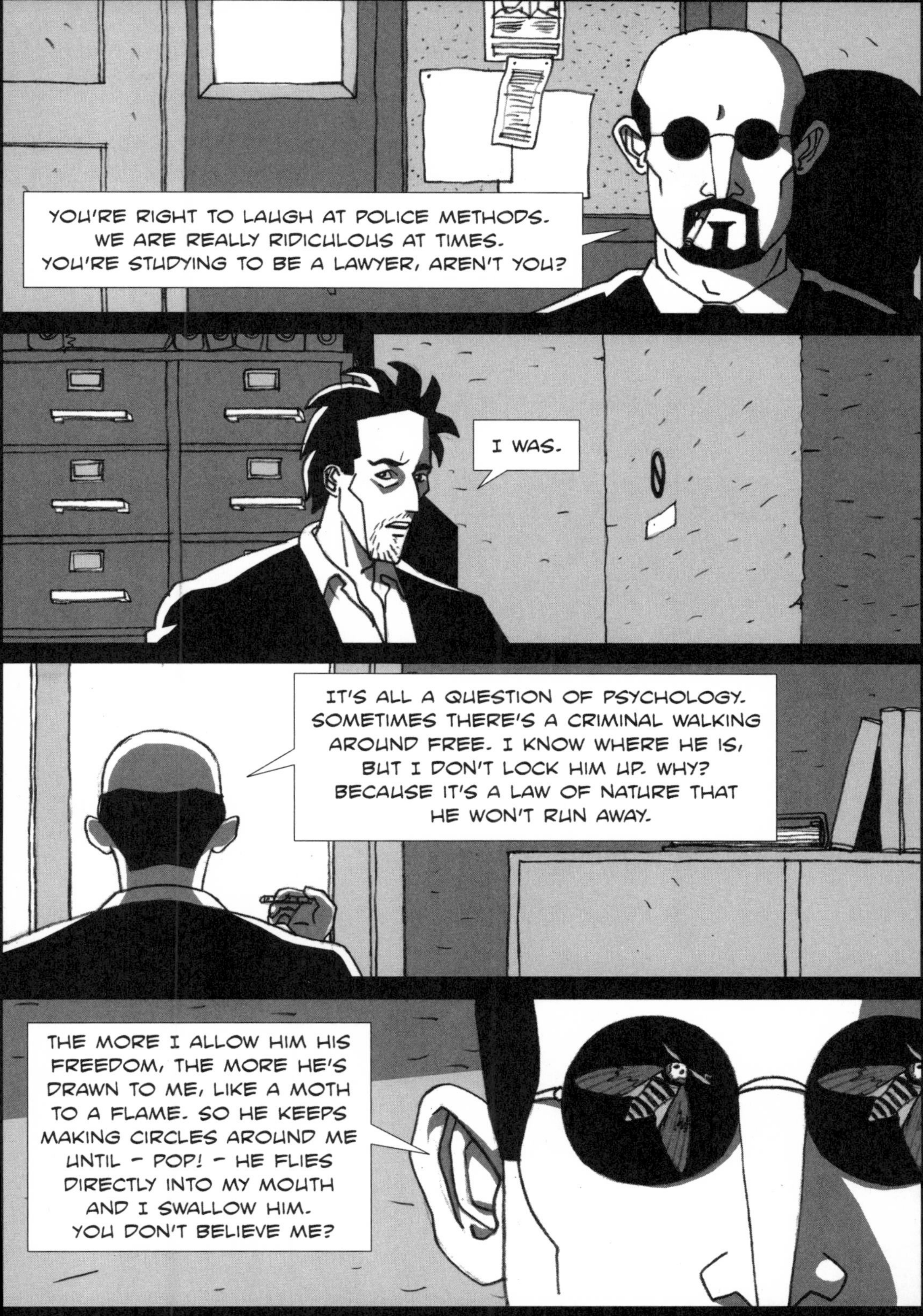
YOU'RE RIGHT TO LAUGH AT POLICE METHODS. WE ARE REALLY RIDICULOUS AT TIMES. YOU'RE STUDYING TO BE A LAWYER, AREN'T YOU?
I WAS.
IT'S ALL A QUESTION OF PSYCHOLOGY. SOMETIMES THERE'S A CRIMINAL WALKING AROUND FREE. I KNOW WHERE HE IS, BUT I DON'T LOCK HIM UP. WHY? BECAUSE IT'S A LAW OF NATURE THAT HE WON'T RUN AWAY.
THE MORE I ALLOW HIM HIS FREEDOM, THE MORE HE'S DRAWN TO ME, LIKE A MOTH TO A FLAME. SO HE KEEPS MAKING CIRCLES AROUND ME UNTIL - POP! - HE FLIES DIRECTLY INTO MY MOUTH AND I SWALLOW HIM. YOU DON'T BELIEVE ME?

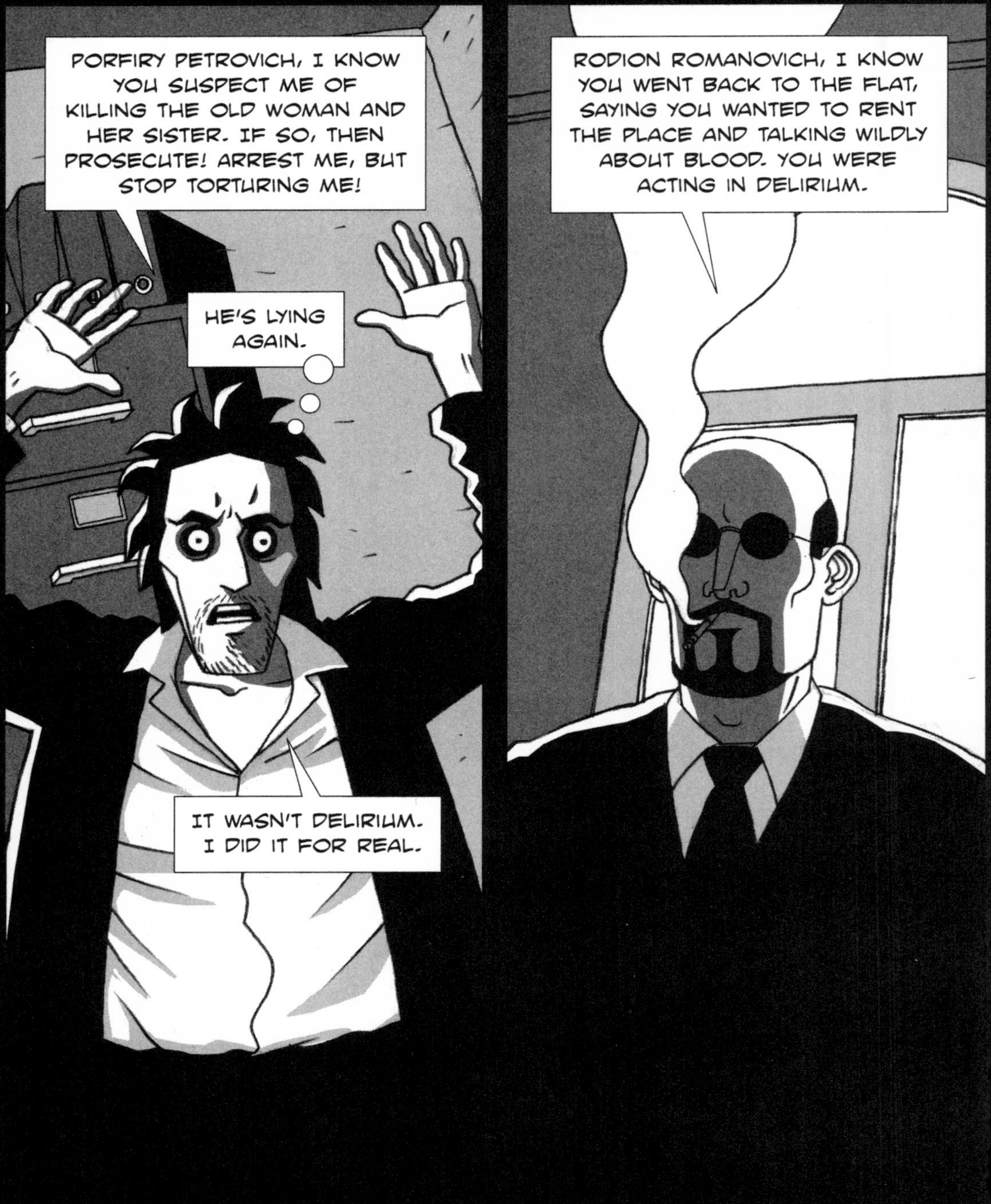
PORFIRY PETROVICH, I KNOW YOU SUSPECT ME OF KILLING THE OLD WOMAN AND HER SISTER. IF SO, THEN PROSECUTE! ARREST ME, BUT STOP TORTURING ME!
HE'S LYING AGAIN.
IT WASN'T DELIRIUM. I DID IT FOR REAL.
RODION ROMANOVICH, I KNOW YOU WENT BACK TO THE FLAT, SAYING YOU WANTED TO RENT THE PLACE AND TALKING WILDLY ABOUT BLOOD. YOU WERE ACTING IN DELIRIUM.

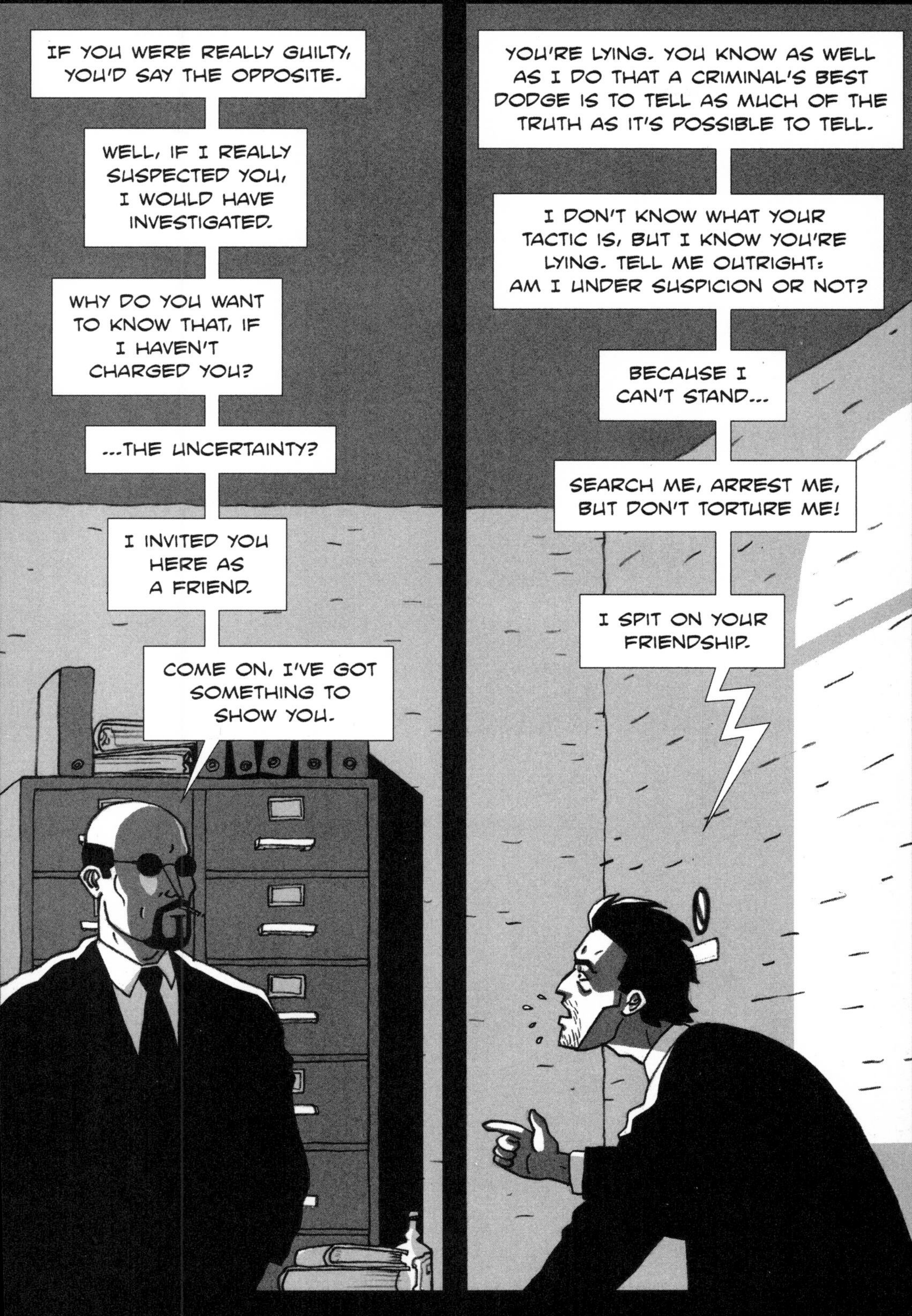
IF YOU WERE REALLY GUILTY, YOU'D SAY THE OPPOSITE.
WELL, IF I REALLY SUSPECTED YOU, I WOULD HAVE INVESTIGATED.
WHY DO YOU WANT TO KNOW THAT, IF I HAVEN'T CHARGED YOU?
...THE UNCERTAINTY?
I INVITED YOU HERE AS A FRIEND.
COME ON, I'VE GOT SOMETHING TO SHOW YOU.
YOU'RE LYING. YOU KNOW AS WELL AS I DO THAT A CRIMINAL'S BEST DODGE IS TO TELL AS MUCH OF THE TRUTH AS IT'S POSSIBLE TO TELL.
I DON'T KNOW WHAT YOUR TACTIC IS, BUT I KNOW YOU'RE LYING. TELL ME OUTRIGHT: AM I UNDER SUSPICION OR NOT?
BECAUSE I CAN'T STAND...
SEARCH ME, ARREST ME, BUT DON'T TORTURE ME!
I SPIT ON YOUR FRIENDSHIP.

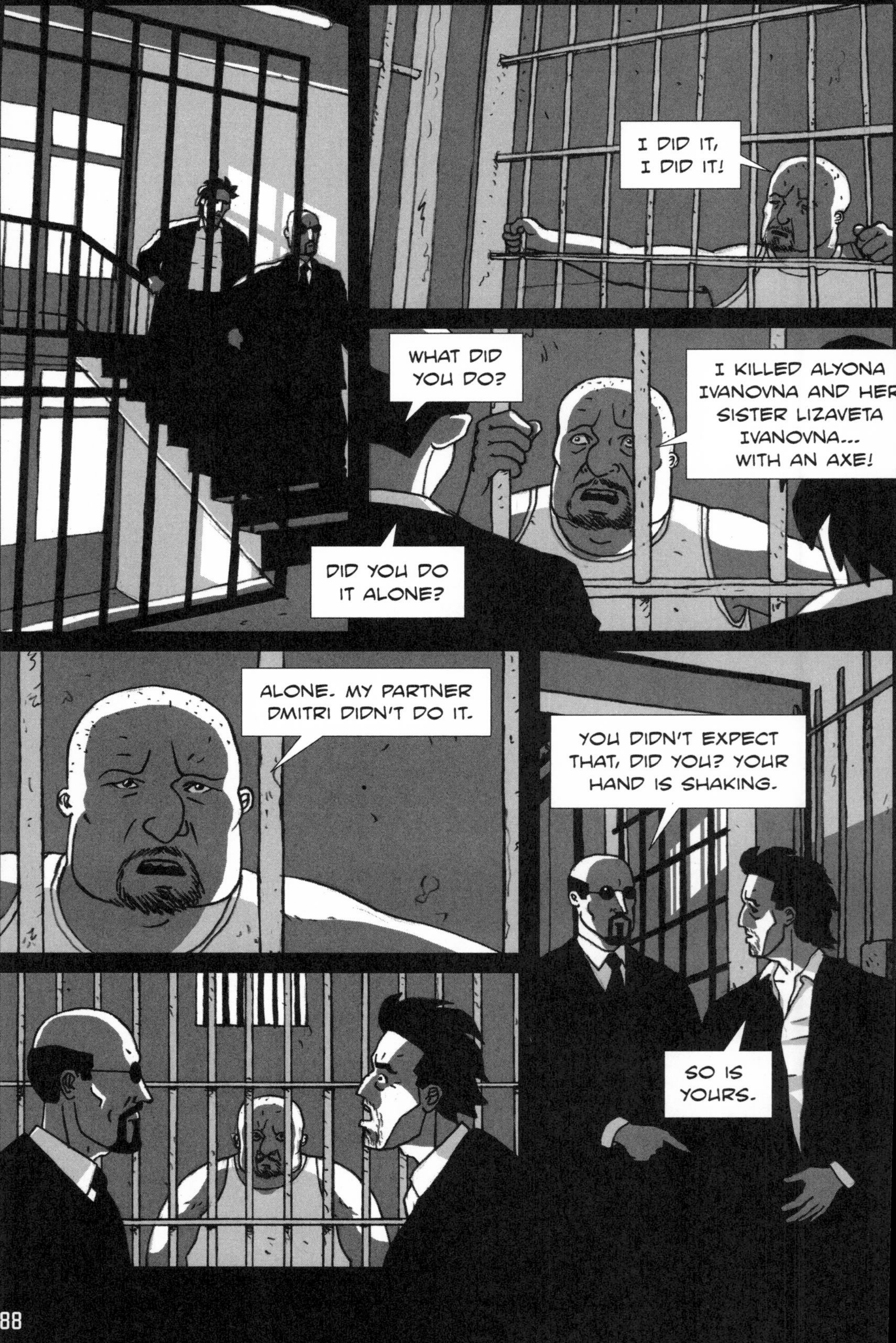
I DID IT,
I DID IT!
WHAT DID YOU DO?
I KILLED ALYONA IVANOVNA AND HER SISTER LIZAVETA IVANOVNA... WITH AN AXE!
DID YOU DO IT ALONE?
ALONE. MY PARTNER DMITRI DIDN'T DO IT.
YOU DIDN'T EXPECT THAT, DID YOU? YOUR HAND IS SHAKING.
SO IS YOURS.

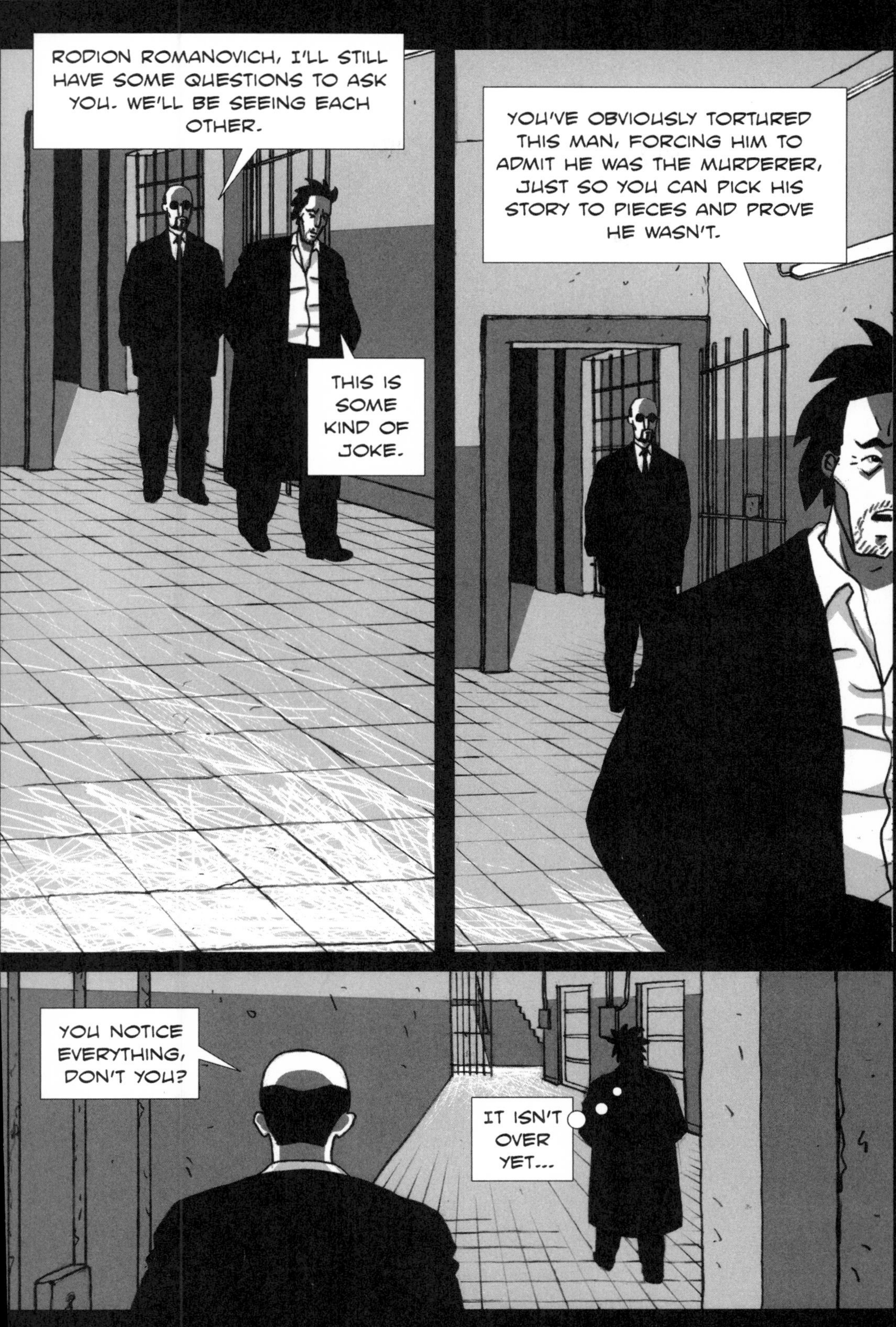
RODION ROMANOVICH, I'LL STILL HAVE SOME QUESTIONS TO ASK YOU. WE'LL BE SEEING EACH OTHER.
THIS IS SOME KIND OF JOKE.
YOU'VE OBVIOUSLY TORTURED THIS MAN, FORCING HIM TO ADMIT HE WAS THE MURDERER, JUST SO YOU CAN PICK HIS STORY TO PIECES AND PROVE HE WASN'T.
YOU NOTICE EVERYTHING, DON'T YOU?
IT ISN'T OVER YET...

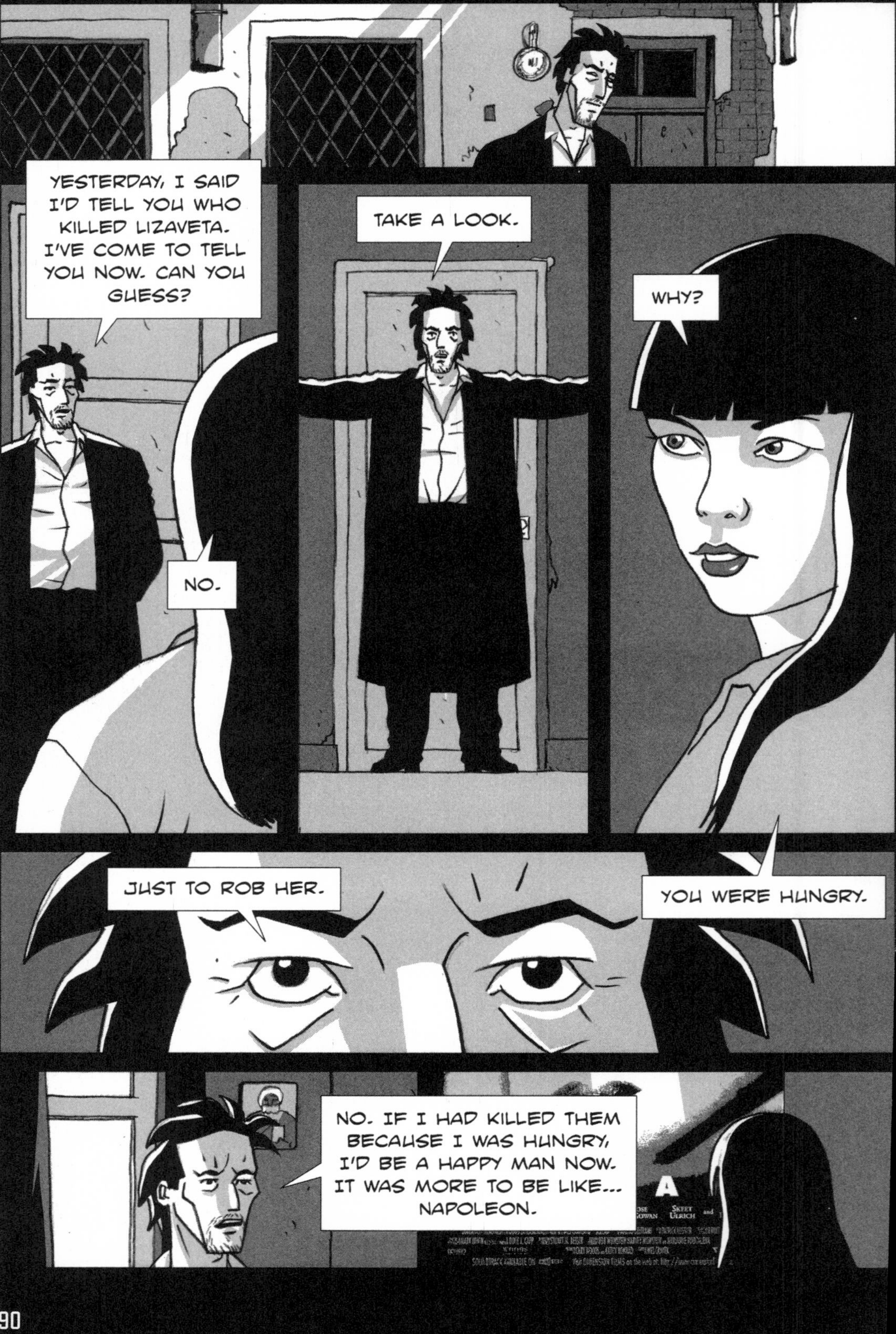
YESTERDAY, I SAID I'D TELL YOU WHO KILLED LIZAVETA. I'VE COME TO TELL YOU NOW. CAN YOU GUESS?
NO.
TAKE A LOOK.
WHY?
JUST TO ROB HER.
YOU WERE HUNGRY.
NO. IF I HAD KILLED THEM BECAUSE I WAS HUNGRY, I'D BE A HAPPY MAN NOW. IT WAS MORE TO BE LIKE... NAPOLEON.

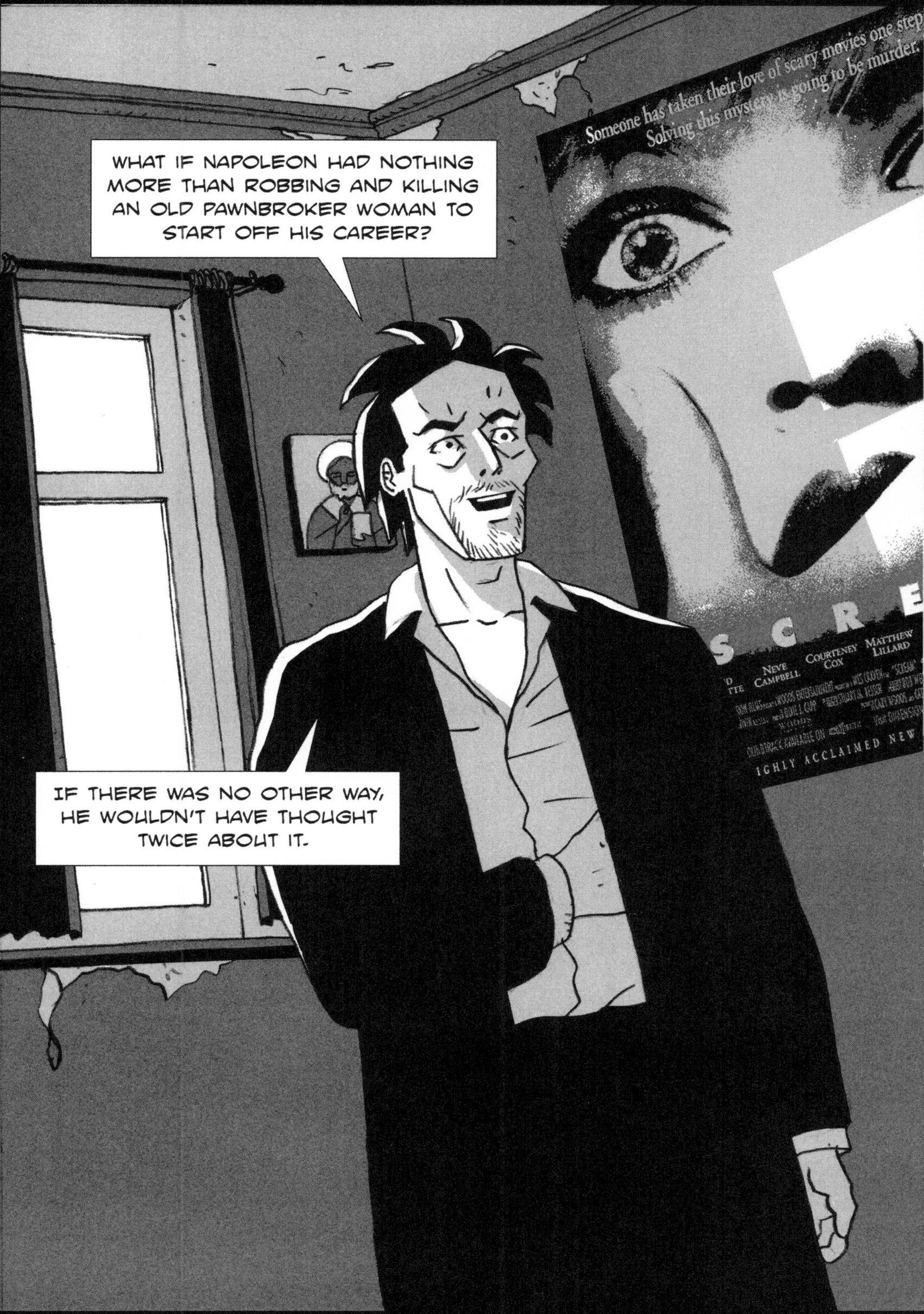
WHAT IF NAPOLEON HAD NOTHING MORE THAN ROBBING AND KILLING AN OLD PAWNBROKER WOMAN TO START OFF HIS CAREER?
Someone has taken their love of scary movies one step
Solving this mystery is going to be murder.
NEVE CAMPBELL
COURTENEY COX
MATTHEW LILLARD
IF THERE WAS NO OTHER WAY, HE WOULDN'T HAVE THOUGHT TWICE ABOUT IT.

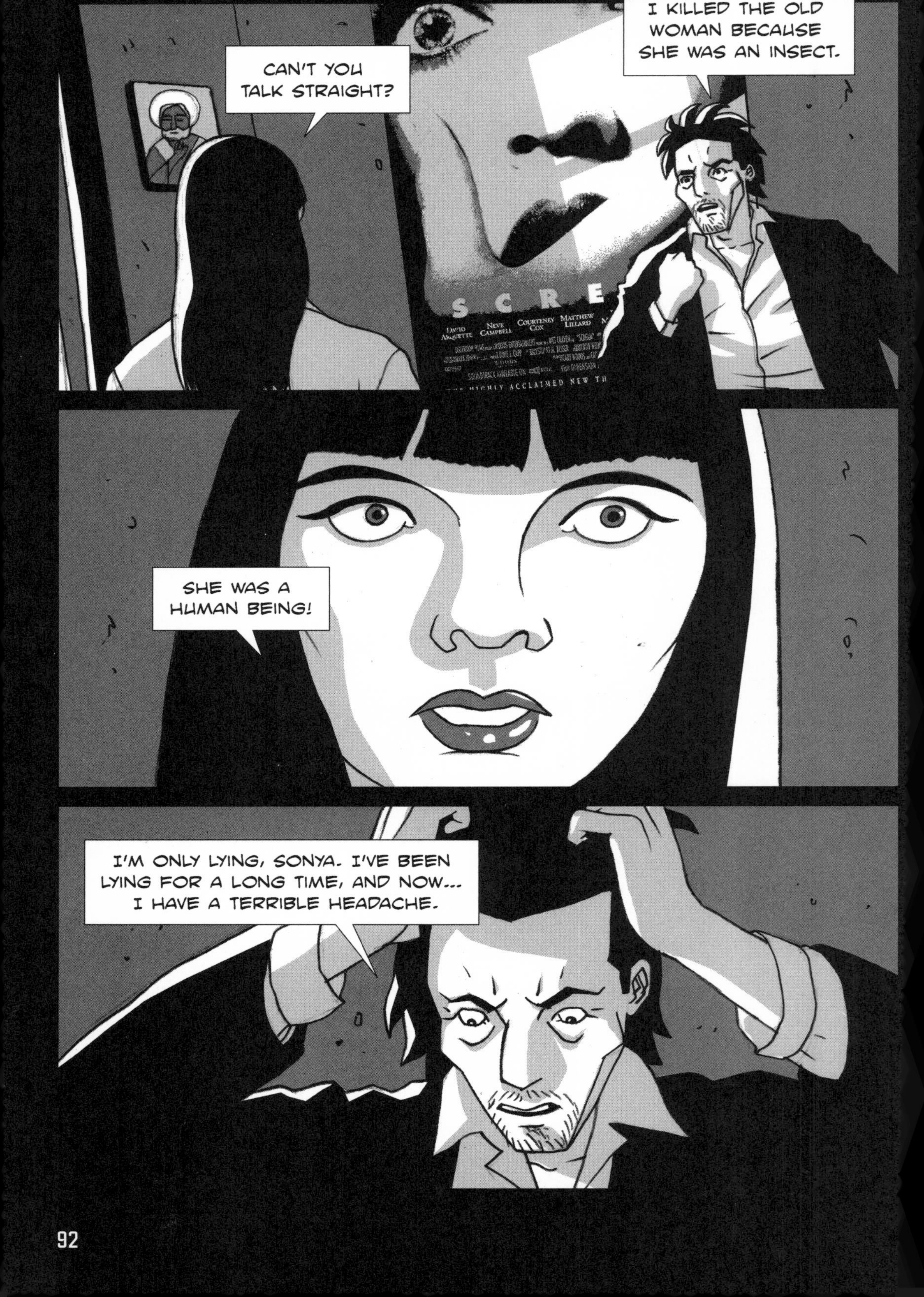
CAN'T YOU TALK STRAIGHT?
I KILLED THE OLD WOMAN BECAUSE SHE WAS AN INSECT.
SCRE
DAVID ARQUETTE
NEVE CAMPBELL
COURTENEY COX
MATTHEW LILLARD
SHE WAS A HUMAN BEING!
I'M ONLY LYING, SONYA. I'VE BEEN LYING FOR A LONG TIME, AND NOW... I HAVE A TERRIBLE HEADACHE.

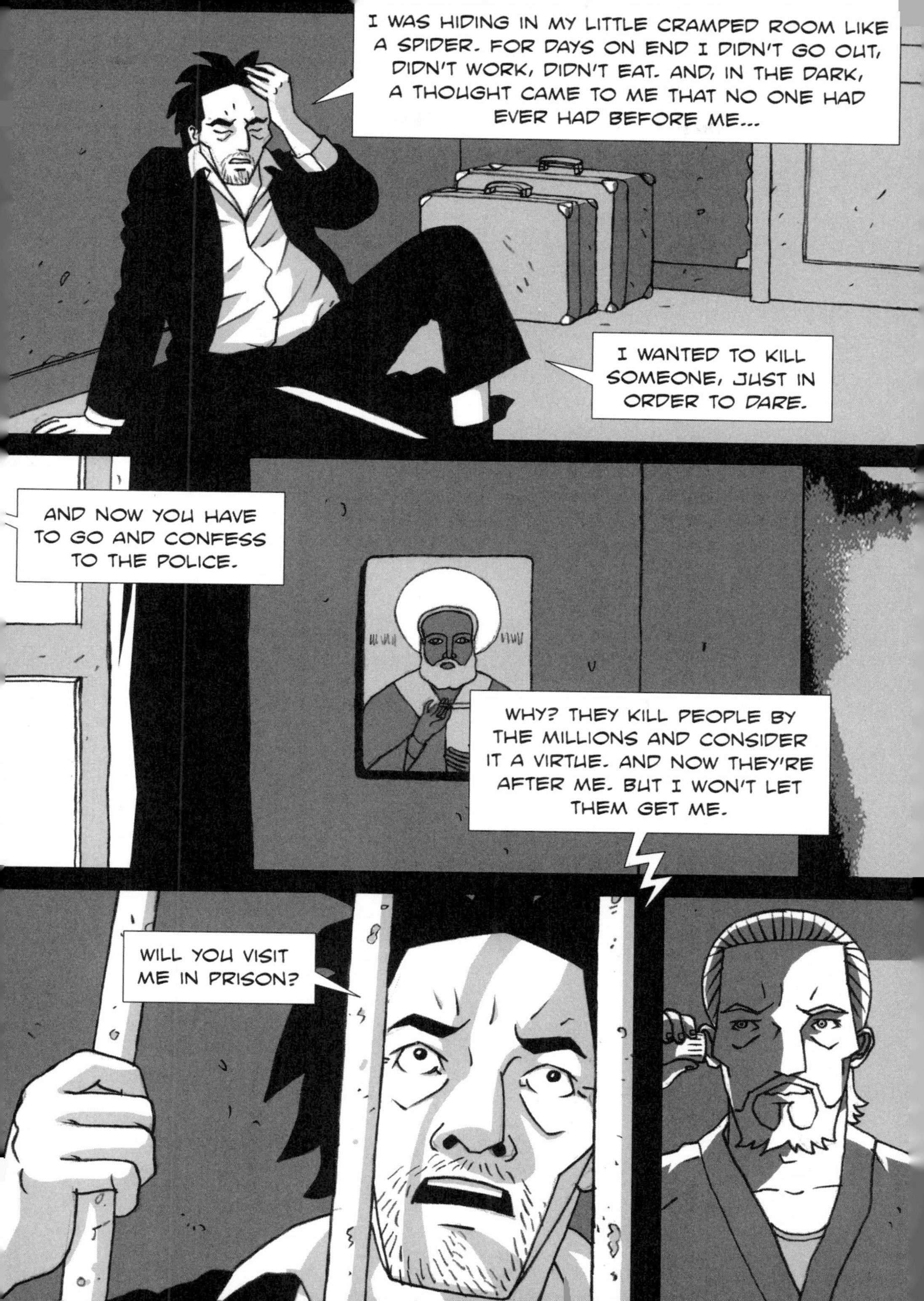
I WAS HIDING IN MY LITTLE CRAMPED ROOM LIKE A SPIDER. FOR DAYS ON END I DIDN'T GO OUT, DIDN'T WORK, DIDN'T EAT. AND, IN THE DARK, A THOUGHT CAME TO ME THAT NO ONE HAD EVER HAD BEFORE ME...
I WANTED TO KILL SOMEONE, JUST IN ORDER TO DARE.
AND NOW YOU HAVE TO GO AND CONFESS TO THE POLICE.
WHY? THEY KILL PEOPLE BY THE MILLIONS AND CONSIDER IT A VIRTUE. AND NOW THEY'RE AFTER ME. BUT I WON'T LET THEM GET ME.
WILL YOU VISIT ME IN PRISON?

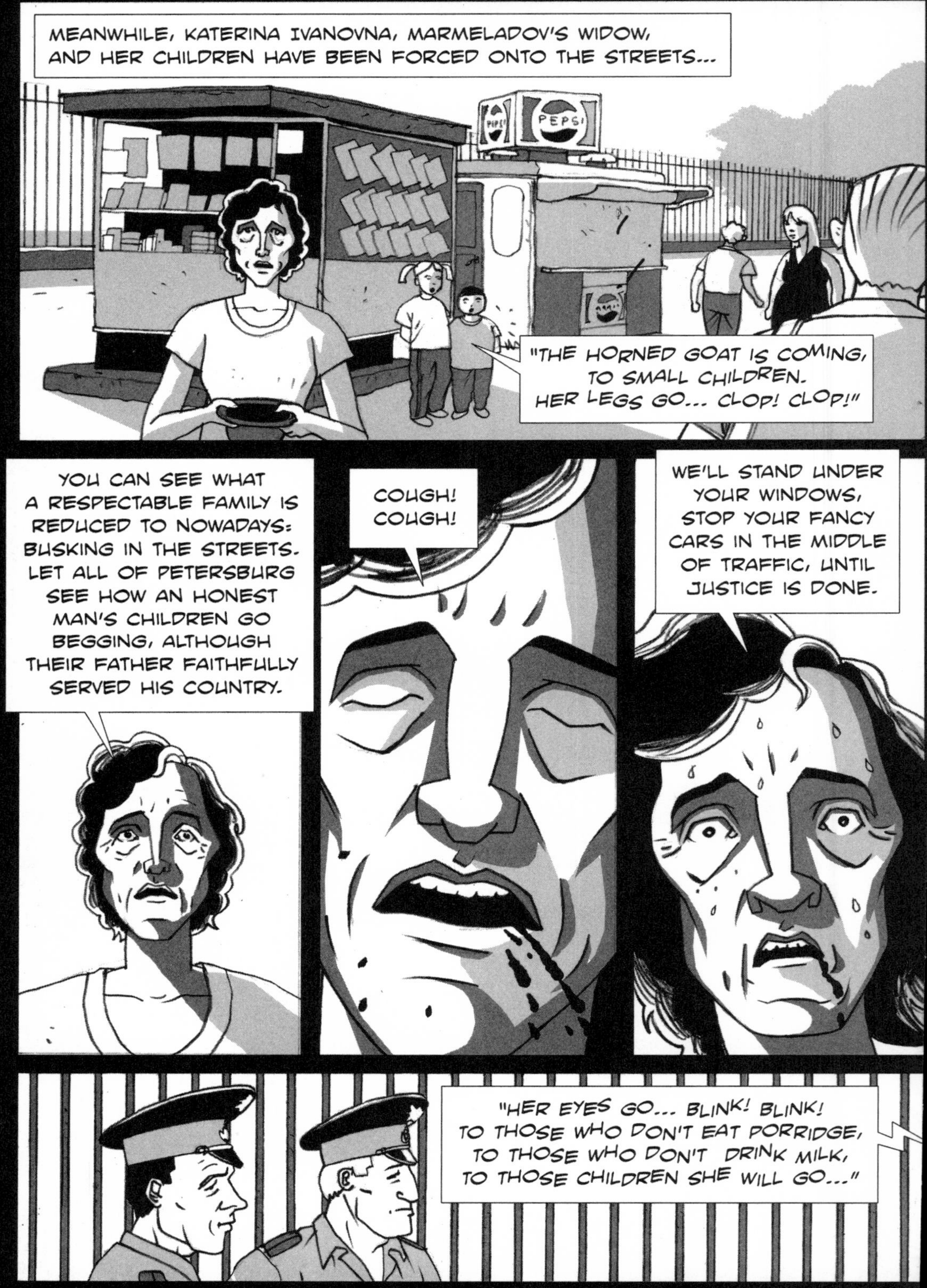
MEANWHILE, KATERINA IVANOVNA, MARMELADOV'S WIDOW, AND HER CHILDREN HAVE BEEN FORCED ONTO THE STREETS...
PEPSI
"THE HORNED GOAT IS COMING, TO SMALL CHILDREN. HER LEGS GO... CLOP! CLOP!"
YOU CAN SEE WHAT A RESPECTABLE FAMILY IS REDUCED TO NOWADAYS: BUSKING IN THE STREETS. LET ALL OF PETERSBURG SEE HOW AN HONEST MAN'S CHILDREN GO BEGGING, ALTHOUGH THEIR FATHER FAITHFULLY SERVED HIS COUNTRY.
COUGH! COUGH!
WE'LL STAND UNDER YOUR WINDOWS, STOP YOUR FANCY CARS IN THE MIDDLE OF TRAFFIC, UNTIL JUSTICE IS DONE.
"HER EYES GO... BLINK! BLINK! TO THOSE WHO DON'T EAT PORRIDGE, TO THOSE WHO DON'T DRINK MILK, TO THOSE CHILDREN SHE WILL GO..."

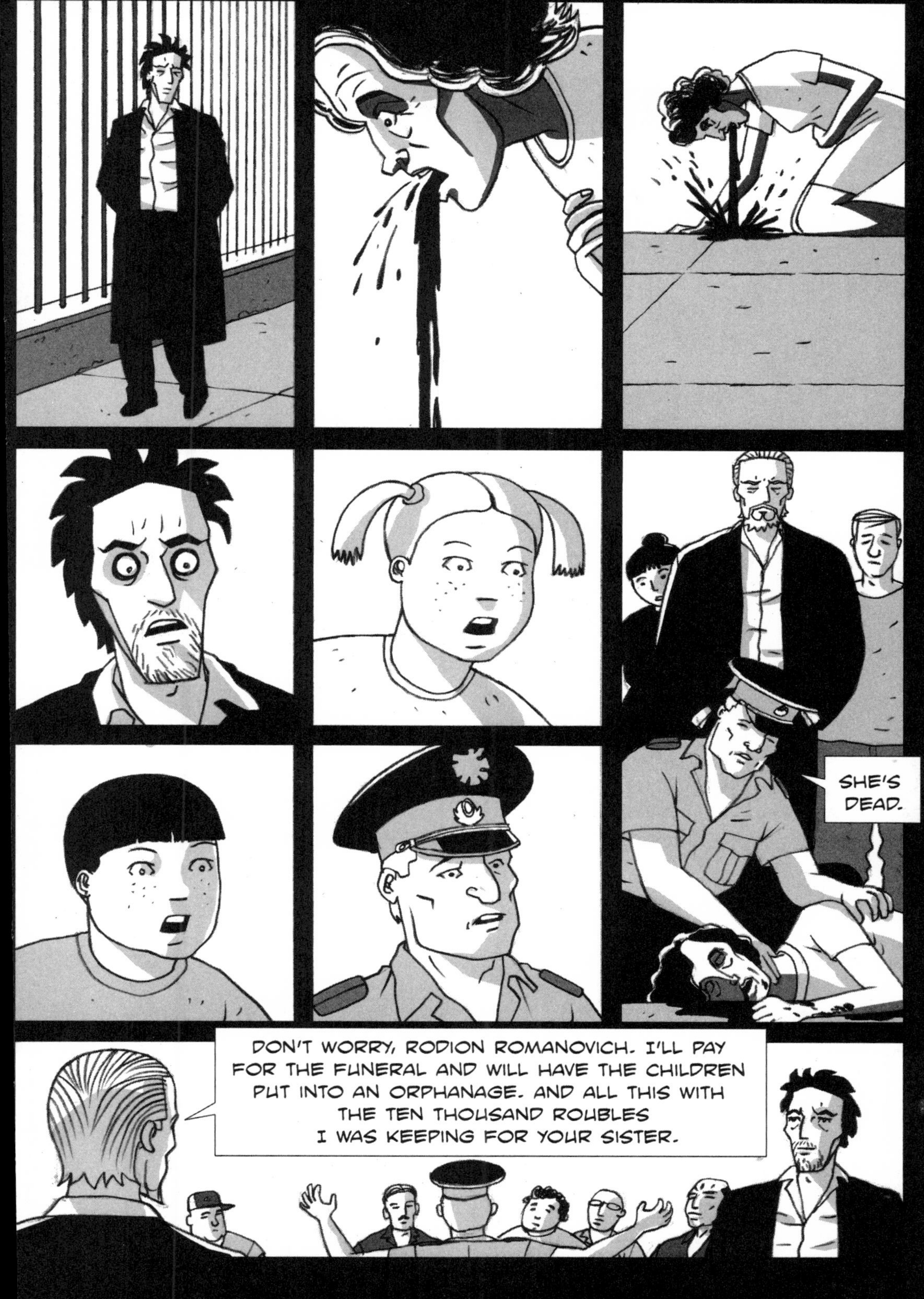
SHE'S DEAD.
DON'T WORRY, RODION ROMANOVICH. I'LL PAY FOR THE FUNERAL AND WILL HAVE THE CHILDREN PUT INTO AN ORPHANAGE. AND ALL THIS WITH THE TEN THOUSAND ROUBLES I WAS KEEPING FOR YOUR SISTER.

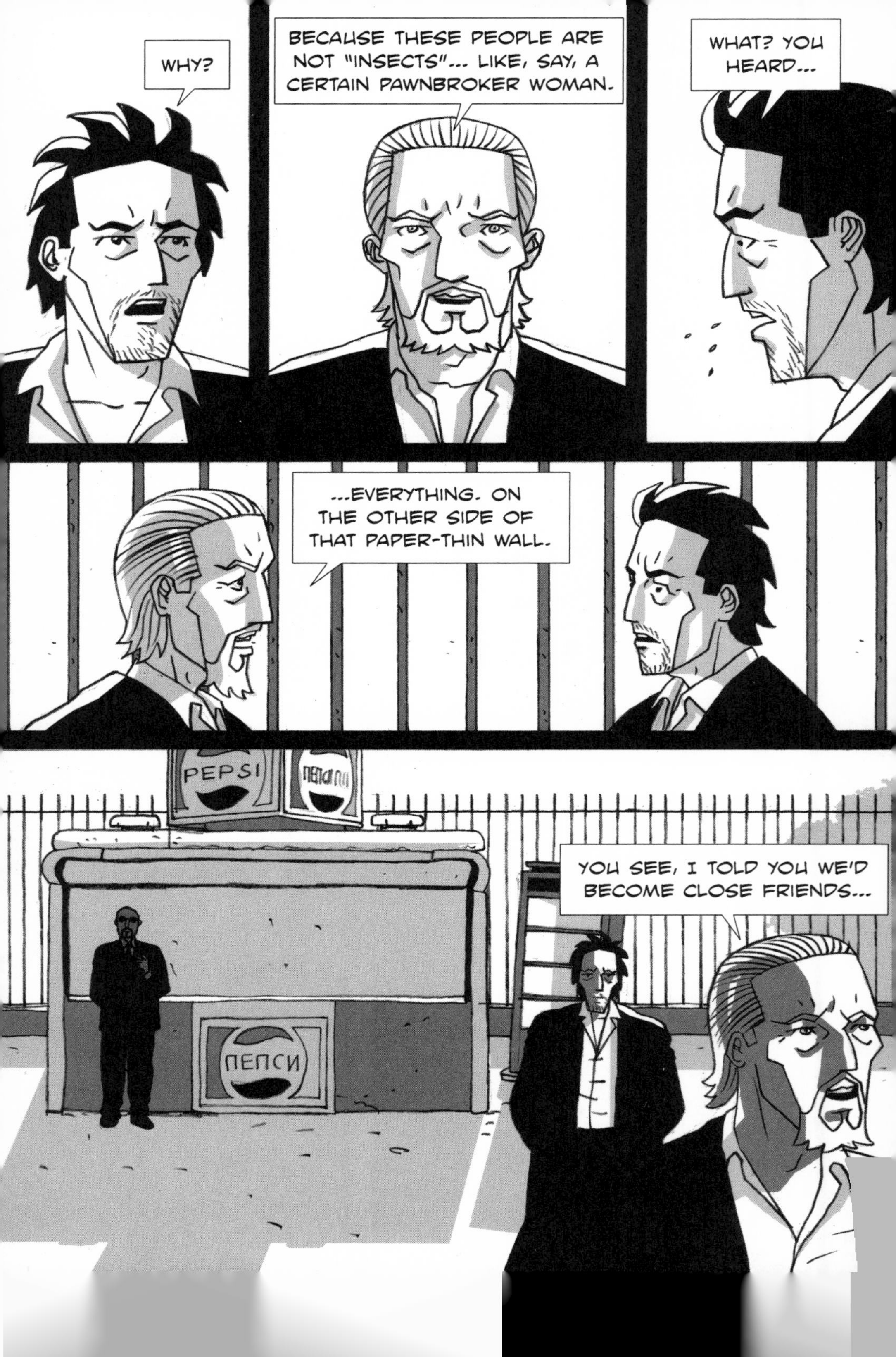
WHY?
BECAUSE THESE PEOPLE ARE NOT "INSECTS"... LIKE, SAY, A CERTAIN PAWNBROKER WOMAN.
WHAT? YOU HEARD...
...EVERYTHING. ON THE OTHER SIDE OF THAT PAPER-THIN WALL.
PEPSI
ПЕПСИ
YOU SEE, I TOLD YOU WE'D BECOME CLOSE FRIENDS...

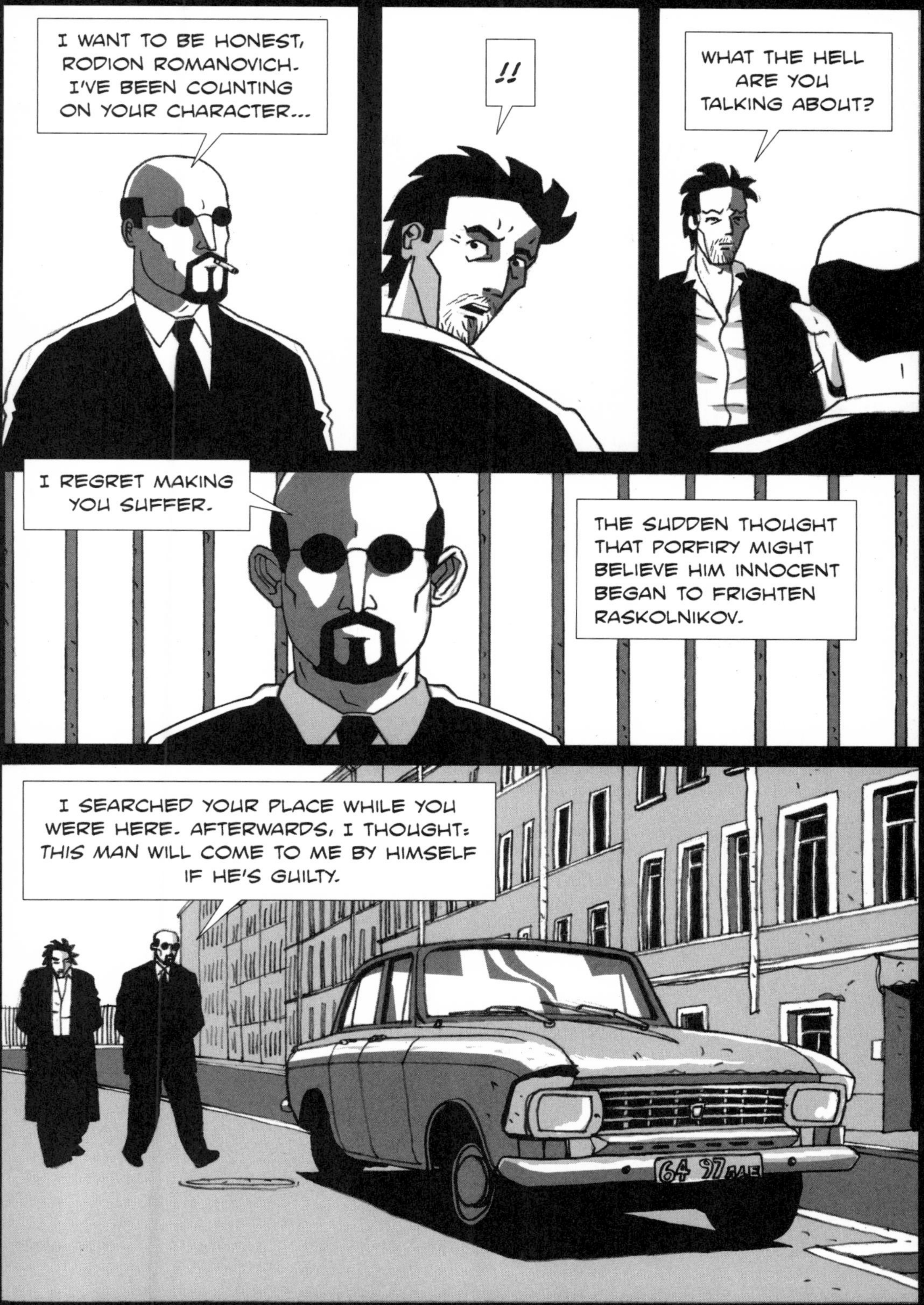
I WANT TO BE HONEST, RODION ROMANOVICH. I'VE BEEN COUNTING ON YOUR CHARACTER...
!!
WHAT THE HELL ARE YOU TALKING ABOUT?
I REGRET MAKING YOU SUFFER.
THE SUDDEN THOUGHT THAT PORFIRY MIGHT BELIEVE HIM INNOCENT BEGAN TO FRIGHTEN RASKOLNIKOV.
I SEARCHED YOUR PLACE WHILE YOU WERE HERE. AFTERWARDS, I THOUGHT: *THIS MAN WILL COME TO ME BY HIMSELF IF HE'S GUILTY.*
64 97

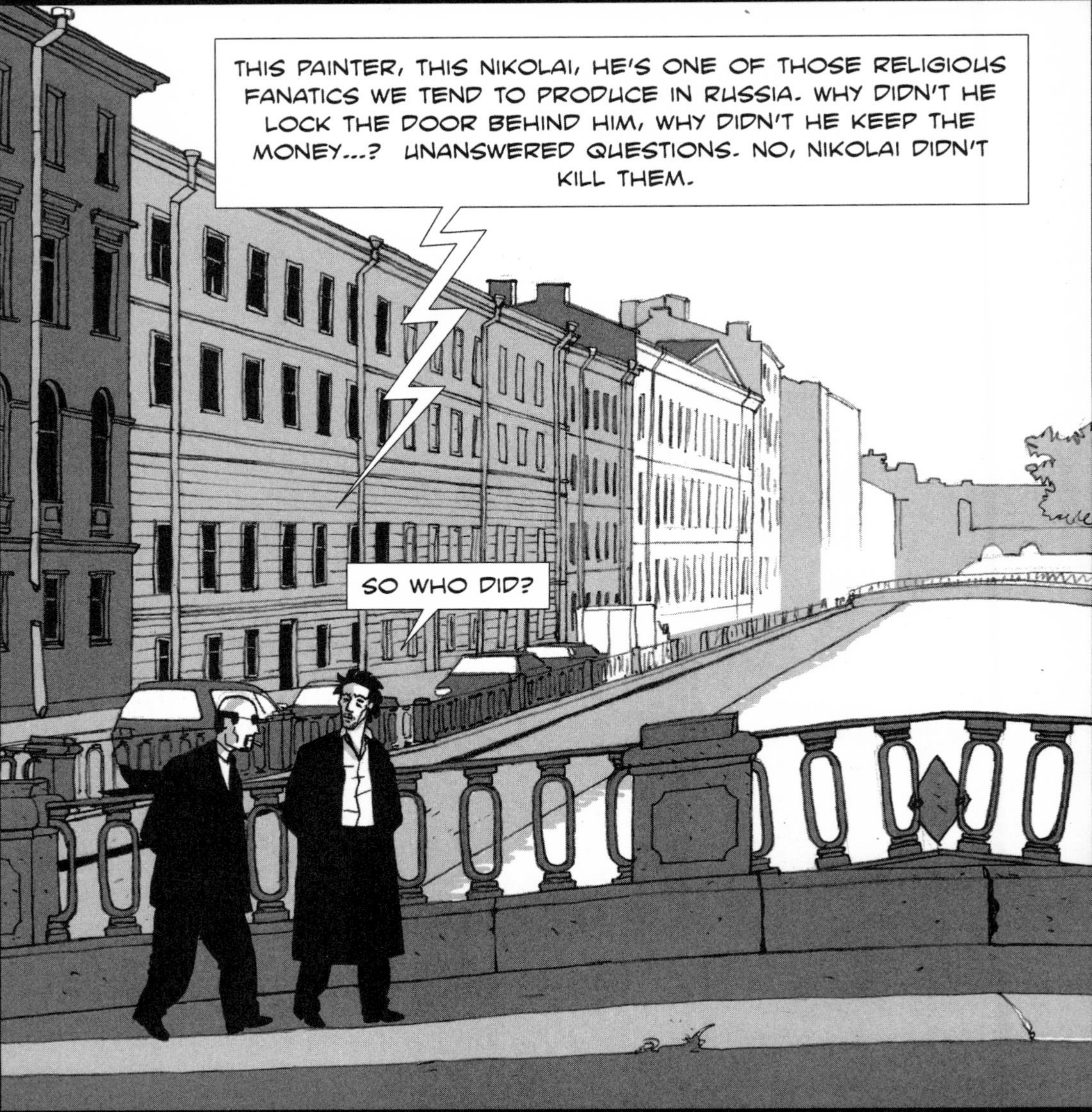
THIS PAINTER, THIS NIKOLAI, HE'S ONE OF THOSE RELIGIOUS FANATICS WE TEND TO PRODUCE IN RUSSIA. WHY DIDN'T HE LOCK THE DOOR BEHIND HIM, WHY DIDN'T HE KEEP THE MONEY...? UNANSWERED QUESTIONS. NO, NIKOLAI DIDN'T KILL THEM.
SO WHO DID?

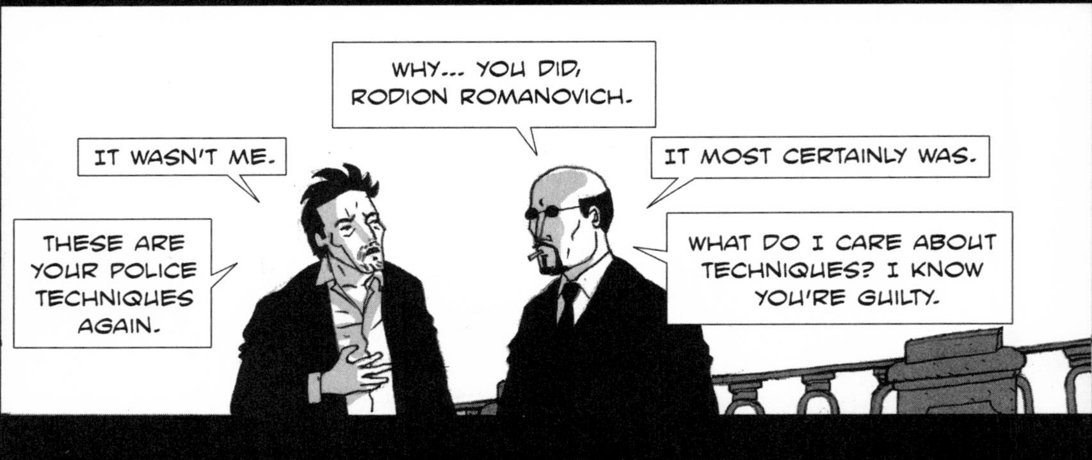
WHY... YOU DID, RODION ROMANOVICH.
IT WASN'T ME.
IT MOST CERTAINLY WAS.
THESE ARE YOUR POLICE TECHNIQUES AGAIN.
WHAT DO I CARE ABOUT TECHNIQUES? I KNOW YOU'RE GUILTY.

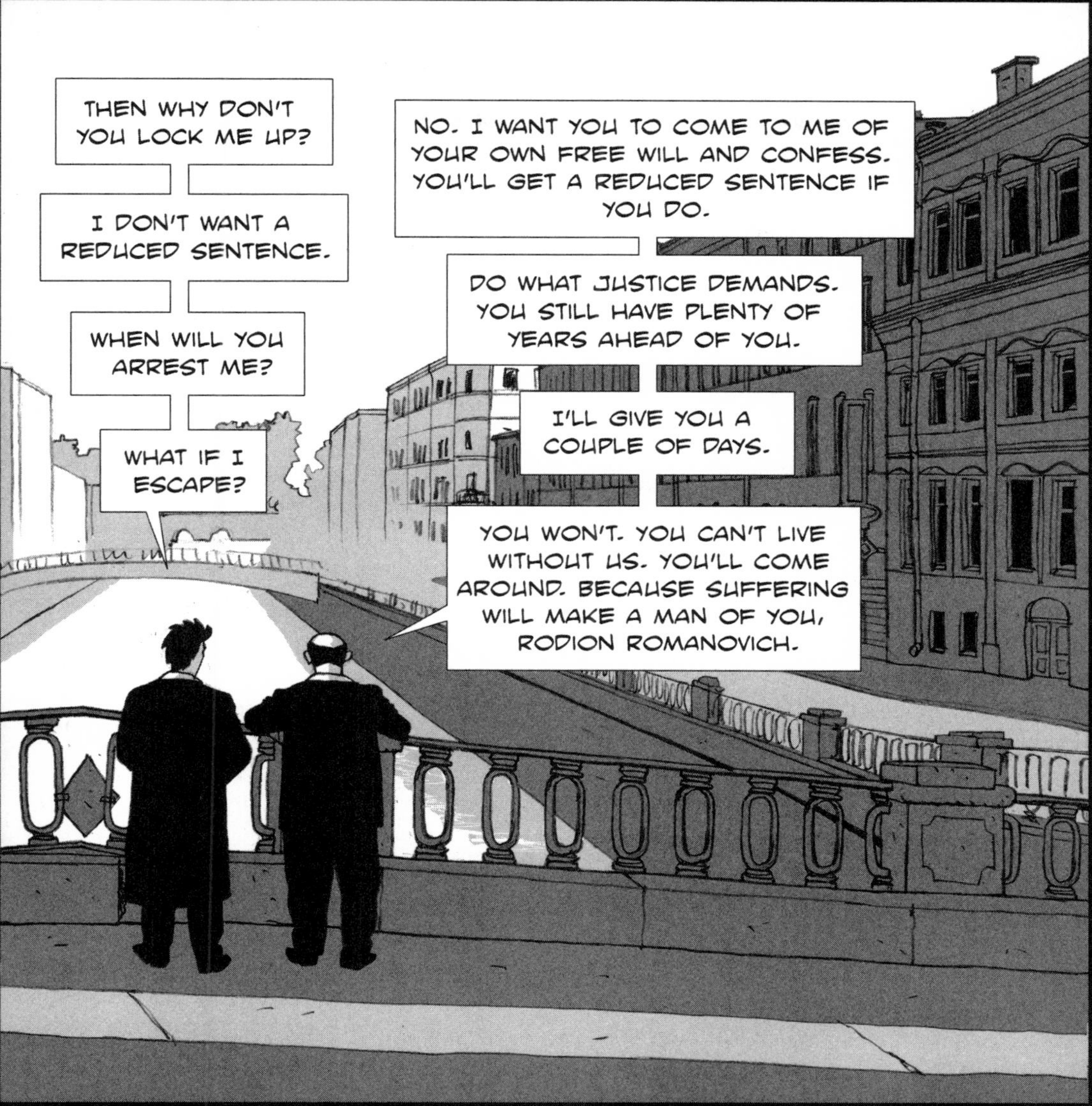
THEN WHY DON'T YOU LOCK ME UP?
NO. I WANT YOU TO COME TO ME OF YOUR OWN FREE WILL AND CONFESS. YOU'LL GET A REDUCED SENTENCE IF YOU DO.
I DON'T WANT A REDUCED SENTENCE.
DO WHAT JUSTICE DEMANDS. YOU STILL HAVE PLENTY OF YEARS AHEAD OF YOU.
WHEN WILL YOU ARREST ME?
I'LL GIVE YOU A COUPLE OF DAYS.
WHAT IF I ESCAPE?
YOU WON'T. YOU CAN'T LIVE WITHOUT US. YOU'LL COME AROUND. BECAUSE SUFFERING WILL MAKE A MAN OF YOU, RODION ROMANOVICH.

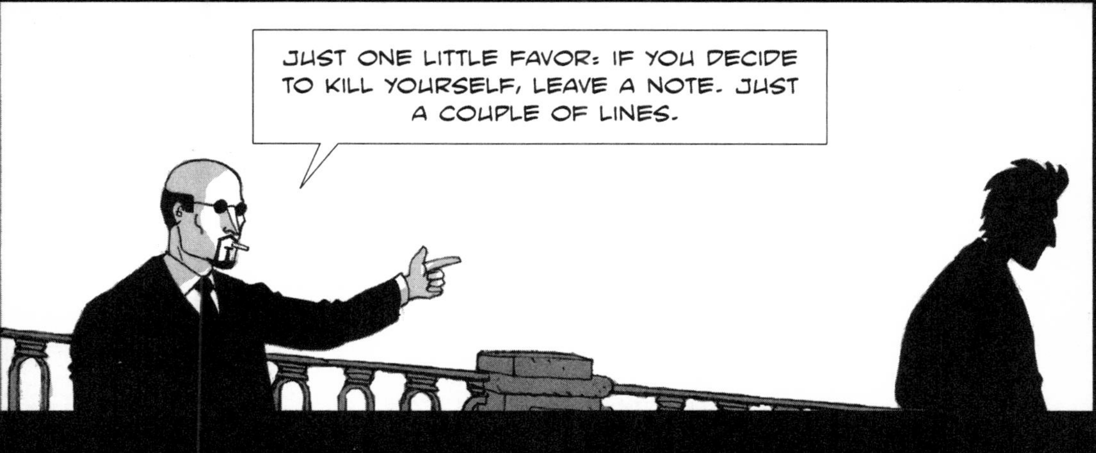
JUST ONE LITTLE FAVOR: IF YOU DECIDE TO KILL YOURSELF, LEAVE A NOTE. JUST A COUPLE OF LINES.

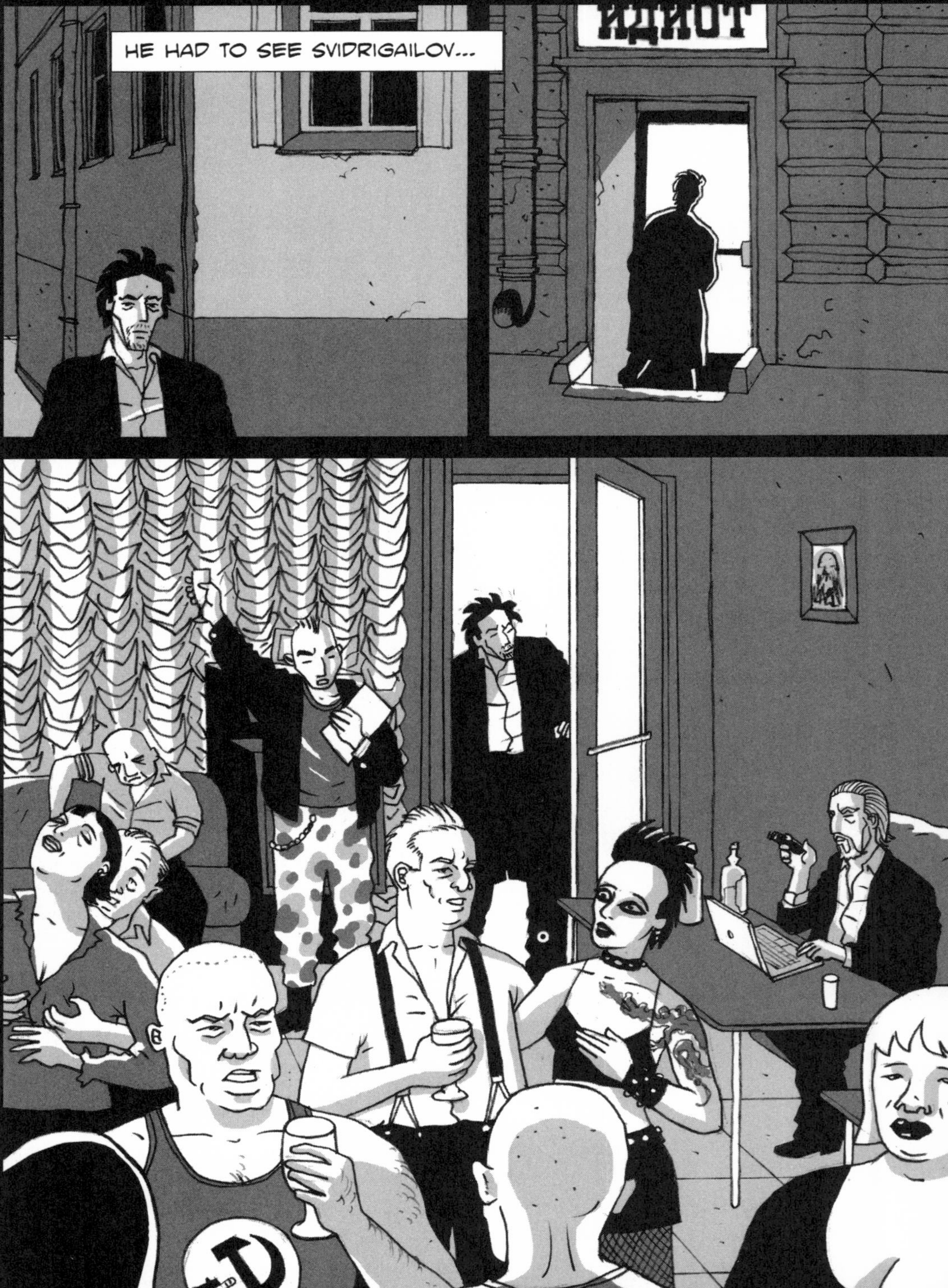
HE HAD TO SEE SVIDRIGAILOV...
ИДИОТ

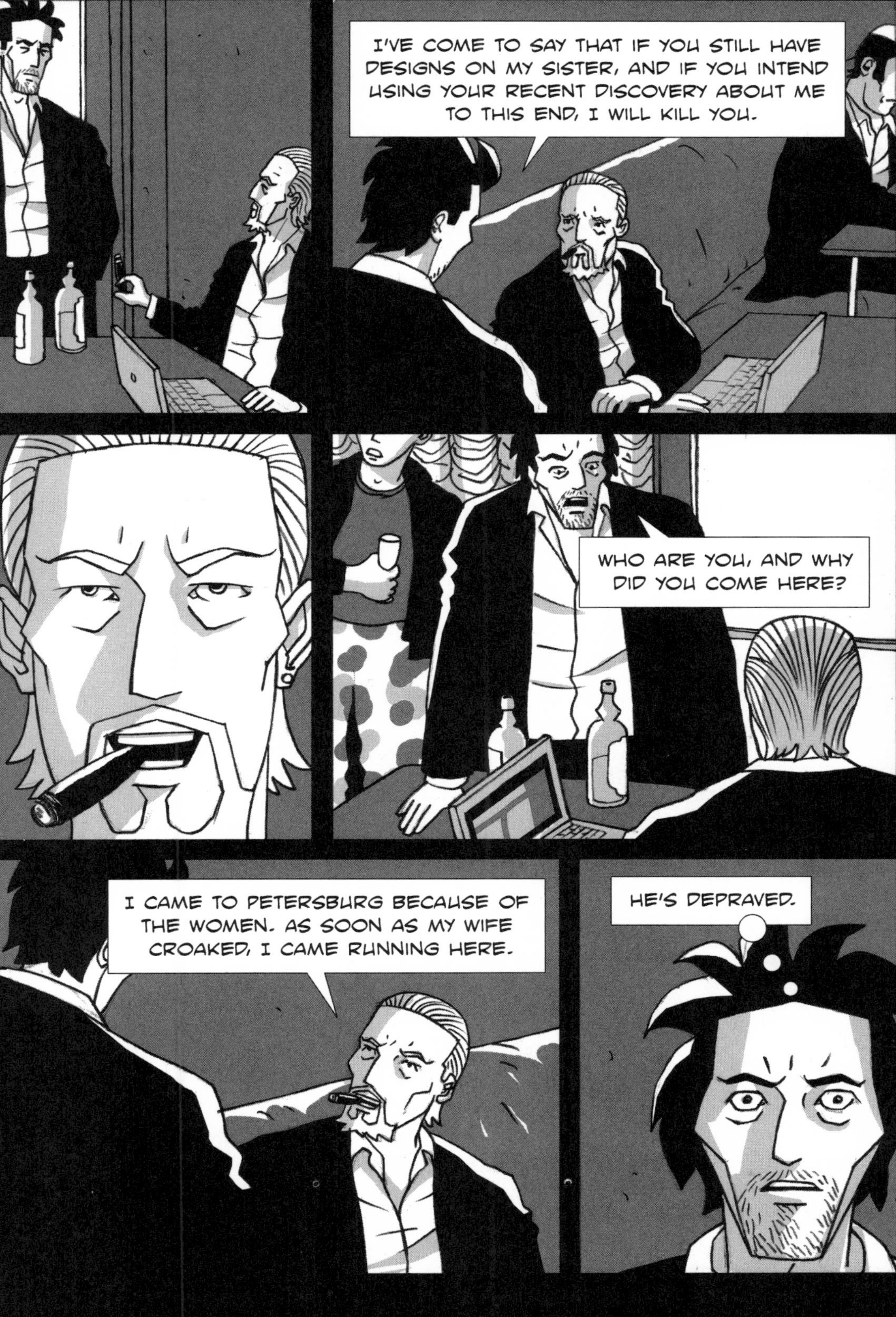
I'VE COME TO SAY THAT IF YOU STILL HAVE DESIGNS ON MY SISTER, AND IF YOU INTEND USING YOUR RECENT DISCOVERY ABOUT ME TO THIS END, I WILL KILL YOU.
WHO ARE YOU, AND WHY DID YOU COME HERE?
I CAME TO PETERSBURG BECAUSE OF THE WOMEN. AS SOON AS MY WIFE CROAKED, I CAME RUNNING HERE.
HE'S DEPRAVED.

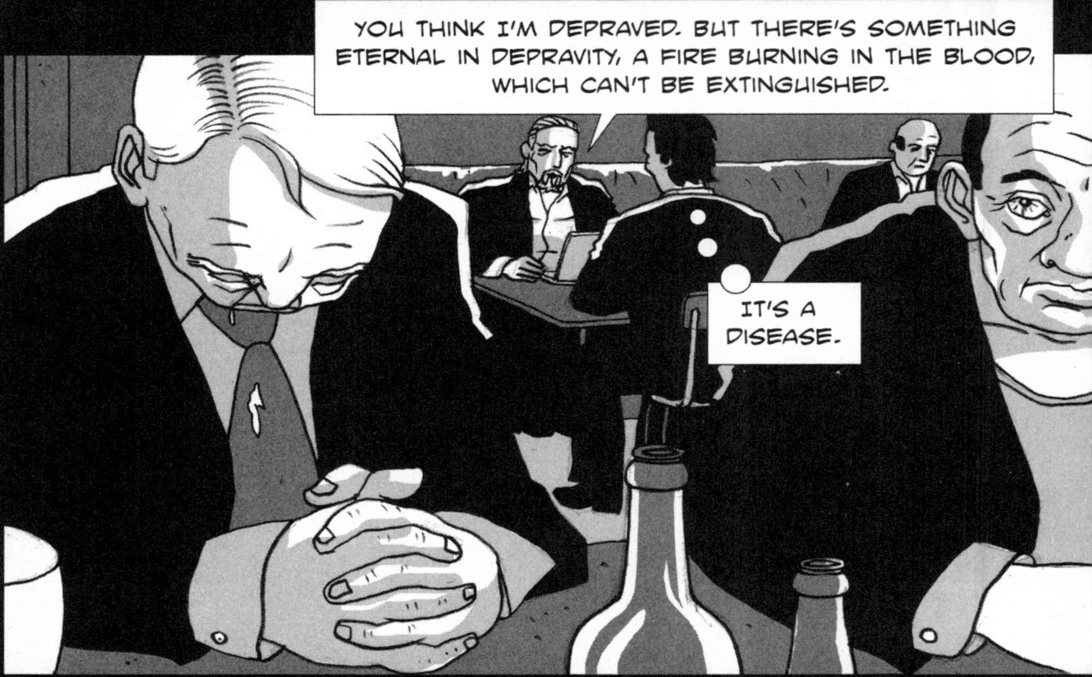
YOU THINK I'M DEPRAVED. BUT THERE'S SOMETHING ETERNAL IN DEPRAVITY, A FIRE BURNING IN THE BLOOD, WHICH CAN'T BE EXTINGUISHED.
IT'S A DISEASE.

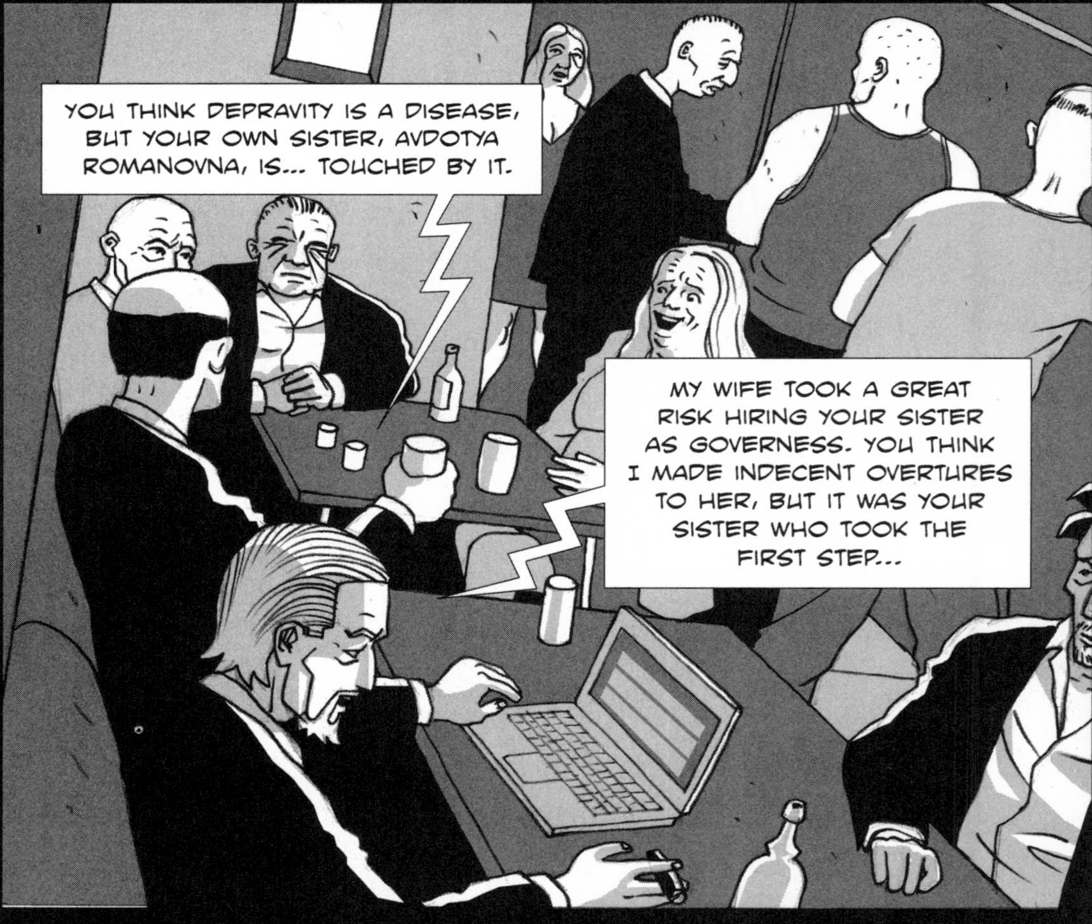
YOU THINK DEPRAVITY IS A DISEASE, BUT YOUR OWN SISTER, AVDOTYA ROMANOVNA, IS... TOUCHED BY IT.
MY WIFE TOOK A GREAT RISK HIRING YOUR SISTER AS GOVERNESS. YOU THINK I MADE INDECENT OVERTURES TO HER, BUT IT WAS YOUR SISTER WHO TOOK THE FIRST STEP...

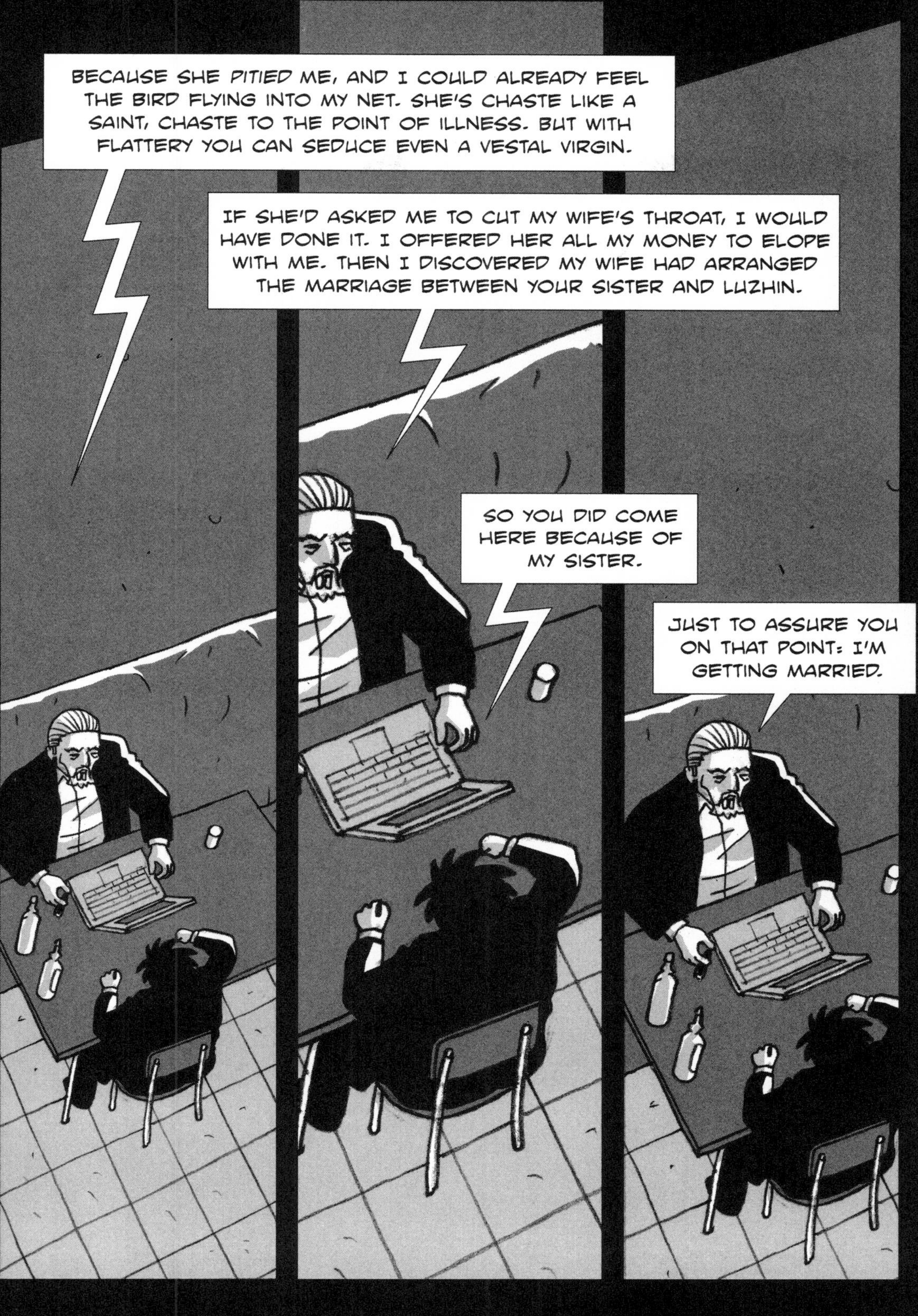
BECAUSE SHE PITIED ME, AND I COULD ALREADY FEEL THE BIRD FLYING INTO MY NET. SHE'S CHASTE LIKE A SAINT, CHASTE TO THE POINT OF ILLNESS. BUT WITH FLATTERY YOU CAN SEDUCE EVEN A VESTAL VIRGIN.
IF SHE'D ASKED ME TO CUT MY WIFE'S THROAT, I WOULD HAVE DONE IT. I OFFERED HER ALL MY MONEY TO ELOPE WITH ME. THEN I DISCOVERED MY WIFE HAD ARRANGED THE MARRIAGE BETWEEN YOUR SISTER AND LUZHIN.
SO YOU DID COME HERE BECAUSE OF MY SISTER.
JUST TO ASSURE YOU ON THAT POINT: I'M GETTING MARRIED.

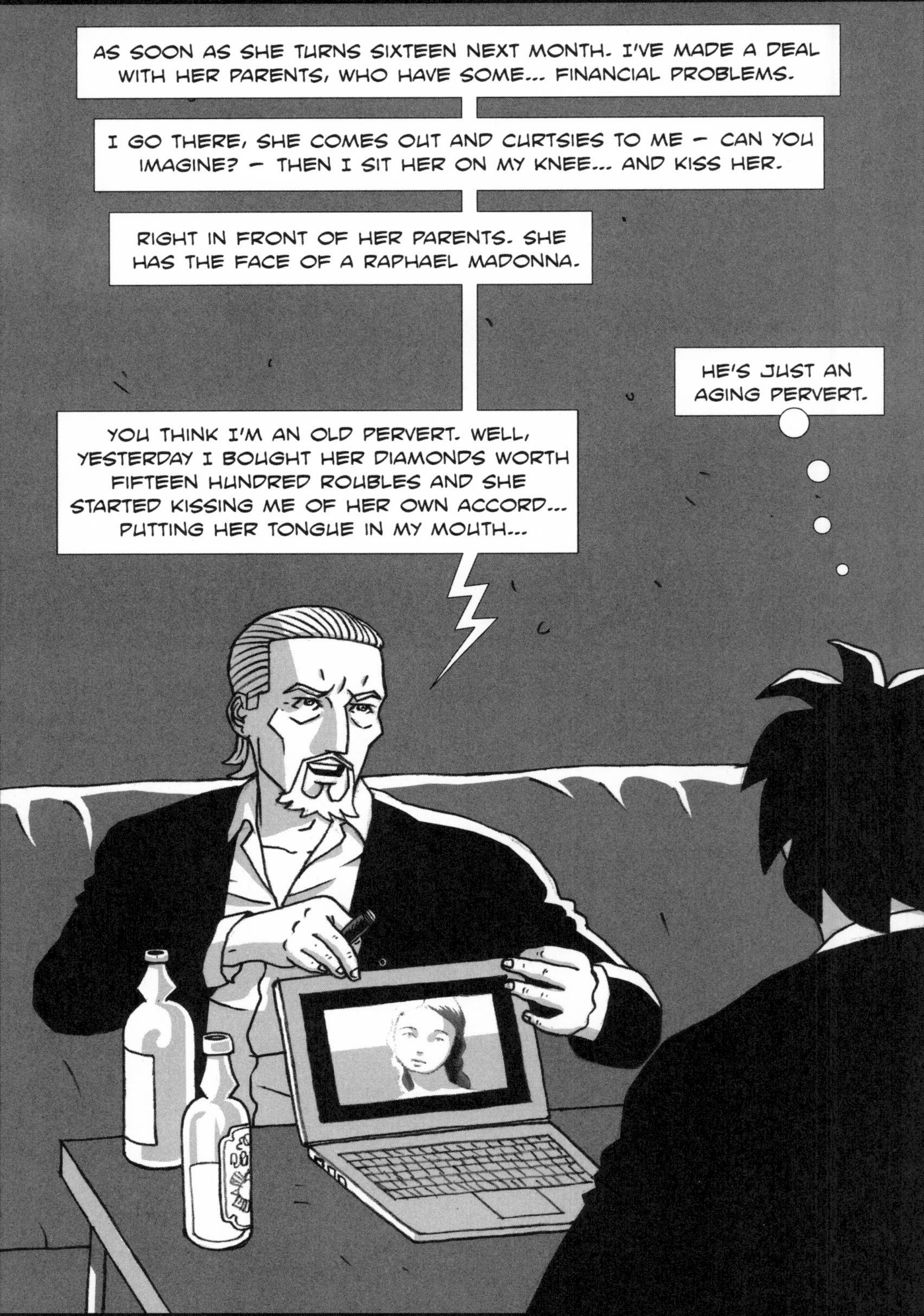
AS SOON AS SHE TURNS SIXTEEN NEXT MONTH. I'VE MADE A DEAL WITH HER PARENTS, WHO HAVE SOME... FINANCIAL PROBLEMS.
I GO THERE, SHE COMES OUT AND CURTSIES TO ME – CAN YOU IMAGINE? – THEN I SIT HER ON MY KNEE... AND KISS HER.
RIGHT IN FRONT OF HER PARENTS. SHE HAS THE FACE OF A RAPHAEL MADONNA.
YOU THINK I'M AN OLD PERVERT. WELL, YESTERDAY I BOUGHT HER DIAMONDS WORTH FIFTEEN HUNDRED ROUBLES AND SHE STARTED KISSING ME OF HER OWN ACCORD... PUTTING HER TONGUE IN MY MOUTH...
HE'S JUST AN AGING PERVERT.

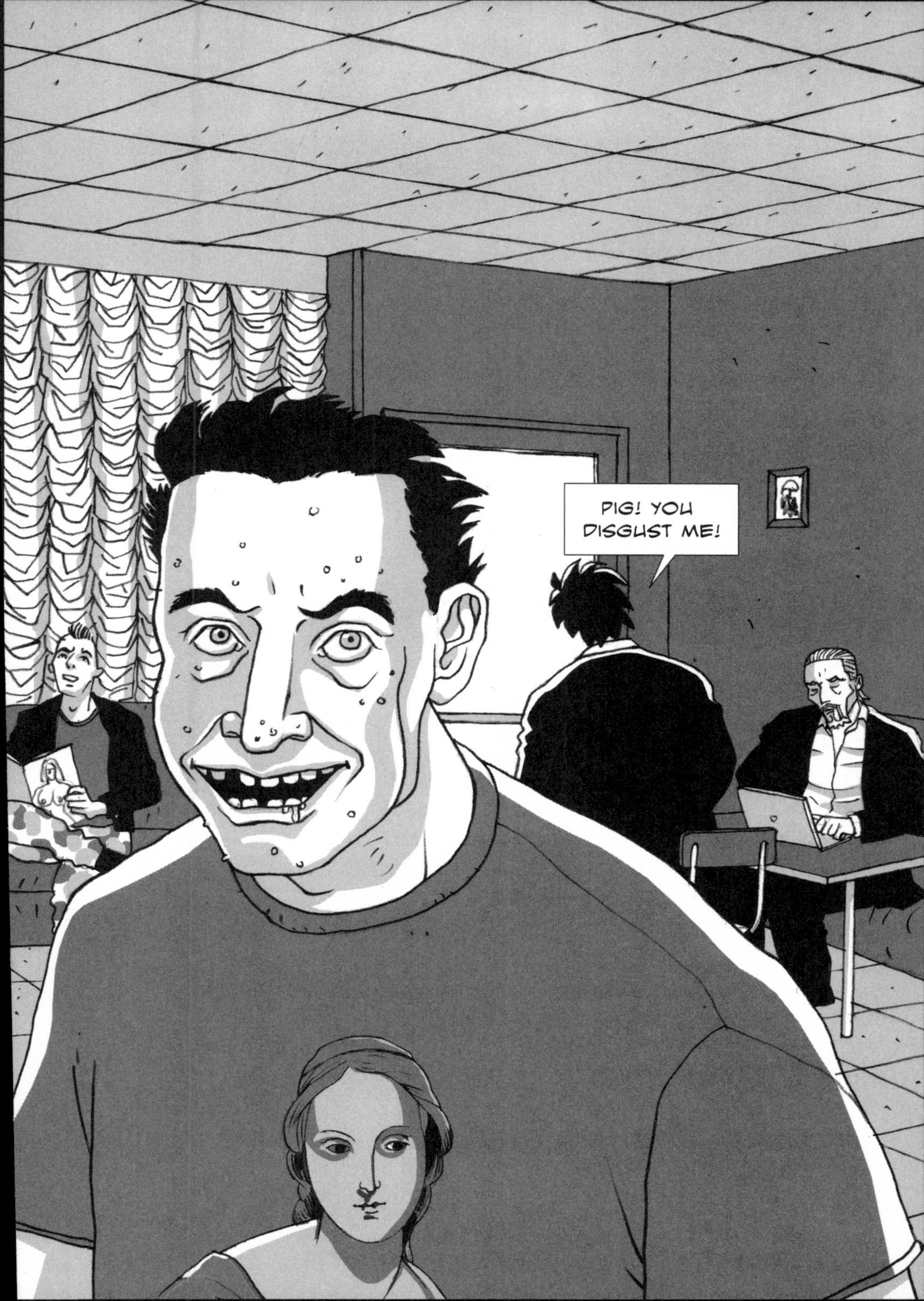
PIG! YOU
DISGUST ME!

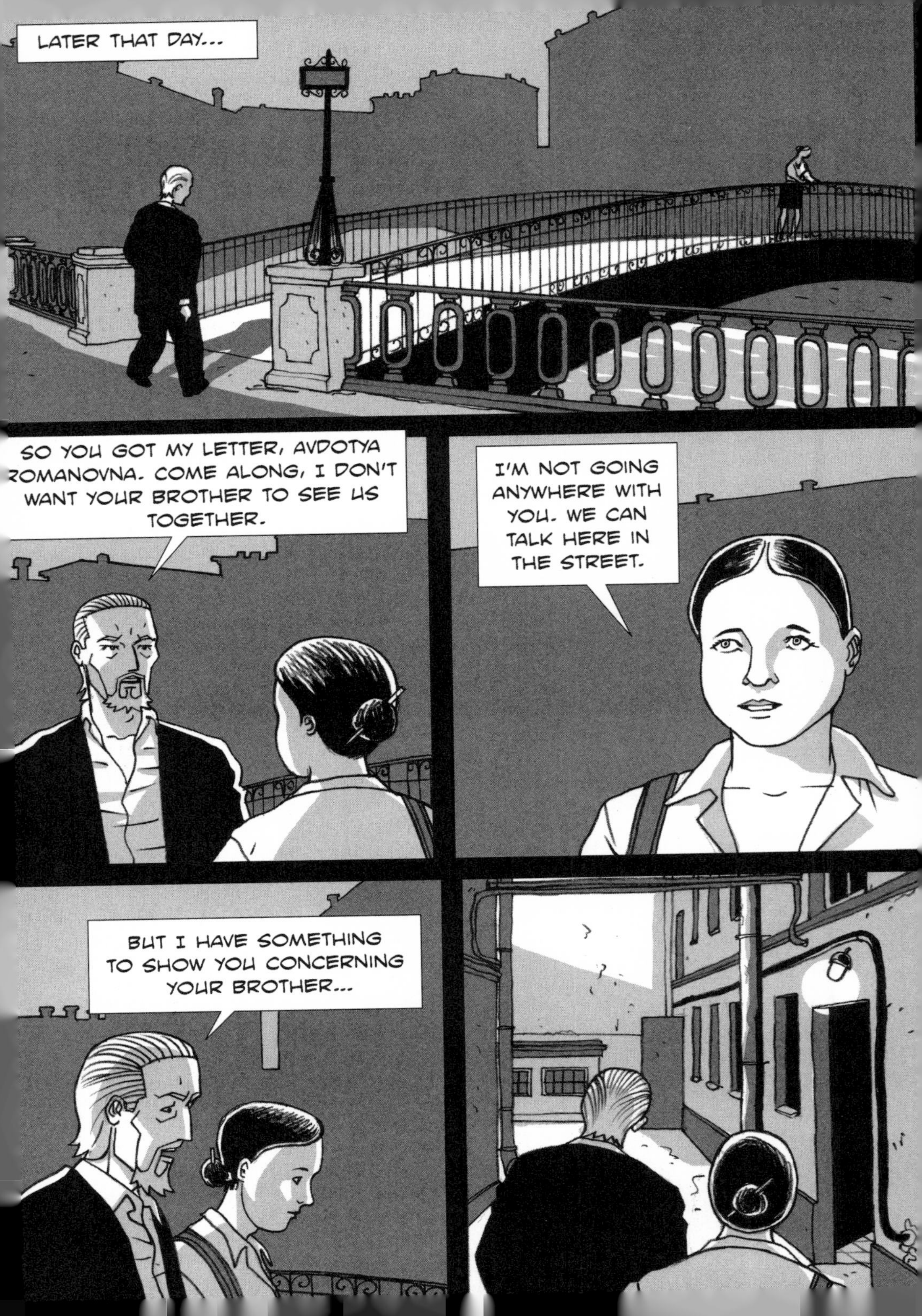
LATER THAT DAY...
SO YOU GOT MY LETTER, AVDOTYA ROMANOVNA. COME ALONG, I DON'T WANT YOUR BROTHER TO SEE US TOGETHER.
I'M NOT GOING ANYWHERE WITH YOU. WE CAN TALK HERE IN THE STREET.
BUT I HAVE SOMETHING TO SHOW YOU CONCERNING YOUR BROTHER...

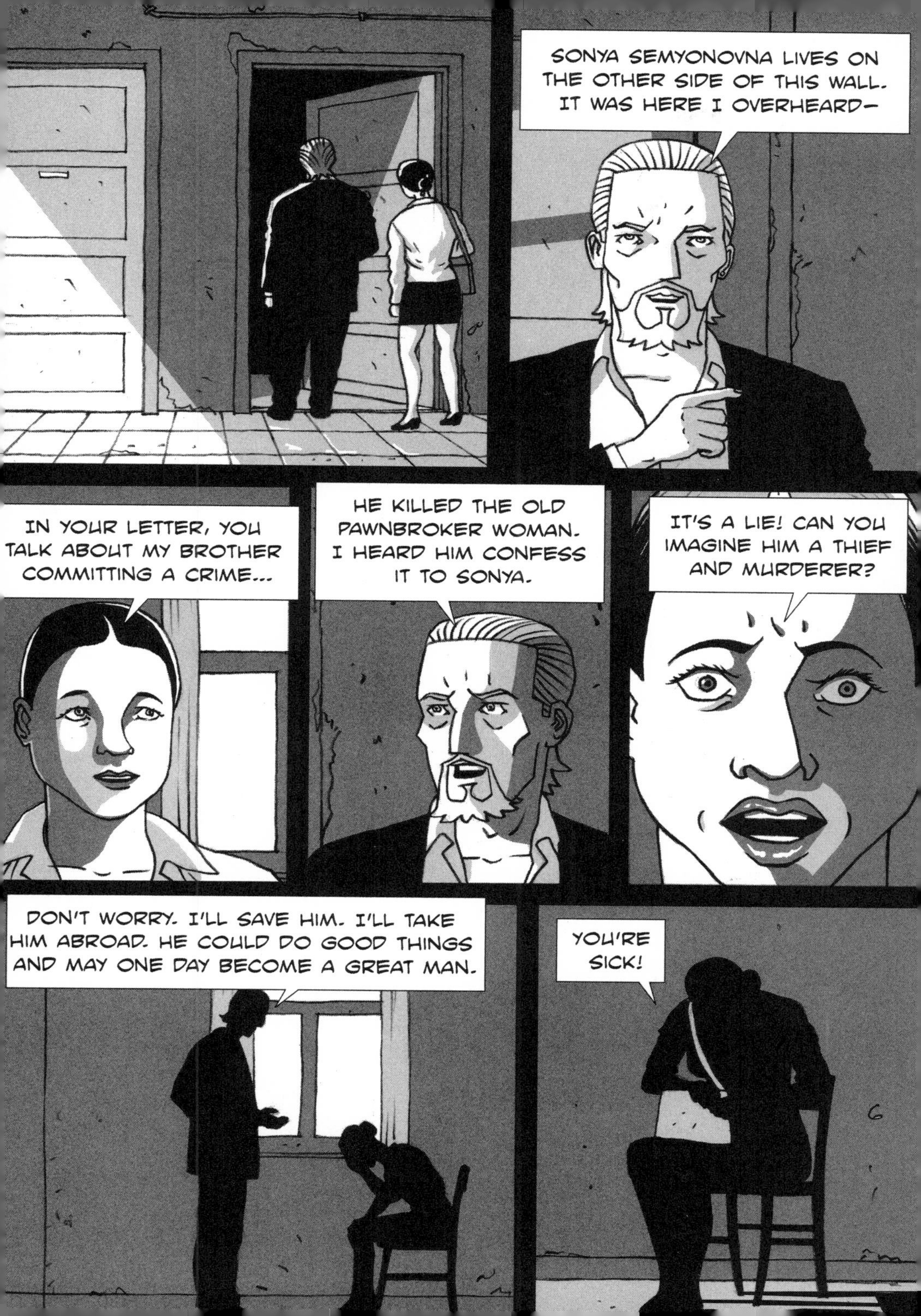
SONYA SEMYONOVNA LIVES ON THE OTHER SIDE OF THIS WALL. IT WAS HERE I OVERHEARD—
IN YOUR LETTER, YOU TALK ABOUT MY BROTHER COMMITTING A CRIME...
HE KILLED THE OLD PAWNBROKER WOMAN. I HEARD HIM CONFESS IT TO SONYA.
IT'S A LIE! CAN YOU IMAGINE HIM A THIEF AND MURDERER?
DON'T WORRY. I'LL SAVE HIM. I'LL TAKE HIM ABROAD. HE COULD DO GOOD THINGS AND MAY ONE DAY BECOME A GREAT MAN.
YOU'RE SICK!

WHY HAVE YOU LOCKED THE DOOR?

ONE WORD FROM YOU, AND YOUR BROTHER IS SAVED. I'LL DO ANYTHING FOR YOU. LET ME KISS THE HEM OF YOUR DRESS...

OPEN IT!

I'VE LOST THE KEY. DON'T MAKE ME FORCE YOU. I'LL BE YOUR SLAVE...

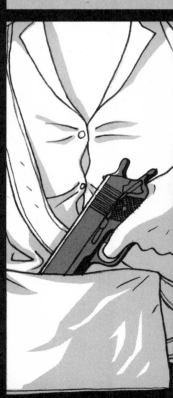

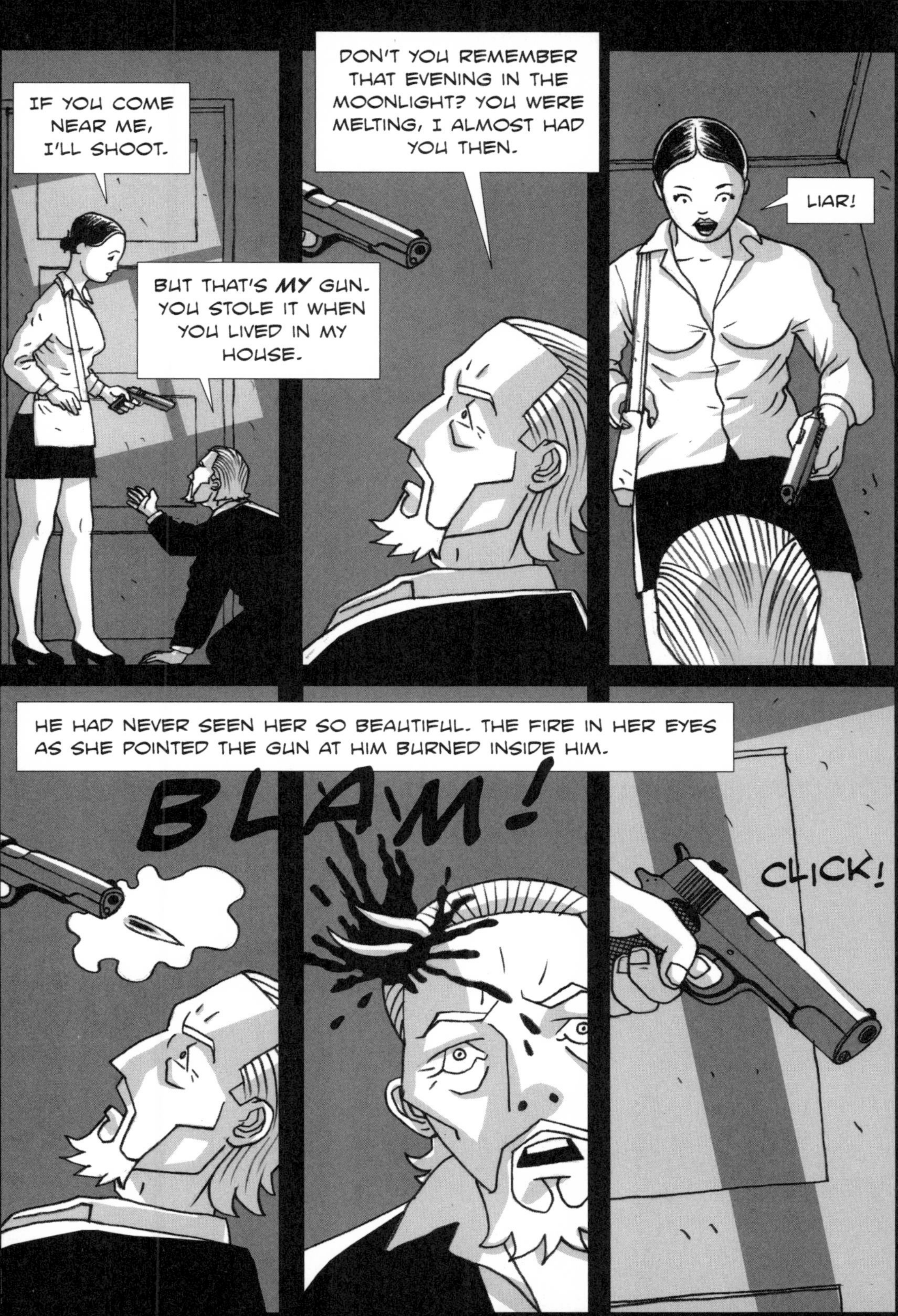
IF YOU COME NEAR ME, I'LL SHOOT.
BUT THAT'S MY GUN. YOU STOLE IT WHEN YOU LIVED IN MY HOUSE.
DON'T YOU REMEMBER THAT EVENING IN THE MOONLIGHT? YOU WERE MELTING, I ALMOST HAD YOU THEN.
LIAR!
HE HAD NEVER SEEN HER SO BEAUTIFUL. THE FIRE IN HER EYES AS SHE POINTED THE GUN AT HIM BURNED INSIDE HIM.
BLAM!
CLICK!

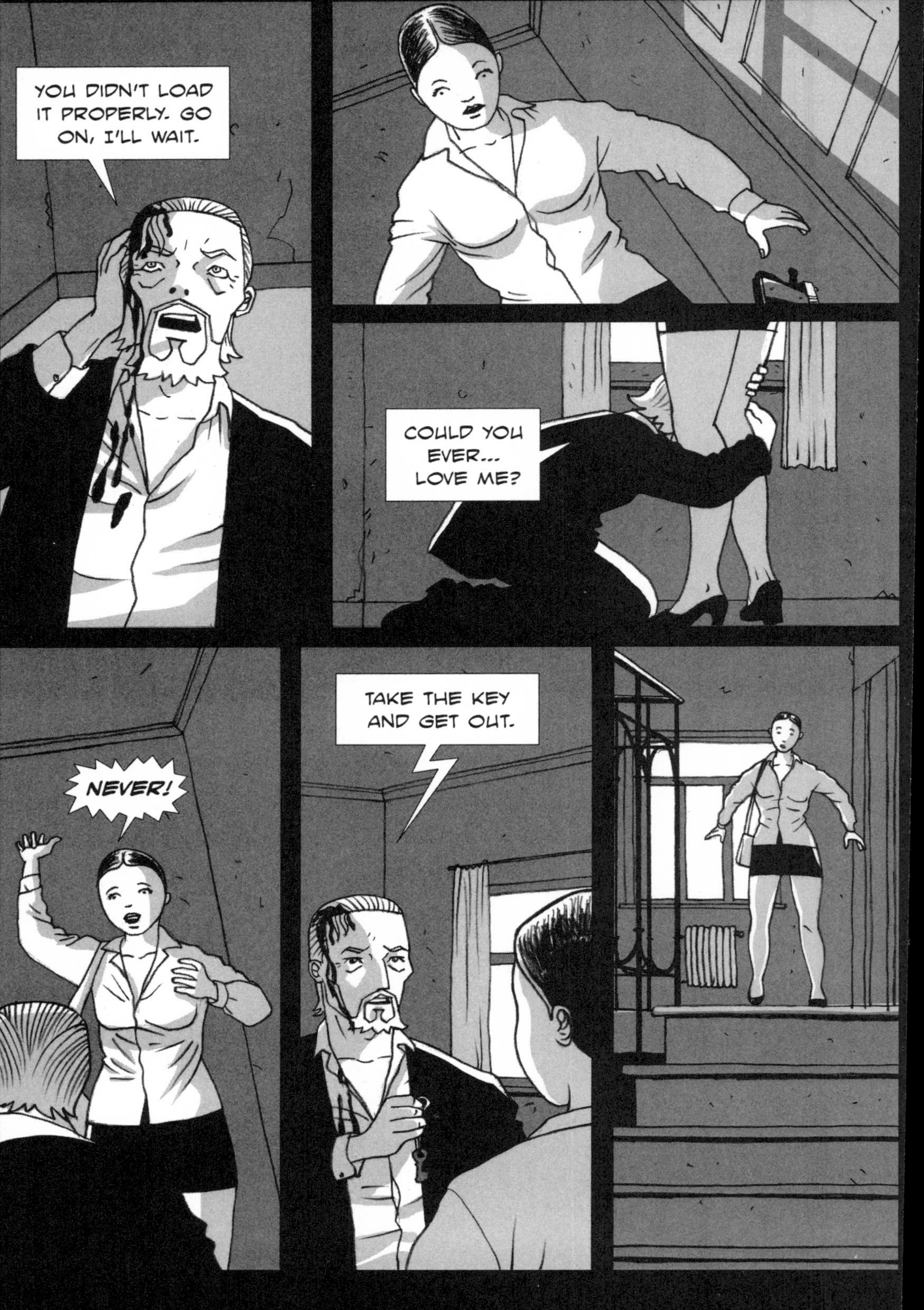
YOU DIDN'T LOAD IT PROPERLY. GO ON, I'LL WAIT.
COULD YOU EVER... LOVE ME?
NEVER!
TAKE THE KEY AND GET OUT.

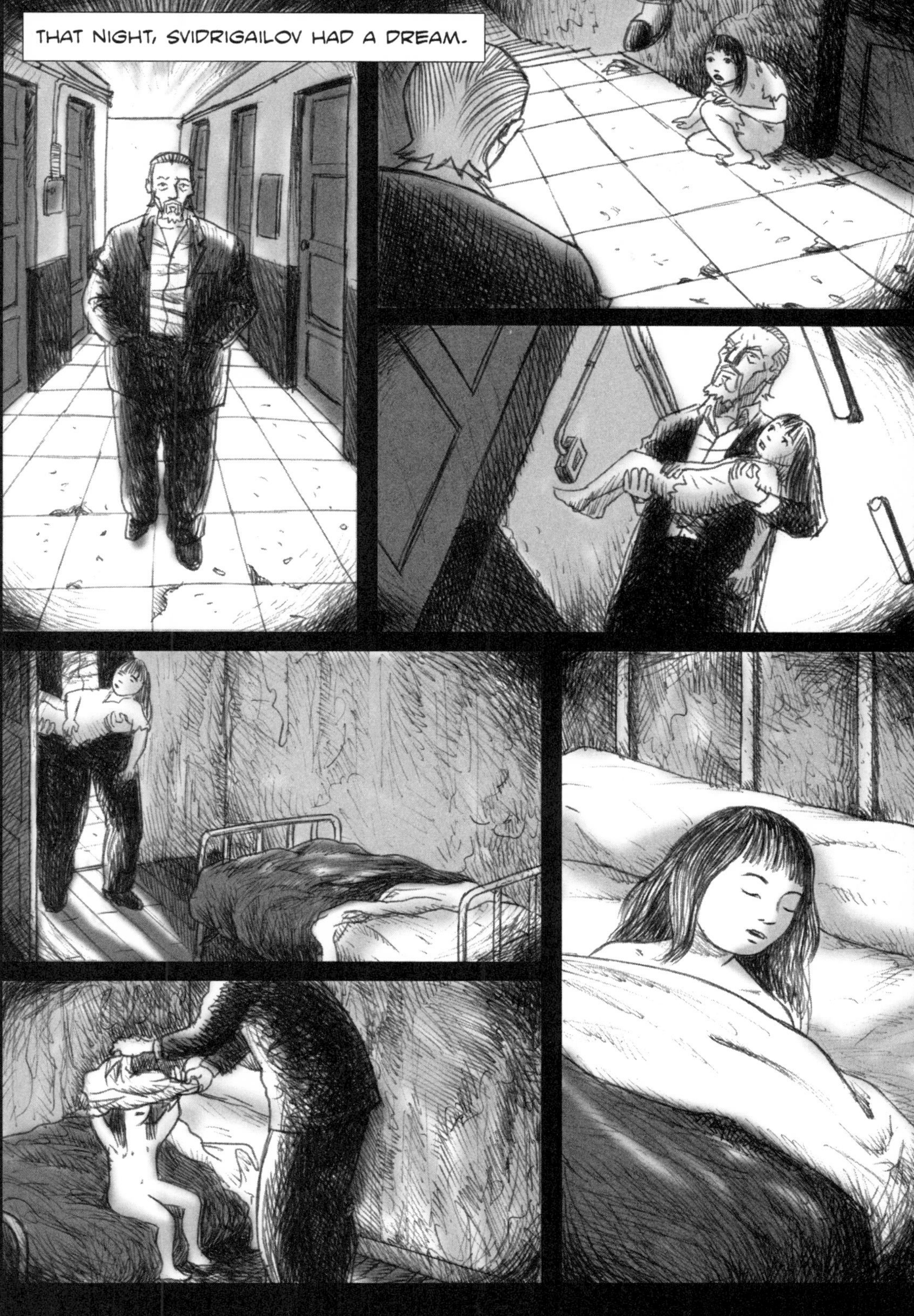
THAT NIGHT, SVIDRIGAILOV HAD A DREAM.

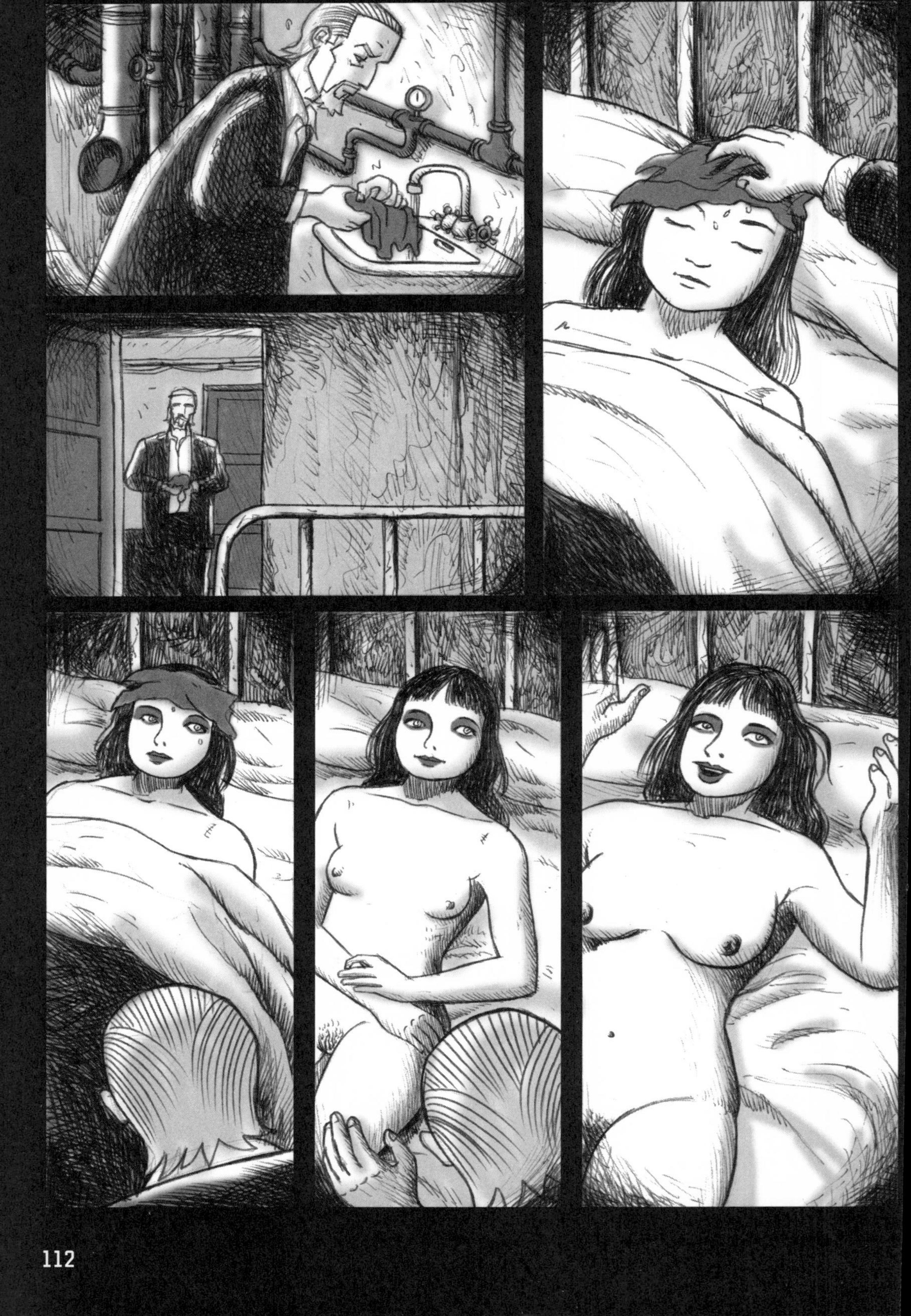

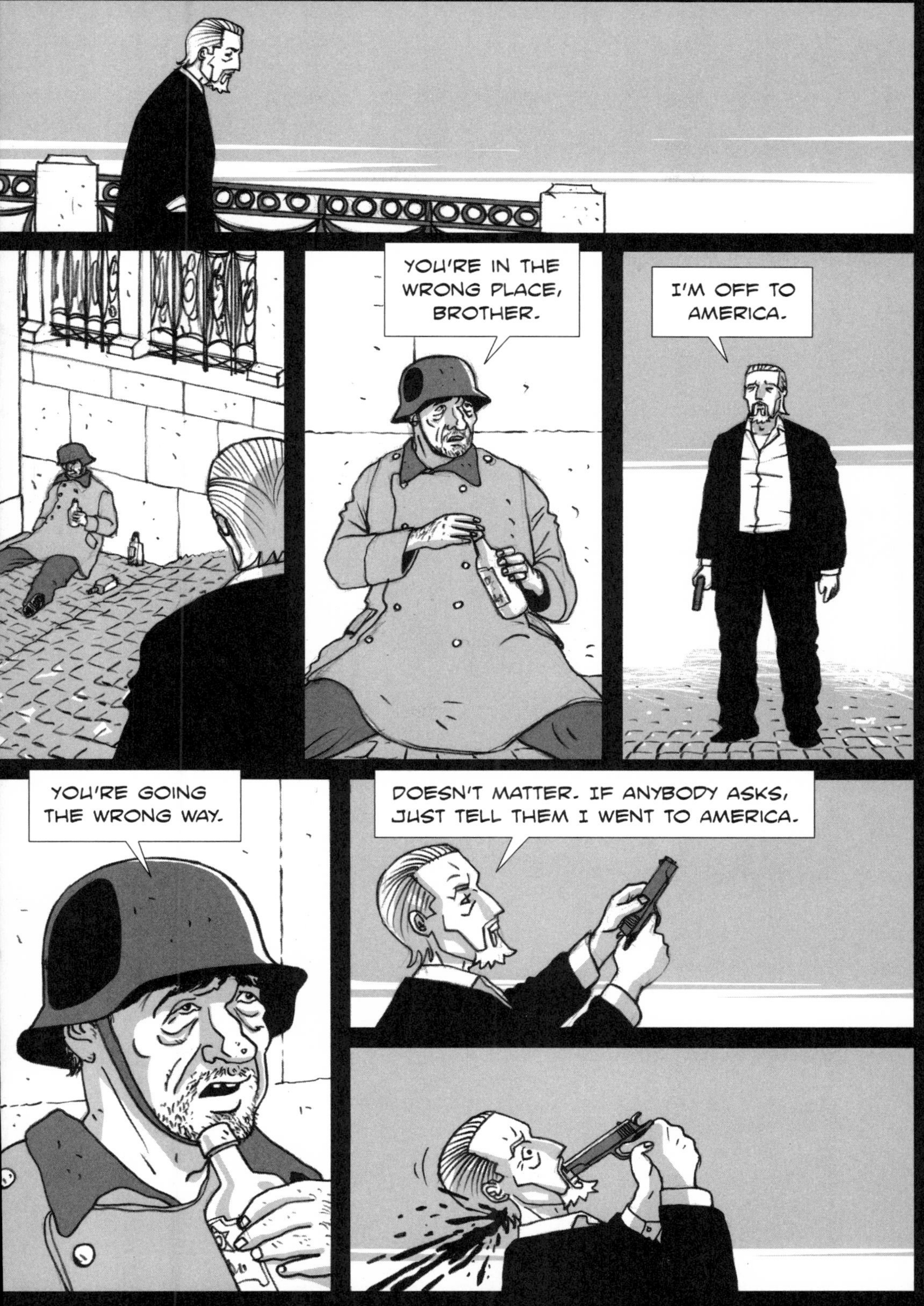
YOU'RE IN THE WRONG PLACE, BROTHER.
I'M OFF TO AMERICA.
YOU'RE GOING THE WRONG WAY.
DOESN'T MATTER. IF ANYBODY ASKS, JUST TELL THEM I WENT TO AMERICA.

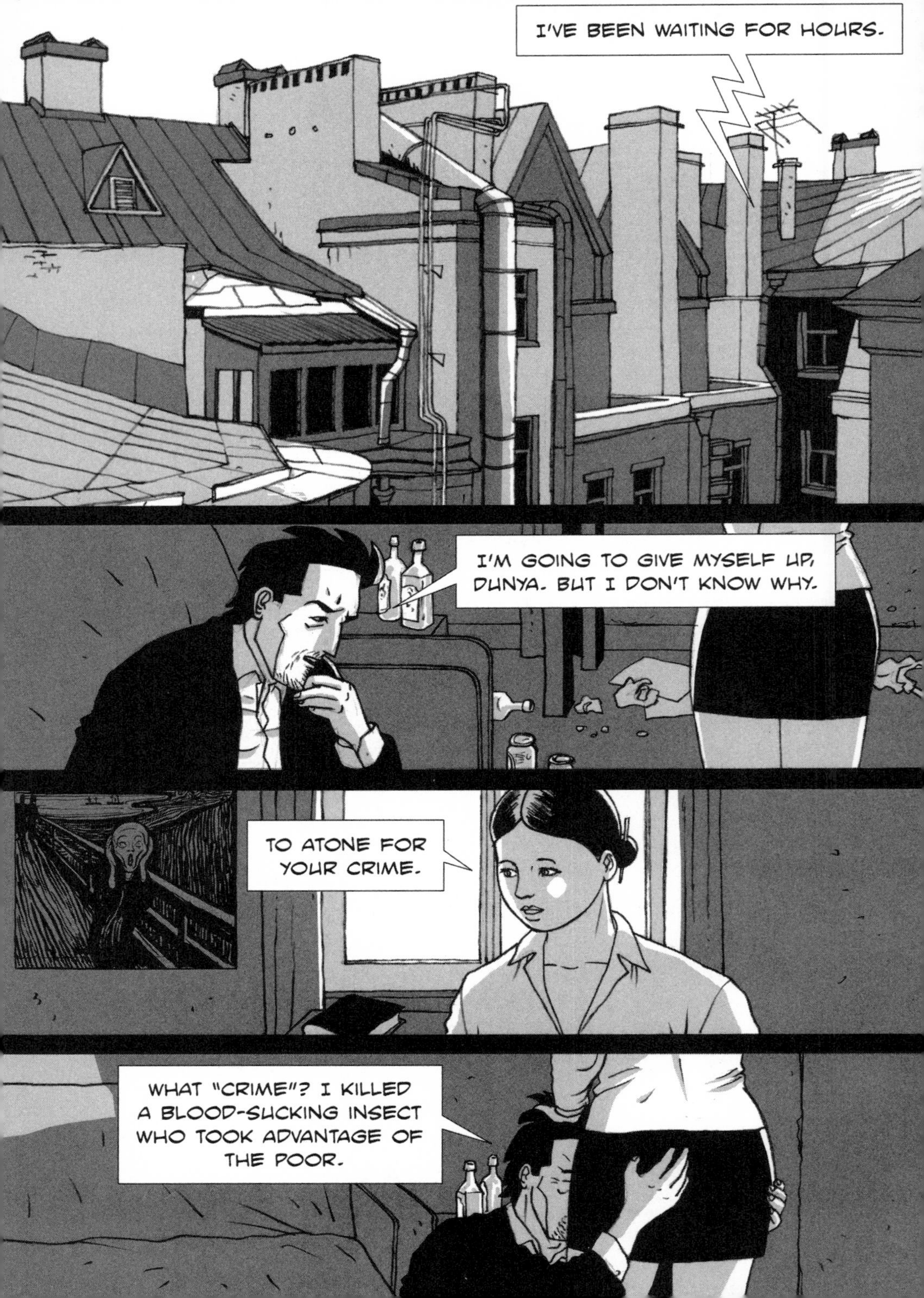
I'VE BEEN WAITING FOR HOURS.
I'M GOING TO GIVE MYSELF UP, DUNYA. BUT I DON'T KNOW WHY.
TO ATONE FOR YOUR CRIME.
WHAT "CRIME"? I KILLED A BLOOD-SUCKING INSECT WHO TOOK ADVANTAGE OF THE POOR.

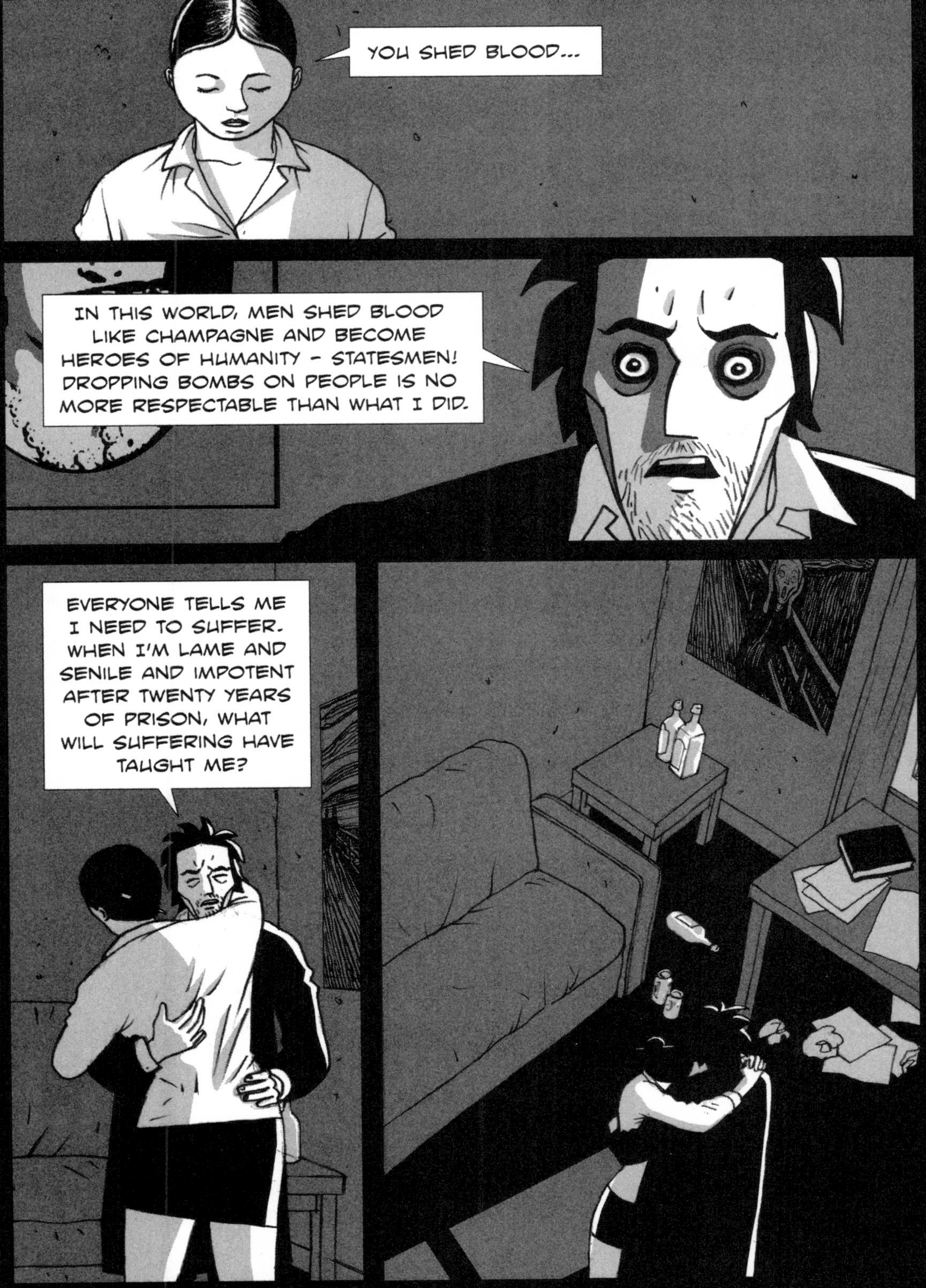
YOU SHED BLOOD...
IN THIS WORLD, MEN SHED BLOOD LIKE CHAMPAGNE AND BECOME HEROES OF HUMANITY – STATESMEN! DROPPING BOMBS ON PEOPLE IS NO MORE RESPECTABLE THAN WHAT I DID.
EVERYONE TELLS ME I NEED TO SUFFER. WHEN I'M LAME AND SENILE AND IMPOTENT AFTER TWENTY YEARS OF PRISON, WHAT WILL SUFFERING HAVE TAUGHT ME?

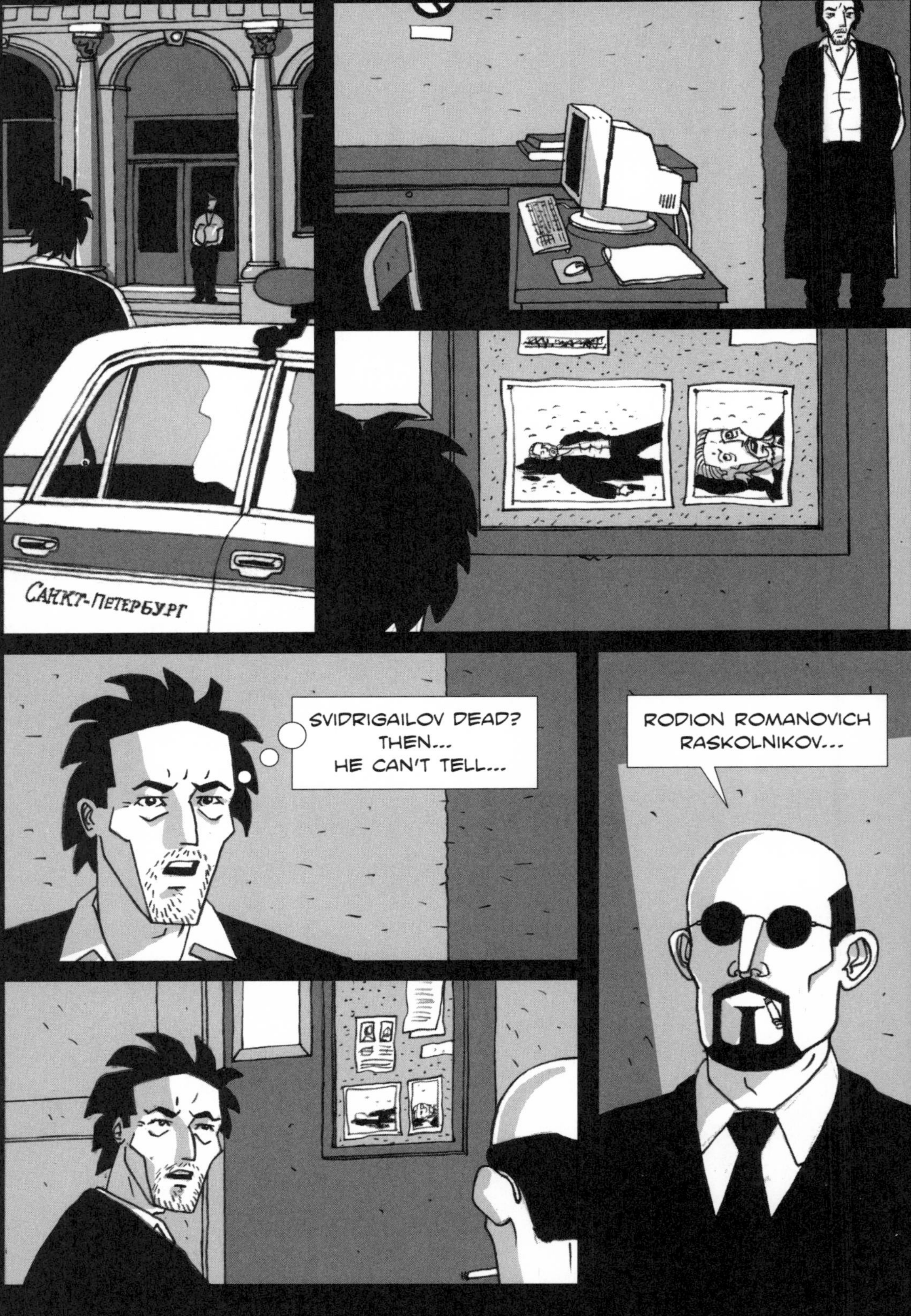
САНКТ-ПЕТЕРБУРГ
SVIDRIGAILOV DEAD? THEN... HE CAN'T TELL...
RODION ROMANOVICH RASKOLNIKOV...

EPILOGUE

RASKOLNIKOV'S SHAME CONSISTED IN THE IDEA THAT HE COULD NOT CONDEMN HIMSELF. INSTEAD, HE HAD TO SUBMIT TO THE "POINTLESSNESS" OF HIS FATE... HIS ONLY "CRIME" WAS THAT HE HAD CONFESSED.

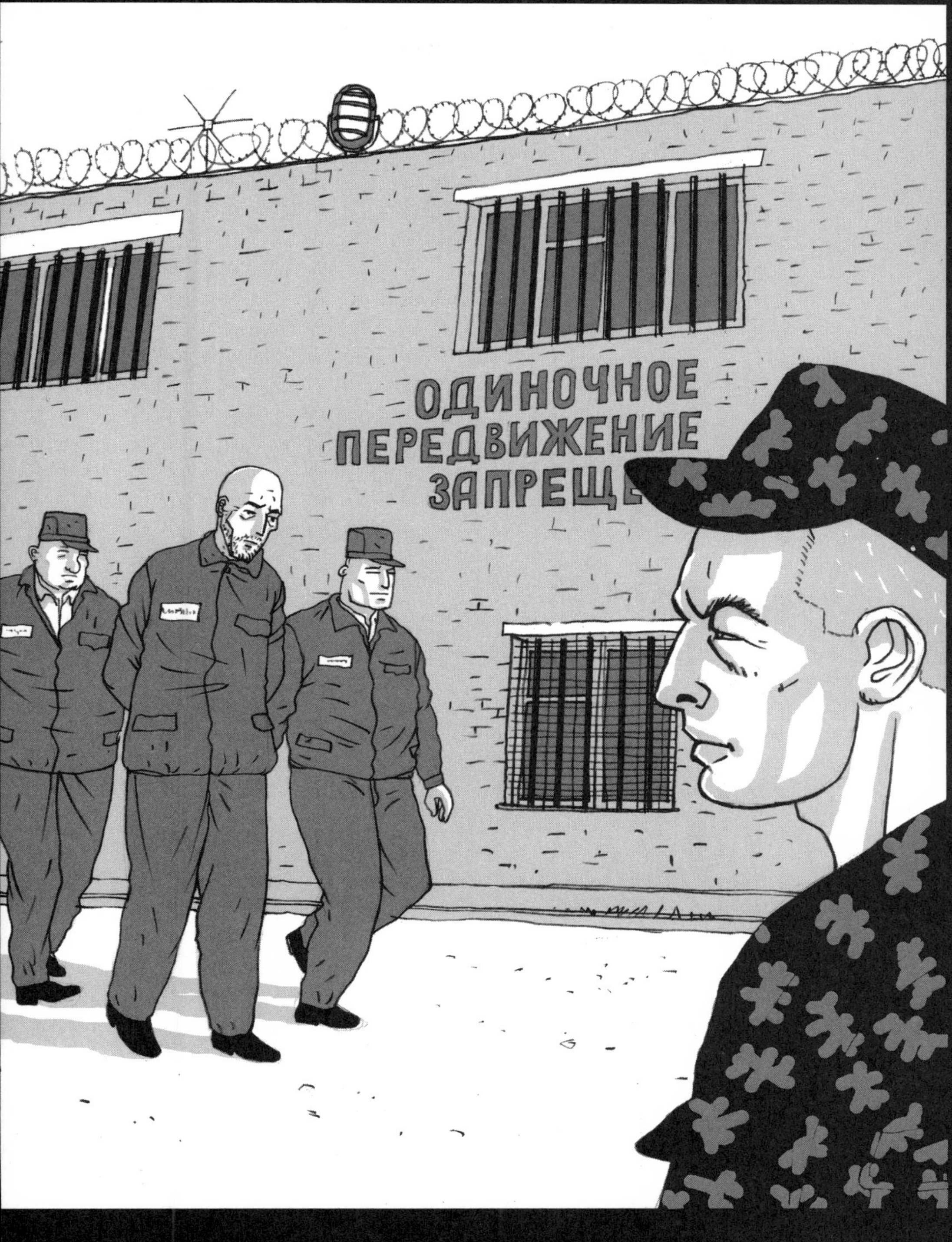
ОДИНОЧНОЕ
ПЕРЕДВИЖЕНИЕ
ЗАПРЕЩЕ

IN HIS ILLNESS, HE DREAMED THAT AN UNKNOWN PLAGUE WAS SPREADING TO EUROPE FROM ASIA. MICROSCOPIC CREATURES HAD WORMED INTO MEN'S BODIES AND BEGUN WIPING OUT MANKIND. THESE CREATURES HAD REASON AND WILL. THOSE THEY ATTACKED BECAME POSSESSED AND CRAZY. IN THIS MADNESS, WHOLE ARMIES FOUGHT IN ORGIES OF ANNIHILATION.

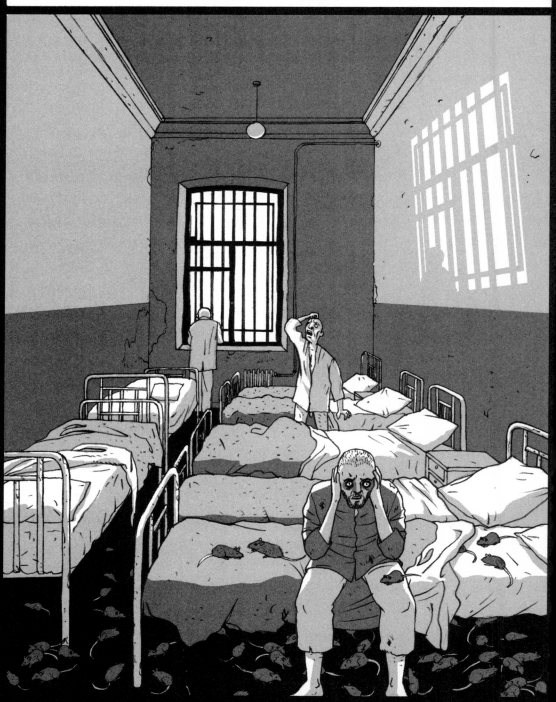

AFTER HIS RECOVERY, RASKOLNIKOV WAS SENT TO A LABOR CAMP. IN THE DISTANCE, ON THE STEPPE, HE COULD SEE NOMADS PASSING, AS IF TIME HAD NOT TOUCHED THEM. THEY SEEMED TO BE FREE, AND RASKOLNIKOV WATCHED THEM IN ANGUISH.

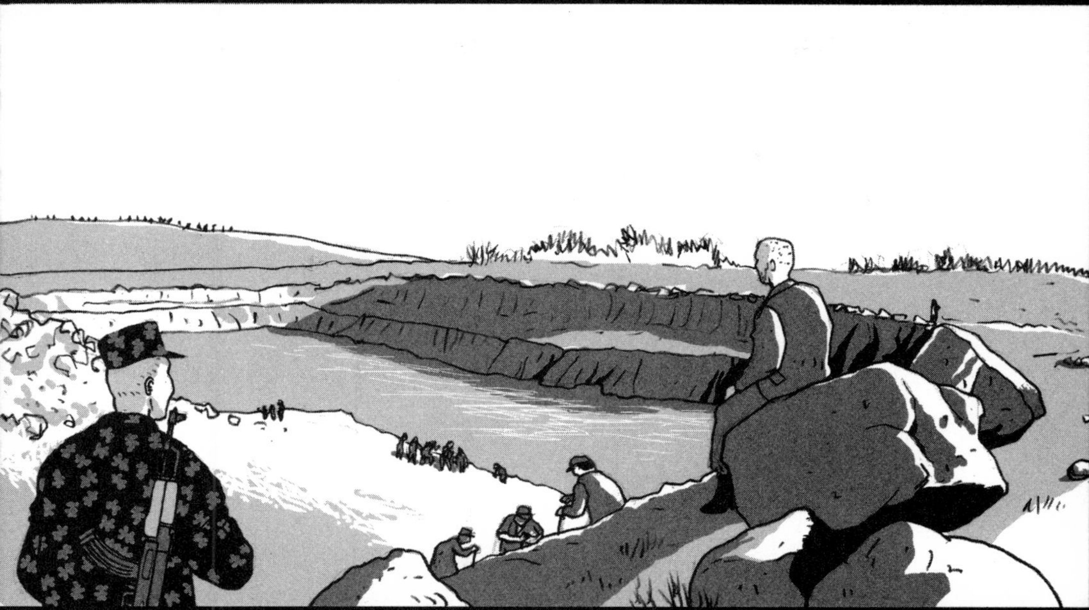

HIS CRIME, HIS PUNISHMENT, SEEMED SOMEHOW OUTSIDE OF HIM, AS IF THEY HAD NEVER OCCURRED. NOW HE WAITED FOR SOMETHING COMPLETELY DIFFERENT TO TAKE PLACE IN HIS BEING.

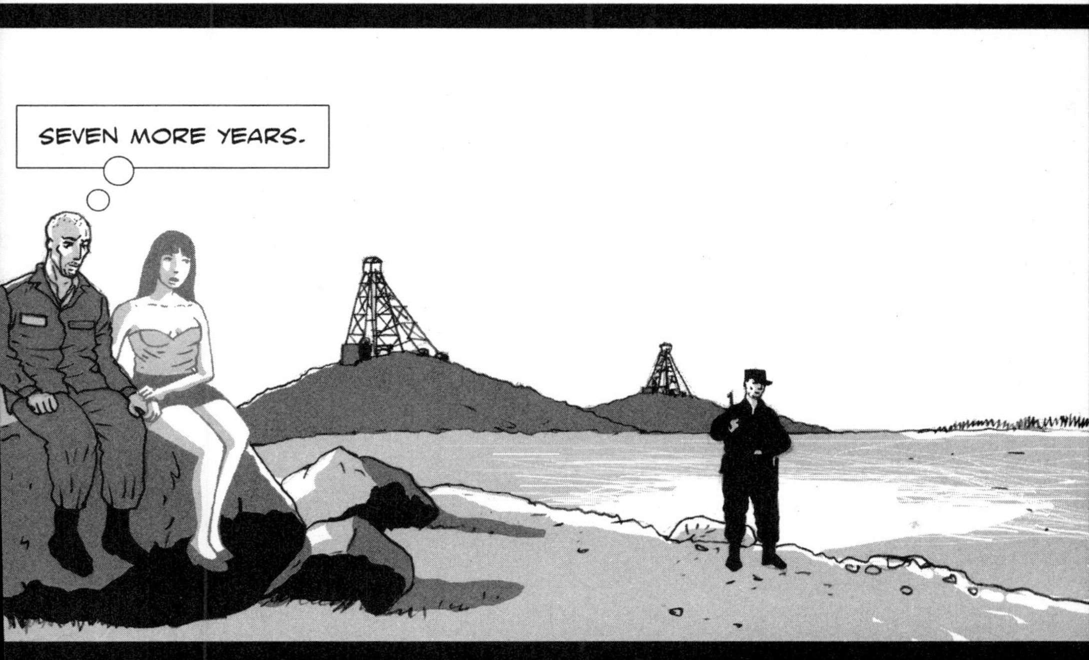
SEVEN MORE YEARS.

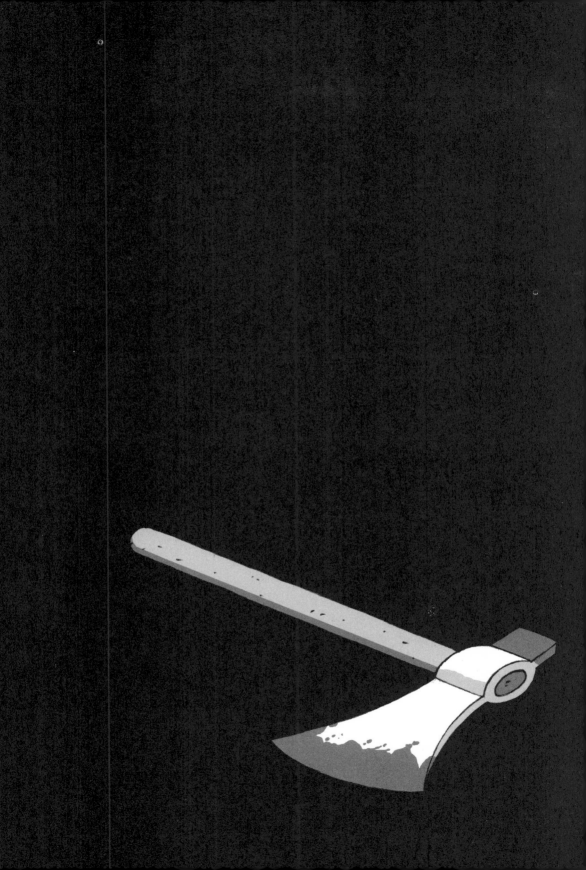

Fyodor Dostoevsky

(1821–1881)

For James Joyce, Fyodor Dostoevsky was the writer who "created modern prose, and intensified it to its present-day pitch": He who added "violence" to the Victorian novel and changed the face of contemporary European literature.

Following the publication of his earliest literary attempts, Dostoevsky was imprisoned for sedition in 1849, one of many arrested in Tsar Nicholas I's Russia for belonging to a forbidden underground organization. He was condemned to death by firing squad, but the execution was commuted at the last minute to four years' hard labor in Siberia.

Prison seems to have stimulated Dostoevsky's orthodox beliefs, and on his release he turned his back on his earlier political stance, now writing against the nihilist movements that had once intrigued him and that he now found utopian and self-destructive (as in his 1872 novel *The Possessed*).

After traveling widely in Europe, including London, Dostoevsky became addicted to gambling, and there is some evidence that he wrote *Crime and Punishment* (1866) quickly because he needed the advance money to service his debts.

In 1876–77 Dostoevsky devoted his energies to the journal *Diary of a Writer*, for which he served as editor, publisher, and sole contributor. Fulminating against Catholics and socialists alike for their materialism, he used its pages to disseminate his increasingly radical political views. He felt that western Europe was in a state of collapse and that the Russian Orthodox Church would create the kingdom of God on earth.

Through his novels, culminating in his masterpiece *The Brothers Karamazov* (1880), Dostoevsky became one of the strongest influences on the century of writers who followed him. The depth and perpetual contradictions of his characters made him unique in his time, winning successive generations of admirers—not least among them Sigmund Freud. Dostoevsky's reflections on the principles and responsibilities of personal freedom anticipate those of a twentieth century anchored in existentialist thinking. (The opening paragraph of Albert Camus' *La Peste* is a paraphrase of the beginning of *The Possessed*.)

He is also the writer who cast a darkness over contemporary fiction from which it has never completely emerged.